DEFENDING
NORTHAMPTONSHIRE

DEFENDING
NORTHAMPTONSHIRE

THE MILITARY LANDSCAPE FROM
PRE-HISTORY TO THE PRESENT

MIKE OSBORNE

FONTHILL

Fonthill Media Language Policy

Fonthill Media publishes in the international English language market. One language edition is published worldwide. As there are minor differences in spelling and presentation, especially with regard to American English and British English, a policy is necessary to define which form of English to use. The Fonthill Policy is to use the form of English native to the author. Mike Osborne was born and educated in England; therefore British English has been adopted in this publication.

Fonthill Media Limited
Fonthill Media LLC
www.fonthillmedia.com
office@fonthillmedia.com

First published in the United Kingdom and the United States of America 2020

British Library Cataloguing in Publication Data:
A catalogue record for this book is available from the British Library

ISBN 978-1-78155-762-4

Typeset in 10pt on 13pt Sabon
Printed and bound in England

Acknowledgements

Thanks are due to Adrian Armishaw for generously sharing information and allowing the use of illustrative material; Graham Cadman, Vivien Davison, Brian Giggins, the Knit & Natter group at Raunds, Ken Nicholl at Greens Norton, Mr Smith at Barnwell Manor, and local studies library staff in Northampton, Higham Ferrers, Rushden and Peterborough; and Tony Smith and the Kettering Evening Telegraph for permission to reproduce a photograph.

My thanks, as always, also go to Alan Sutton, Jay Slater, and Joshua Greenland at Fonthill Media for their consistent enthusiasm and professionalism.

Once again, my wife, Pam, has helped with research, encouragement, interest, and technical support, for which I am, as ever, grateful.

Contents

List of Abbreviations

AA	Anti-aircraft
AAA	Anti-aircraft Artillery (US Army)
AALMG	Anti-aircraft light machine-gun
ACF	Army Cadet Force
ADGB	Air Defence Great Britain
AFDD	Air Force Distribution Depot (fuel)
AFRD	Air Force Reserve Depot (fuel)
AM	Air Ministry
AP	Aerial photography
ARC	Army Reserve Centre (formerly TAC)
ARG	Airfield Research Group
ARP	Air Raid Precautions
ASP	Aircraft Servicing Platform
A/T	anti-tank
ATA	Air Transport Auxiliary (civilian ferry pilots)
ATC	Air Training Corps
ATS	Auxiliary Territorial Service (1938–49, then WRAC)
AW	Albright & Wilson (phosphorus bombs)
AWA	Armstrong Whitworth Aircraft
BEF	British Expeditionary Force
BHQ	Battle Headquarters
BSA	Birmingham Small Arms
CBA	Council for British Archaeology
CCF	Combined Cadet Force (successor to OTC)
CD	Civil Defence
CFS	Central Flying School
CFS	Central Fire Service
COD	Central Ordnance Depot
CRU	Civilian Repair Unit (aircraft repair workshops)
DFW3	Directorate of Fortifications & Works, Department 3

DL	Defended Locality
(E & R)(S)FTS	(Elementary & Reserve)(Service) Flying Training School
ESR	Essential Service Route
FANY	First Aid Nursing Yeomanry
FFI	Force Francaise Interieure (Free French army)
GCI	Ground Control Intercept (radar system, Second World War onwards)
GDA	Gun-Defended Area (AA defences)
GHQ	General Headquarters (GHQ Line, GHQ Reserve, etc.)
GOC	General Officer Commanding
GPO	General Post Office
GS	Grammar School
HAA	Heavy Anti-aircraft
HCU	Heavy Conversion Unit (pilot training)
HE	High explosive
HER	Heritage Environment Record (formerly SMR)
HF	Home Forces (First World War)
HG	Home Guard
HT	Horse Transport
ICBM	Inter-Continental Ballistic Missile (e.g. POLARIS)
IRBM	Intermediate-Range Ballistic Missile (e.g. Thor)
ITC	Infantry Training Centre
KRRC	King's Royal Rifle Corps
LAA	Light Anti-Aircraft
LADA	London Air Defence Area (AA scheme, First World War onwards)
LDV	Local Defence Volunteers, later Home Guard
LG	Landing ground
LMS	London-Midland-Scottish (pre-nationalisation rail company)
MAFF	Ministry of Agriculture, Fisheries & Food (post-Second World War)
MAP	Ministry of Aircraft Production (Second World War)
MI	Military Intelligence (MI5, MI9, etc.)
MOLA	Museum of London Archaeology (in Northampton)
MoS	Ministry of Supply
MT	Motor Transport
MU	Maintenance Unit (RAF)
NAAFI	Navy, Army and Air Force Institute
NCC	Northamptonshire County Council
NFF	National (shell-) Filling Factory
NORSOG	Norwegian Special Operations Group
NRA	National Rifle Association
OC	Officer commanding
OCTU	Officer Cadet Training Unit
OP	Observation post
ORP	Operational Readiness Platform
OSS	Office of Strategic Services (US equivalent of SOE)
OTC	Officer Training Corps (school or university cadet corps)
OTU	Operational Training Unit (RAF Bomber/Training Commands)

(P)AFU	(Pilots') Advanced Flying Unit
PBX	Private Branch Exchange (telephones)
pdr	pounder (as in weight of projectile) 1 pound = 454 grams
Pluto	Pipeline under the ocean
QM	Quartermaster
RA	Royal Artillery
RAuxAF	Royal Auxiliary Air Force (until 1957)
RAE	Royal Aircraft Establishment (Farnborough, Hampshire)
RAF	Royal Air Force (from 1 April 1918)
RAFVR	Royal Air Force Volunteer Reserve
RAMC	Royal Army Medical Corps
(R)AOC	(Royal from 1918) Army Ordnance Corps (until 1993)
(R)ASC	(Royal from 1918) Army Service Corps
RCHM(E)	Royal Commission on Historical Monuments (England)
RE	Royal Engineers
REME	Royal Electrical and Mechanical Engineers (formed 1942)
RFA	Royal Field Artillery
RFC	Royal Flying Corps (up to 31 March 1918)
RGA	Royal Garrison Artillery
RHA	Royal Horse Artillery
RHQ	Regimental Headquarters
RNAS	Royal Naval Air Service (until 31 March 1918)
(R)OC	(Royal from 1941) Observer Corps
ROD	Royal Ordnance Depot
ROF	Royal Ordnance Factory
RSJ	Rolled steel joist
RSM	Regimental Sergeant-Major
RVC	Rifle Volunteer Corps (from 1859)
SAA	small arms ammunition
SAC	Strategic Air Command (USAF)
SF	Special Fires (Bombing Decoy—'Starfish')
SIP	Self-Igniting Phosphorous (grenade)
S/L	searchlight
SMLE	Short Magazine Lee Enfield (0.303-inch rifle)
SMR	Sites & Monuments Record (now HER)
SOE	Special Operations Executive
STS	Special Training School (SOE)
TA	Territorial Army (from 1920–39 and 1947–2014)
TAC	Territorial Army Centre (drill hall 1947–2014, *see* ARC)
TAFA	Territorial & Auxiliary Forces Association
tb	temporary brick (single brick with buttresses in RAF buildings)
TCG	Troop Carrier Group (USAAF)
TDS	Training Depot Station (1917–20)
TF	Territorial Force (from 1908–1918)
TNA	The National Archive (formerly Public Record Office)
u/g	underground

UHF	Ultra High Frequency (radio wavelength)
UKWMO	United Kingdom Warning & Monitoring Organisation
USAAC	United States Army Air Corps (Second World War)
USAAF	United States Army Air Force (Second World War)
USAF(E)	United States Air Force (Europe) (post-Second World War)
VAD	Voluntary Aid Detachment (First World War)
VCR	Visual Control Room (atop watch office)
VHF	Very High Frequency (radio wavelength)
VP	Vulnerable Point
VTC	Volunteer Training Corps (First World War Home Guard equivalent)
WAAF	Women's Auxiliary Air Force (later WRAF)
WLA	Women's Land Army
WRAC	Women's Royal Army Corps (from 1949–92)
W(R)VS	Women's (Royal) Voluntary Service
W/T	Wireless telegraphy
YWCA	Young Women's Christian Association

Introduction

In 1974, shortly after having quit London and moving to the Peterborough area, an early priority was a visit to Rockingham Castle. My family was shown round by Commander Michael Saunders-Watson, RN, who would then have been around forty years old, married to an admiral's daughter, and with three young children. Coming from the English county furthest from the sea, paradoxically, his was the fourth generation to produce senior naval officers. That same remoteness from the coast, however, decided the location for the vast ordnance depot at Weedon Bec, whose grand pavilion, if only in popular legend, was intended to provide sanctuary for George III in the event of a French invasion by Napoleon's armies. Successive waves of incomers have settled in this accessible county, establishing Northamptonshire as an archetype for England's shire counties with its prehistoric camps, Roman towns, Norman castles, and fortified houses, demonstrating the developments of local defence over the centuries. Many of these locations are closely associated with the most famous of historical personages: King John; Richard III; Mary, Queen of Scots; and Oliver Cromwell. Northamptonshire battlefields saw Edward IV gain a throne and Charles I lose one. Military sites range from the Iron Age hillfort of Hunsbury to the genuine castles of Barnwell and Rockingham and the militia barracks in Northampton built as a pastiche fortress. More recently, hurriedly built concrete pillboxes, defending against a very tangible anticipated assault, gave way to Thor missile sites, insuring us all against the more abstract threat of mutually assured destruction in the Nuclear Age.

This land-locked county is bordered by eight other counties, as well as the City of Peterborough, since 1997 a unitary authority but until 1963 part of Northamptonshire. At the other end of the county, Banbury, lying just over the border in Oxfordshire, has equally influenced events that impinge on our county's military history.

Given the reductions in archaeological and museum services caused by continuing austerity, it is important to record the efforts of those voluntary groups and societies that work to increase our general knowledge of those themes explored in this book. These include the Castle Studies Group with its research arm, the Castle Studies Trust; the Fortress Study Group; the Pillbox Study Group; and the Airfield Research Group, as well as the many local history and archaeology groups, all of which are accessible via the internet.

This book is the ninth in a county series I started in 2010, and while there are, inevitably, similarities across those nine counties, each one exhibits individual characteristics. These are determined by factors such as landscape, population, communications, or serendipity. I have greatly enjoyed exploring Northamptonshire's past and present, and while much of the military past is disappearing as brownfield sites go under housing or commercial development, there are still discoveries to be made and reported to the County Heritage Environment Record. I hope this book may stimulate interest in what remains and contribute to the record of what once was.

Mike Osborne
Market Deeping, 2018

1

Northamptonshire before the Norman Conquest

Prehistoric Earthworks: Camps and Hillforts

Despite the apparent importance of the trackway that ran along the Jurassic Ridge, extending from the Cotswolds, along the Northamptonshire Heights, and through Rockingham Forest, north-east to the Lincolnshire Wolds and the Humber Estuary, prehistoric Northamptonshire cannot boast anything on the scale of the great hillforts of South West England or other regions of the British Isles. It is now thought that causewayed enclosures such as those at Briar Hill, Dallington, and Southwick were meeting or market sites, later used for burials, rather than settlements, their enclosing banks pierced by multiple gaps, thereby removing defensive capabilities. A defended settlement excavated at Draughton (SP778775) was surrounded by a single bank and ditch, forming a circular enclosure 100 feet (30 metres) in diameter around a farmstead, consisting of three huts, 20 feet (6 metres) and 33 feet (10 metres) in diameter. From *c*. 400 BC, settlements appear in the hillier southern half of the county at a number of sites where hillforts were built. Constituting the northernmost lands of the Belgic Catuvellauni tribe, centred on St Albans and Colchester, early in the first century BC, Northamptonshire was border country, with the Iceni of East Anglia to the east and the Corieltauvi of Leicestershire to the north.

There is still some doubt as to the purpose of hillforts given that they may have fulfilled different roles at different times: as venues for tribal gatherings and seasonal celebrations; for the centralisation of food production and markets; as secure places for the storage of agricultural surplus; as places of refuge for people and animals in times of conflict; or as dominant symbols of authority. It is possible that, over time, hillforts performed all these functions. Where typical early Iron Age hillforts were appearing in Northamptonshire, they were located on whatever eminence the local topography afforded. Hunsbury stands 300 feet (90 metres) above sea level, and Borough Hill, Daventry, at 600 feet (180 metres). Usually, a ditch was dug around the lip of a hill or across the neck of a spur or promontory, and the spoil was heaped inside the line of the ditch to form a rampart, enclosing an area of anything from 2.5 acres (1.2 ha) at Egg Rings to 150 acres (60 ha) at Borough Hill. The rampart would often consist of rubble and earth heaped up around and inside a box-framework of timber posts sunk in at ground level. In Northamptonshire, examples at Hunsbury, Guilsborough, Rainsborough, and Castle Yard, Farthingstone, were built in the tradition of the hillforts of the south-west. Such constructions were subject to decay over time and often required refurbishment as evidenced at Rainsborough, Hunsbury, and Guilsborough. The fort at Crow Hill, Irthlingborough, now ploughed out but revealed by aerial photography, was found to have been refurbished with a palisade in the late Iron Age. The difficulty of dating earthworks in the absence of excavation evidence or finds means that even identification can be difficult. Arbury Hill near Badby, for instance, has long been regarded as a roughly square Iron Age hillfort, with sides of 200 yards. It appears to have had a single rampart, but little trace remains of either this or the associated former ditch. However, the RCHM(E) casts doubt on this interpretation, assigning any discernible earthworks to natural causes: earth movement through the natural forces of weathering or to later agricultural activity. It is mentioned in a charter of 944 where it is described as a fortified site, but there have been no finds to support this designation. There is significant uncertainty over the origins of the earthworks at Harringworth, Rothersthorpe, Wadenhoe, and Arbury Banks, near Chipping Warden. Each one could have originated as either an Iron Age or a later Danish or Anglo-Saxon settlement. Equally, each could represent both possibilities, an Iron Age fort taken over and refurbished temporarily by raiders or more permanently by a group of incoming settlers.

Borough Hill is a prominent hillfort standing on the eastern edge of Daventry. It may date from before the Iron Age and therefore would be earlier than most others in the county. Here, a bank and ditch enclose 150 acres (60 ha) on the 600-foot (180-metre) contour line, with a double line of defences on the south, and a possible entrance to the south-east, with triple ditches. It may have contained roundhouses within the defences. Assigned to the middle Iron Age is a smaller, discrete hillfort at the north end, partly under the golf course, enclosing 12.5 acres (5 ha). This has a much more substantial

Cross-section of a typical hill-fort bank and ditch

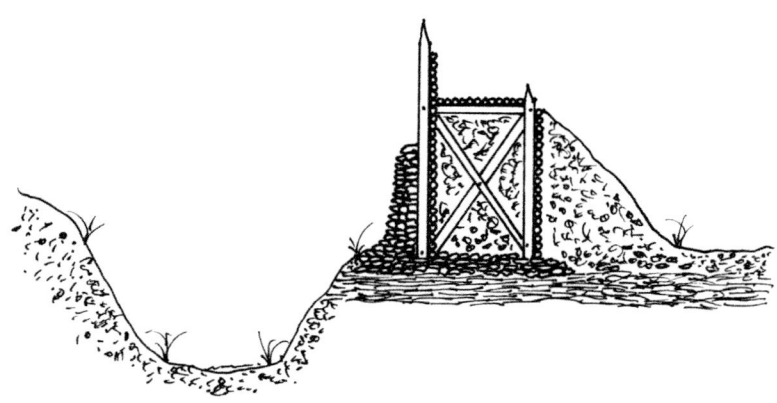

Hunsbury hillfort: a cross-section of the rampart, a typical design of the period.

rampart and ditch and a counterscarp bank. However, erosion, agricultural use, and landscaping have more or less obliterated most of the details, but it is possible to get an impression of the strength of the site by walking around the hilltop.

Hunsbury hillfort stands on the southern edge of Northampton, and quite close to Duston Mill, thought to have been a prehistoric crossing of the Nene. It is a much-damaged, roughly circular Iron Age hillfort on the 300-foot (90-metre) contour line covering 4 acres (1.6 ha). Inside the ramparts were discovered around 300 circular pits, between 13 and 26 feet (4 and 8 metres) across, and 8 and 11 feet (2.5 and 3.5 metres) deep, suggesting that one of the camp's functions was the storage of foodstuffs, particularly grain. The fort was surrounded by a ditch, 18 feet (5.5 metres) deep, crossed by a causeway at the western entrance, and with a counterscarp bank on the east. An entrance to the south-east may be original. The rampart, which in places is built on a shelf of natural rock, stands up to 13 feet (4 metres) above the ground level of the interior and was constructed in at least two phases. The earlier bank constructed in the sixth to fifth centuries BC was probably of the timber box design and consists of a clay and rubble bank with timber revetment to front and back and a stone facing wall about a metre high. Subsequently, a new bank of loam was raised in front of this earlier rampart, swallowing up the revetment. Excavations in 1952 and 1988 may have uncovered evidence for further ditches.

At Castle Yard, Farthingstone, the Iron Age hillfort stands at 520 feet (160 metres) above sea-level. It is roughly rectangular with double banks and ditches, and shared Hunsbury's building style. Excavations have revealed a stone-faced box rampart, and a 3-foot-high (90-cm-high) counterscarp bank of dumped stiff clay. Burrow Hill camp, Guilsborough, at a height of 535 feet (165 metres), has a rectangular shape with single bank and ditch, long sides of 500–600 feet (155–185 metres) and short sides of around 300 feet (90 metres). This regular footprint was misidentified in the eighteenth century as that of a Roman camp. The two earthwork enclosures at Harringworth are both roughly circular. One has a much-eroded bank, now about 1 metre high, and a shallow ditch, while the other is completely ploughed out. Traces of another circular ring fort, 325 feet (100 metres) in diameter, and defended by a bank and ditch, and attributed to the Iron Age, have been found at Thrapston

Rainsborough Camp, Newbottle, an oval early Iron Age hillfort excavated in the 1960s, offers tantalising insights into the warlike aspect of a fort. The three-tiered rampart was faced with turf or dry-stone revetments and topped with a timber palisade. There was a V-shaped ditch and a counterscarp bank. The western entrance, approached by a causeway over the ditches, was in-turned in order to channel attackers into a narrow passage commanded from the ramparts, and guardrooms were built into the walls backing the gates. These had been burned down in the early fourth century BC, and a casualty of this presumed battle was found under charred roof timbers in the southern guard chamber. Late in the second century BC, the camp was refortified with a simple double bank and U-shaped ditches. Once again, the entrance was given strong defences, as a bridge over the ditch led to a gate passage, flanked by bastions. The fighting platform on the palisade was carried over this gate passage on a timber bridge. In the AD fourth century, a building, 10 feet (3 metres) square, was built over the backfilled ditch and the entrance passage was remodelled. Now hardly anything, beyond the dominant situation of this fort, can be seen. On a totally different scale, Egg

Rings, Hartwell, Salcey Forest, is a kidney-shaped defended enclosure, probably a small hillfort, with a single rampart rising about 5 feet (1.5 metres) above the bottom of the ditch, enclosing an area of only 2.5 acres (1.2 ha). On the east side are two gaps in the defences, the more northerly one of which appears to have in-turning banks, perhaps representing the original entrance.

Apart from those sites suspected of having much later origins, many confirmed Iron Age camps enjoyed prolonged occupation, as we shall see. The hillfort at Whittlebury, in Old Tun Copse, thought to be the precursor of Towcester as a military centre, saw royal use in Anglo-Saxon times. Later Iron Age settlements typically comprised single farmsteads with a few roundhouses enclosed within a banked and ditched enclosure, affording only minimal defensive capability. They were intended as much to keep livestock in and predators out as to defend against aggressors. Undefended prehistoric settlements at Towcester, Irchester, and Titchmarsh later evolved into Roman towns. Like Whittlebury, Crow Hill was reoccupied in the Anglo-Saxon period as the centre of a possibly royal estate.

One particular anomaly from this period is The Larches at Church Stowe, a triple-ditched linear earthwork extending 300 yards up Church Stowe Lane from Upper Stowe Road. It may be early Iron Age or, more probably, associated with later medieval field systems. No other linear earthwork features, as are common in many other border areas, have been recorded in the county. Duston has been suggested as the possible site of an *oppidum*, or tribal centre, but there is no real evidence for any such site in Northamptonshire. However, the site at Duston has long been destroyed so no traces of the characteristic dykes, associated with such *oppidum* sites as Colchester (Essex), have ever been found.

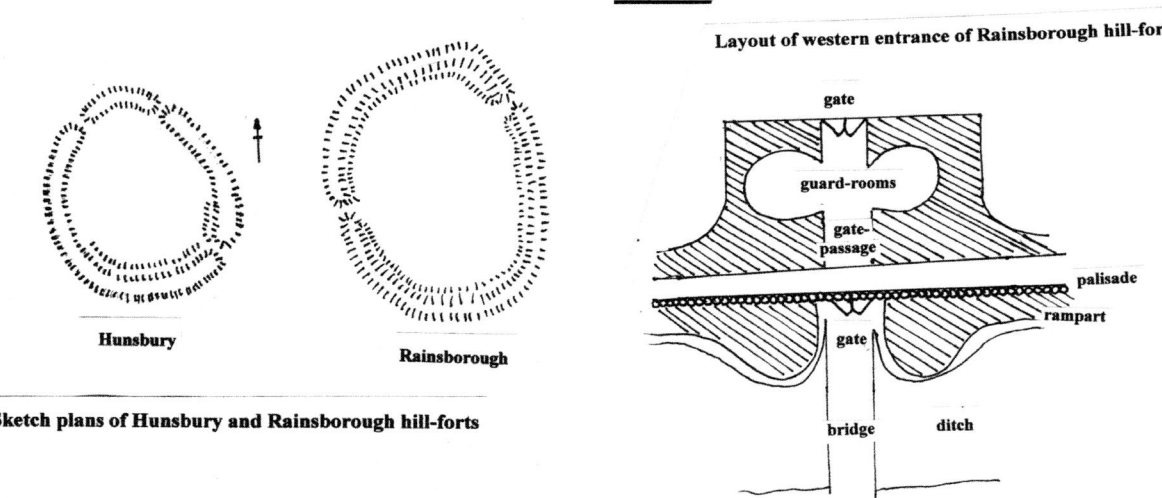

Above left: Hunsbury and Rainsborough hillforts: sketch plans of the ramparts. (*After Allcroft*)

Above right: Rainsborough hillfort: a sophisticated gateway layout. (*After a plan drawn for the Prehistoric Society*)

Roman Forts and Defended Towns

After the Roman invasion of AD 43, Ermine Street formed the western boundary of the invaders' settlement, and provided a baseline for further conquest. Under Roman rule, the north-eastern fringes of the county prospered, benefiting from the industry centred on the lower Nene Valley. Sandwiched between provincial capitals at Leicester (*Ratae*) and St Albans (*Verulamium*), central Northamptonshire was a land of villas and farms rather than important towns or military centres. Two significant Roman roads, Watling Street (linking London to Chester) and the Gartree Road (which ran from Leicester to Godmanchester, near Huntingdon), traversed the county. Remains of a first-century Roman bridge over the Nene on the road between Titchmarsh and Aldwincle were found in 1966. It probably collapsed after the Romans left and its replacement was built at Thrapston where the river was more easily forded. The original bridge was constructed on piles sunk into the river bed, on which were laid massive, 20-foot-long (6-metre-long) beams with mortices cut to hold crossbeams, but it was subsequently twice patched up with less robust structures.

The formerly accepted sequence of events in the defences of Northamptonshire's three walled towns was that earthen ramparts were raised sometime in the AD second century, and then remodelled with stone walls in the third or fourth centuries, with some artillery bastions being added soon after. Charmian Woodfield argues that the line formed by the defended towns of Alchester (Oxfordshire); Towcester, Irchester, and *Bannaventa* (Northamptonshire); Water Newton (Cambridgeshire); and Great Casterton (Rutland) together may have formed a co-ordinated line of defence, marking the old frontier of the Catevellauni, rather than representing isolated local strongpoints, and was well-established by *c.* AD 175. Woodfield cites widespread examples of the burning of villas, such as at Weldon, Bozeat, and others in the region of Towcester, in the final third of the second century as evidence for violence and unrest on a large scale. A token of the urgency surrounding this ambitious fortification project is the fact that Towcester was actually walled ten years or more before London. Some time in the fourth century, corner bastions were added: two externally at Towcester and one internally at Irchester. These may well have been designed to carry artillery, similar provision being made at Great Casterton, suggesting the presence of regular garrisons at each of these places. These later refurbishments may have included recutting the ditches. It has been pointed out that the extensive extra-mural settlements would have gained little benefit from these town defences, and they would actually have constituted an impediment to an effective defence by providing cover for attackers.

Towcester (*Lactodorum*) stands midway between St Albans (*Verulamium*) and Wall (*Letocetum*) on the road from London to North Wales and Chester (*Deva*). It is possible that it originated as a short-lived legionary fortress during the early years of Roman conquest. The second-century defences extended each side of Watling Street, enclosing an area of 29 acres (11.75 ha), with a circuit of walls almost a mile (1.5 km) in length. Although by the fourth century the defences were decaying, they were refurbished at that time. The multiple ditches, with their saucer-like profile, quite conventional in their marshy situation, will have been subject to a regular cycle of silting up followed by maintenance, and so were periodically recut at different times. The evidence of overlaying structures suggests a construction date of AD 170–175. Inside the ditch, the bank was a generous 12 yards in width with a stone wall 3 yards wide. With the wet ditches and counterscarp bank, the combined width of the defences extended to 200 feet (60 metres). One factor that contributed to this width was the internal bank built up against the wall as it was being built. The walled area did not take in all the existing domestic development so may have acted as a citadel. It has been suggested that such a strong defence indicates Towcester's high civic status. Unusually, there is clear evidence that the bank and wall were coeval, unlike many fortified settlements where a stone wall was cut into an existing bank anything up to 200 years later. Apart from a recutting of ditches, the main improvement to Towcester's defences in the fourth century was the addition of two external square turrets or bastions to the north-west and north-east corners, which may have been designed to carry artillery. The town had at least three gates, of which one may lie under the Norman motte. Even accounting for later modifications to the defences in Norman and Civil War times, it would appear that double ditches were already present in Roman times.

Irchester stands at the junction of two Roman roads, which both originated in Cambridgeshire. One comes down from Water Newton (*Durobrivae*), to the north, and continues on southwards to link with Watling Street, while the other, from Godmanchester (*Durovigutum*), arrives from the east. The town defences consisted of a banked and ditched enclosure measuring 715 × 850 feet (220 × 275 metres), and covering an area of 20 acres (8 ha). These late second-century defences, similar to those at Towcester, appear to overlay an earlier fort, now forming the northern half of the town. The walls of the southern half of the walled town appear to be at a slight angle to the upper half, producing an irregular, sub-rectangular shape, and these two halves were separated by an east-west ditch, presumably that of the earlier fort. The road layout conforms to the normal pattern except that no road appears to approach from the west, but excavations have shown that there was, nevertheless, a West Gate, and it was a substantial stone structure, subsequently blocked. Some time, probably in the fourth century, an internal, trapezoidal corner bastion was built at the south-west angle. The rampart was 40 feet (12 metres) wide, built of earth with a stone core. At some time, the front face was cut away for the insertion of a limestone wall, over 6 feet (2 metres) thick. At the base of the wall there was a berm, extending some 16 feet (5 metres) as far as a 6-foot-deep (2-metre-deep) ditch. In places, a triple ditch, possibly Iron Age in origin, girdles the town.

The third of Northamptonshire's Roman walled towns was *Bannaventa*, at Whilton Lodge near Norton, straddling Watling Street. This walled town, covering an area of 10–11 acres (4.5 ha), is an irregular quadrilateral with sides of 500–600 feet (170–200 metres). It is surrounded by a 14-foot-wide (4.5-metre-wide) earth and gravel rampart and ditch. At some time, possibly in the third century it has been suggested, the front of the rampart was overlain by a bank of clay as a foundation for a new stone wall, at least 8 feet (2.5 metres) thick. The original ditch was filled with earth and clay and fresh external triple ditches dug. The site was abandoned in the late fourth century. Given a number of questions over dating this sequence of events raised by archaeological excavation, and taking into account both the apparent upheavals of the last quarter of the second century and the evidence of Towcester's defences, Woodfield argues that it is wholly possible that the defences of both Irchester and *Bannaventa* were also achieved in a single operation, around 170–175. There are examples of small walled towns in

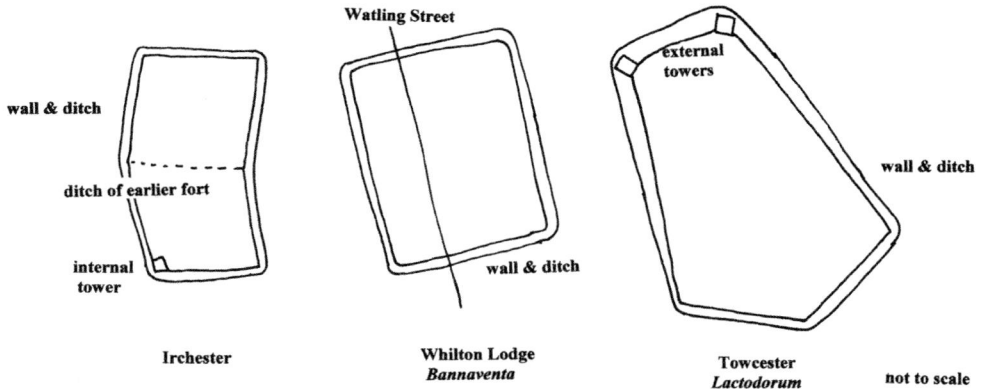

Sketch-plans of Northamptonshire Roman town defences

Roman towns in Northamptonshire: comparative plans of the defences of the county's three defended Roman towns.

Roman Britain that were given coeval rampart and wall defences at later dates than the three under examination here, and of towns where walls were much later cut into ramparts, so all permutations are plausible.

While the provision of defences was once regarded as the major criterion for being awarded the status of town, it is now recognised that a large number of undefended Roman towns flourished in Britannia. These included the Northamptonshire examples of Ashton by Oundle, where several settlements covering over 60 acres (24 ha) were occupied from 60–375; the possible former *oppidum* of Duston; King's Sutton, Little Houghton, Kettering, Higham Ferrers, and Titchmarsh.

Anglo-Saxon and Danish Northamptonshire

After the Romans had left, bands of German mercenaries were enlisted to protect what remained of the country's trade and industry, and by *c.* 500, most of the land between Ermine Street on the east and Watling Street on the west had been occupied by the Angles. Just as an iron-working industry survived in Rockingham Forest right from pre-Roman times through into the medieval period, further evidence of continuity of use in settlement sites is also gradually emerging, such as the presence of Saxon burial sites at former Roman settlements. Anglo-Saxon pottery has been found inside Hunsbury hillfort, and Anglo-Saxon timber buildings were constructed inside the ruins of Roman villas at Brixworth, Nether Heyford, and Stanwick. Danish battle-axes and spearheads of the ninth or tenth centuries were found on Borough Hill at Daventry. The Anglo-Saxons tended to establish dispersed farms on only the most favourable locations, abandoning the less productive lands and either displacing or absorbing any British inhabitants. Towards the end of the seventh century, Mercia, under Penda, had been established as a kingdom, containing clan or tribal groups owing allegiance to their king. The grave of the leader of such a group has been discovered at Wollaston, containing evidence of martial association: a decorated steel sword and an elaborate helmet. A hierarchy of settlements was evolving, which included single farms often descended from Roman villa sites; expanded settlements, which would become villages; larger regional centres, which would grow into market towns; and full-fledged boroughs. Royal estates were established, and these would later form the basis for administrative areas, possibly known as 'sokes'. These sokes were grouped into three areas centred on Northampton, King's Sutton, and Oundle, all together eventually forming the shire. The Soke of Oundle appears to have consisted of eight hundreds, extending along the Nene Valley from Kettering to Peterborough. From the eighth century, Northamptonshire, along with the counties of Bedfordshire, Huntingdonshire, and Cambridgeshire, had formed an Outer Mercia, and would later constitute an Outer Danelaw. Each of their county towns represented important settlements based on crossings of the rivers Nene, Great Ouse, and Cam. Besides Northampton itself, there were, within Northamptonshire, Mercian settlements at Irthlingborough, Brixworth, Oundle, and Towcester. A move from dispersed to nucleated village sites occurred in the later Saxon period, and many isolated early and middle-Saxon sites had disappeared by *c.* 850, evidenced by a dateable change in the form of pottery to wheel-thrown pots. The Anglo-Saxon royal estate centre of Kettering was granted to Peterborough Abbey in 963.

Northampton enjoyed a similar evolution to Nottingham; it was on a navigable river and set in the familiar D-shaped enclosure, open to the waterfront, and favoured by the Danish settlers, who still liked to maintain an easy escape route. Although the concept of the 'Five Boroughs' only surfaced in the *Anglo-Saxon Chronicle* for 942, such a grouping has traditionally been regarded as exclusively York, Lincoln, Derby, Nottingham, and Stamford. However, sharing most of the relevant characteristics, Northampton has been claimed as the 'Sixth Borough' of the Danelaw. It appears to have developed through the Middle Saxon period as a Mercian town with a stone Minster church and a royal palace. Close to St Peter's church, built over the Minster site, a seventh-century hall of timber was superseded during the next century by a larger hall raised on stone footings. This, with accompanying structures—all contained within an enclosure entered through a gateway—has been suggested as a Mercian royal palace site, but others have seen it as possibly monastic rather than secular. The earlier hall, 98 feet long × 30 feet wide (30 metres × 9 metres) was replaced *c.* 820 by a hall measuring 120 feet long × 37 feet wide (37.6 metres × 11.4 metres), roughly the same size as the Saxon nave of Brixworth Church, and built of reused ironstone and limestone slabs, along with Roman tile. By the end of the tenth century, this hall had been abandoned and its stone robbed. A second church, St Gregory's, stood further to the east of the hall.

If historical periods can be characterised by particular forms of fortification, then the Anglo-Saxon era is symbolised by the *burh*. This has usually been interpreted as a large, essentially public fortification defending a substantial settlement such as a town. Northampton appears to have been given new defences, probably in the early 900s, but whether under Danish or Saxon direction remains unknown. A clay bank, 6 feet 6 inches (2 metres) high, with a width of 20 feet (6 metres) with timber revetments was raised and a wide ditch was dug, enclosing an area of 80 acres (32 ha) in what would become the south-western quarter of the much larger medieval walled town.

The western entrance to the *burh* was defended by a timber gatehouse. Excavations in Green Street and between Bath and Scarletwell Streets, uncovered a section of these town defences, here consisting of the clay bank with its timber revetment, inside a ditch 40 feet wide (13 metres wide) and 10 feet deep (3 metres deep). Edward the Elder's *burh* at Towcester lay on the south-western edge of the Danelaw. As recorded by the *Anglo-Saxon Chronicle* in 920, following a Danish attack, the Roman walls were refortified by being refaced in stone and, most probably, having the ditch scoured or completely re-dug. Older defended sites, whether refortified or not, also retained significance. The fort on Crow Hill, Irthlingborough, for instance, was reoccupied, and in 780, the presence there of King Offa of Mercia was recorded. The hillfort of Whittlebury, 3 miles south of Towcester, provided the venue for King Athelstan's royal Witan, or council meeting, in 930. Excavation of the hillfort on Borough Hill, Daventry, carried out in 1823, uncovered, as we have seen, Anglo-Saxon or Danish weapons. The fort was described as a *burh* in the tenth century but appears to have been used chiefly as an enclosure for livestock.

In 873, a Danish invasion had seen the break-up of Mercia, and by 877, a Danish army had settled much of Northamptonshire from Northampton and Towcester to the River Welland. However, the Danish advance was curtailed by their defeat by Alfred, in 878, which led to the establishment of the Danelaw. This consisted of the Five Boroughs plus land to the south containing Danish *burhs* at Northampton, Bedford, Cambridge, and Huntingdon, each generally defended by a palisade and ditch. In 914, Viking raids were launched from Northampton, penetrating as far south as Luton. The boundary of the Danelaw was Watling Street, cutting Northamptonshire in two. Edward the Elder, son of Alfred, established *burhs* at Stamford, south of the River Welland, and at Towcester. This latter site was refortified in 920 with a stone wall, the only recorded instance of such provision at a new *burh*. The Danes, often known as 'Vikings', made incursions into Saxon territory from the ninth century onwards, producing another type of communal defence: the fortified camp, often semi-circular in form with a river bank forming the straight side. Boats could be beached inside the ramparts for the host to winter in safety. At Harringworth, there is a roughly circular enclosure, around 325 feet (100 metres) across. Material from the ditch has been radio-carbon dated to 980+ or –60. Around 300 yards away lies another, similar camp. Both may be of Danish origin as a Dane is known to have held land in Harringworth. Danish place names appear from the 850s. Naseby, for instance, is interpreted as the 'fortified place of Hnaef'. Nineteen 'Thorps', meaning a piece of land or an estate, for instance, have been listed in Northamptonshire in the period up to Domesday, in 1086, with a further fifteen added by 1300. Of these, some twenty-six lay within the Danelaw, which took in three-quarters of Northamptonshire. Only those parts south-west of a line drawn between Daventry and Towcester, basically following Watling Street (now the A5), lay outside.

In the early 900s, the process of reclaiming the Danelaw was initiated by Edward the Elder, but in 913, a Danish army from Northampton and Leicester went on the rampage. Following his capture of Bedford in 915, Edward received the submission of the Danish Jarls of Northampton. In 917, Towcester was besieged by Danish forces but its defences held. After the death of Athelstan in 939, Olaf Gothfrithson, King of Dublin, invaded England. After capturing York, he went on to besiege Northampton in 940, where his progress was arrested by English forces under Edmund I, who then retook the five boroughs, cornering Olaf at Leicester and forcing him into a peace treaty. Further raids in 991, under Swein Forkbeard, forced the county into raising Danegeld in a vain attempt to buy off the raiders. This tax was collected by local officials, reinforcing the growing perception of them as landlords, but even these crippling sums failed to provide the promised protection. After the Battle of Ringmere (Norfolk) in May 1010, the victorious Danes advanced westwards from East Anglia, ravaging Oxfordshire and Buckinghamshire, and burning Northampton before moving down into Wiltshire. In 1065, Earl Morcar defeated Tostig, and as he made his way south with his Welsh and Northumbrian troops, Northampton was once again sacked.

The recent growth of castle studies (or 'castellology') has continued to be bedevilled by definitions going back to Mrs Armitage in 1912. Castles, the received wisdom dictates, were a by-product of the Norman Conquest, providing a defensible dwelling for a knight with his soldiers, and a locus for government, the collection of taxes, and the administration of justice. A few important royal, ducal, or episcopal castles were built in stone, while the majority—of a type known as motte and bailey castles—consisted of timber buildings surrounded by earthworks, moats, and timber defences. These structures will be explored in the next chapter, but it can be argued that their precursors could be found in England (and all over much of Europe) long before the Normans arrived in 1066. It has been convenient to visualise Norman castles in this stereotypical way despite strong evidence to show that, no less in Normandy than in England, they were built in a wide range of styles. Although tradition, often backed up by archaeological evidence, identifies a group of pre-Conquest earthwork castles built by French expatriates, mainly around Hereford but with the odd additional example elsewhere, there is a strong case for the existence of home-grown private, defensible, domestic structures built by the, by-now indigenous, Anglo-Saxon thegns, or their Danish counterparts.

As early as 757, the *Anglo-Saxon Chronicle* records an action centred on a hall, evidently surrounded by a wall or fence, whose gate was defended against attackers. Across the country, enough examples have come to light to suggest that fortified royal or thegnal residences were not uncommon. Many of these went on to become castles after the Conquest. One of the most persuasive examples is Sulgrave. Here, a timber structure dates from late in the tenth century; it measured 80 feet (24 metres) in length and 18 feet (5.5 metres) in width, contained an open hall 55 feet (16.75 metres) long and service rooms, which were accessed via a screen wall at one end. At the other end was a cross-wing, possibly of two storeys and built on stone footings. In line with this main block was a square detached timber building, probably a kitchen. Around AD 1000, the hall-block was remodelled on stone footings, and a stone building—possibly a two-storey tower with walls 2 feet (60 cm) thick and measuring 25 feet × 12 feet internally (7.6 metres × 3.6 metres)—was built alongside. This structure later served as a gatehouse when the new Norman owner built a ringwork castle, so it must have presented as a serviceable defence work. The pre-Conquest site was defended by an apparently unfinished turf bank and a ditch 15 feet (4.6 metres) wide and 3 feet (90 cm) deep, which could only have had a defensive function. It has been suggested that the church, whose west tower incorporates a Saxon triangular-headed doorway, may at some time have occupied an outer earthwork enclosure. A Saxon tract of the eleventh century lays down certain duties, rights, and responsibilities of both landowners and peasants. The peasant is required to help to erect the hedge (a generic term for rampart, barricade, or wall) and dig the defensive ditch around his lord's *burh*, or fortified house. This would appear to be analogous to the requirement to construct the defences of the local *burh*, in Wessex or Mercia, and to man them if summoned to repulse an attack. The lord, on his part, if his income justified it, would build a hall and a tower, thus gaining for himself the status of thegn. This tower could either be described as a *burhgeat*, literally the gate defending access to the fortified enclosure, or alternatively as a belfry or bell-tower, etymologically still implying a fortification. Such towers may have had multiple functions as a lookout, a refuge, or as a platform for religious or civic ceremonial. Saxon churches often lay inside the enclosure of the manor, another criterion for thegnly status, and their towers often had doors at first-floor level, facing either outwards, as at Earls Barton, or connecting with an internal gallery as at Brixworth. At Earls Barton, the pre-Conquest church tower, usually dated to 950–1000, lies on a spur bearing all the hallmarks of a promontory fort, cut off at the west end by a high mound and a deep ditch. Here, it is very easy to see the church tower fulfilling a defensive role. The manor was held by one of the leading thegns of the Danelaw and was the centre of a large estate, which included local villages but extended into neighbouring counties. It is unlikely that the Normans would erect a motte, dominated by the earlier church tower. It would seem more likely, therefore, that the church was built inside the enhanced earthworks of an existing Iron Age fort, in order to maximise the defensive potential of an already strong site.

Furnells manor, Raunds, was an early Saxon site occupied from the seventh to the ninth centuries and superseded by development on an adjacent site. Excavations have shown that this eighth-century farm was itself abandoned prior to being resettled in the mid-tenth century as the centre of a manorial complex. Four rectangular timber buildings, the largest of which may have been a hall, lay in an enclosure, an acre (0.4 ha) in area, and bounded by a substantial ditch. After *c*. 900, a stone church was added within the ditched enclosure, which contained the rebuilt timber aisled hall, and its associated stables, barns, and other out-buildings. Other enclosures, probably for livestock, adjoined this central nucleus, and other, smaller ones occupied the area around, possibly representing dependant farmsteads. It would appear that such a centre represents the establishment of an estate held by a thegn, representative of a newly emerging landowning elite, ruling over tenant smallholders. Furnells was held by an important thegn with extensive landholdings in three counties. A second Raunds manor was held by the wife of the earl of the East Midlands in 1050, and was called 'Burystead', a clear reference to a fortified site. A similar manorial complex existed at West Cotton, but there the timber hall was rebuilt in stone soon after 1066. Further comparable, but often less extensive developments consisted of a timber hall with attached living accommodation, barns, a mill, and a small, often single-cell, church, all contained within a ditched enclosure with further ditches enclosing stockyards. There are over 350 recorded Saxon settlement sites in Northamptonshire, and many will have conformed to the model described above.

Northamptonshire is rich in Saxon churches that may have fulfilled a role in this relationship between manor and church, and there survives in the county a particular parish church plan in which the tower is 'clasped' by a short, three-bay nave, thereby precluding any westward extension of the nave. The aisles may then overlap the nave,

Left: Earls Barton: the church tower dating back to the tenth century and dominating the promontory cut off by impressive earthwork defences.

Below: Earls Barton: the tower seen above the castle earthworks.

terminating in a west wall in line with that of the tower. The church at King's Sutton is of this type, and may contain the ghost outline of the Anglo-Saxon church. Others include Brigstock, Nassington, Culworth, Flore, Watford, and Chipping Warden. It has been suggested that King's Sutton was the centre of a Soke, and that the church enjoyed the status of a Minster, but no associated royal hall has yet been discovered. Brixworth is the largest Anglo-Saxon church in Britain, measuring 148 feet long × 30 feet wide (45 metres × 9 metres). It was built in the late eighth or early ninth century to the basilica plan, reusing Roman tiles and masonry from still extant ruins. A narthex, the width of the nave plus the *porticus*, formed the centre part of a western fore-building, later reduced to a double-height porch as the basis for the tower. A semi-circular stair turret was added and it was dated (on the evidence of its construction) to between 1000 and 1200. This was an early monastic site from the seventh century, and the church precinct was defined by a V-shaped 2-metre-deep boundary ditch, dated to 710, plus or minus eighty years. The monastic complex was one of several in the area targeted by the Danish attacks of 870. A doorway, its arch of Roman brick, in the interior face of the tower either provided access from the nave by a ladder or allowed access from the fore-building to a gallery across the west end of the nave. This doorway is now blocked with a triple-arched opening inserted above, probably at the time the present tower was built. A further example may be Nassington, where the Prebendal manor house is said to contain evidence of a Late Saxon structure and may previously have formed a single house with the adjacent royal manor. Nassington church, the core of whose west tower represents either an Anglo-Saxon tower or a tall western porch, also has a blocked triangular-headed doorway above the tower arch. Further possible candidates include Oundle, Gretton, and Rothwell. Oundle was the probable capital of a Mercian province and had an abbey in the eighth century, which was destroyed by the Danes in the ninth century, and remained in royal possession until given to Peterborough Abbey in 963. Gretton was the possible centre of a Saxon royal estate; Rothwell was another royal estate centre and its church is a possible 'minster'; another possible defended residence was at Desborough. Other high-status middle-Saxon sites were Yardley Hastings and Higham Ferrers. More Anglo-Saxon churches can be found at Brigstock, where the Saxon tower has a semi-circular stair turret of the late tenth century or early eleventh century, similar to that at Brixworth; Geddington showing traces of Anglo-Saxon work in the nave and at the base of the tower arch; Greens Norton with its Anglo-Saxon nave; and Radstone, where the lower level of its west tower dates from the eleventh century. At Church Stowe or Stowe Nine Churches, the two elements of the Anglo-Saxon church tower and an adjacent, possibly contemporary, defensive earthwork may be seen together. The ringwork at Culworth, adjacent to a church with Saxon features and held by a landowner who also held land at Sulgrave, may well have its origins in an earlier work. Suggested by the excavator of Sulgrave, yet another possible example of this pre-Conquest ringwork: church relationship is Weedon Lois, with its cruciform plan and crossing tower.

Four further defensive earthworks of indeterminate date, but all proposed as likely Anglo-Saxon sites exist in the county at Daventry, Rothersthorpe, Wadenhoe, and Arbury Banks, near Chipping Warden. At Burnt Walls, outside Daventry excavations have suggested that this triangular-banked and ditched enclosure may have been a Late Saxon defensive site and possibly a development of an Iron Age enclosure. It had been

Brixworth: the east wall of the tower showing the former opening, now blocked, which gave access onto an interior gallery overlooking the nave in this church, dating from the late eighth or early ninth century.

Brixworth: the lower two storeys of the late eighth- or early ninth-century tower with the stair turret added after AD 1000.

Brigstock: the horseshoe-shaped turret attached to the tower of this late tenth- or early eleventh-century church appears to be larger than a mere stair turret.

Wadenhoe: the massive earthworks of this fortified site alongside the Nene with the later Norman church in the background.

abandoned and its purpose forgotten by 1255; it was used in later medieval times for stock-keeping purposes. The rampart is 6 feet, 6 inches (2 metres) high, with a 6-foot, 6-inch-deep (2-metre-deep) ditch and a counterscarp bank. Any masonry, present in the rampart, has been robbed out. The Berry, lying north-east of Rothersthorpe church, is a roughly triangular or heart-shaped enclosure with bank and ditch, measuring 90 × 120 yards. It has no assigned date but may possible be Anglo-Saxon. There are possible traces of buildings and of a stone wall on the bank. Wadenhoe, deriving from an Anglo-Saxon named 'Wada', occupies a spur with a dry valley on one side and the River Nene to the south. There are remnants of a once-continuous limestone rampart following the edge of the slope, which has been scarped on all sides. Known in 1793 as 'Castle Close', it is traditionally thought of as a castle site, albeit with no documentary evidence, but it is equally likely to be pre-Conquest in origin. It is tempting to imagine it a Danish over-wintering camp, with the long ships beached on the banks of the Nene underneath the towering rampart. In places, these ramparts have been cut into by buildings and quarrying, but they are still very impressive, particularly from the riverside. At the end of the enclosure stands the church with its Norman tower, and the whole site lies within the deer park, of *c*. 1300. Arbury Banks may be a Danish reworking of an Iron Age enclosure, and Arbury Hill, its prehistoric origins now challenged, may have become further confused by the boundary ditches of Bishop Aelfric in Saxon times.

2

Northamptonshire in the Middle Ages 1066–1500

We have seen how the development of castles may not be as clear cut as was once believed, with the Norman invasion of 1066 no longer so firmly thought of as a clear watershed between the public *burh* and the private fortress. The obvious relationship of church and castle in many Northamptonshire villages is one clue, and another is the construction of fortified sites such as Sulgrave, Long Buckby, and Culworth, on Greenfield sites, abutted by cultivated land, rather than being superimposed on established settlements, suggesting that some of these early sites predated the growth of their villages. An accurate assessment of the density of castles in a county is always difficult to reach due to differences in definitions. According to one source, Northamptonshire had twenty-six castles and fortified manor houses with a further seven possible candidates from the evidence of place names or documents. These include, for example, eighteenth-century references to Irthlingborough's 'Castleyard' and 'Castle Lane' in Rothwell. Other sources cite totals of thirty-five and thirty-nine. This present writer employing, admittedly, the most liberal of criteria, has listed thirty-five castles, sixteen fortified manor houses, two Tudor strong houses, two circuits of town defences, thirteen hunting lodges or keepers' lodges, thirteen ecclesiastical sites, and fifty-one moated sites. Additionally, four sites are rejected. For an inland county, this reveals quite a significant nod to defence over a long period of time. It is worth noting, however, that only eight of those sites, in a time span of 500 years, were called upon seriously to fulfil their warlike potential, a ratio not dissimilar to those found across the country.

Castles of the Conquest

The majority of castles in the immediate post-Conquest landscape were of earth and timber, generally taking one of two forms. A conical earthen mound with a flat top, the motte, would be surrounded by a deep ditch and might carry a timber tower, and if the top were large enough, its lip might be surrounded by a timber palisade with a fighting platform. The ditch would be spanned either by a timber bridge, crossing the moat at ground level and leading to steps ascending the motte, or by a flying bridge, carried on trestles to the top of the motte. Where possible, natural mounds would be scarped to provide the optimum slope: normally close to 40 degrees. Northampton's early motte was given a covering of clay to improve its stability, but at Little Houghton, one side of the motte appears to have collapsed possibly never having been effectively stabilised. The alternative to the motte was the ringwork, a bank and ditch enclosing a courtyard in which a hall, kitchen, barns, stables, and chapel might be built, and pretty much what some Saxon thegns appear to have been building prior to the Conquest (see Chapter 1). Both mottes and ringworks could have one or more additional banked and ditched enclosures known as baileys. The motte would often only have room for a tower, so all the domestic buildings would be located in the bailey. The motte offered greater height for both vigilance and dominance, but the ringwork afforded more spacious accommodation. The choice of style appears to have been arbitrary. In Northamptonshire, there were twice as many mottes as there were ringworks, and it is fairly clear that those castles built between 1066 and 1086 by the incoming Normans, and in the next century as their grip on the country was consolidated, were of these two types. Northampton was both, starting as a small motte, which was then subsumed into the ringwork. Of the same period, Little Houghton, Fotheringhay, and Rockingham, all sited to command river crossings rather than towns, had larger mottes. The work of the Round Mounds Project has recently dated the mottes at Fotheringhay and Little Houghton by radio-carbon dating techniques finding a date for both castles as from mid- to late eleventh century to mid-twelfth century. These early castles were intended to dominate their setting, reinforcing royal authority and representing the local seat of power.

Northampton gained its importance by virtue of where it sat in the Midlands at the junction of several Roman roads, and close to Watling Street (now the A5) for long, one of England's most important arteries. It linked London to Chester and North Wales, the ports of the north-west, and represented one of the two main routes into Scotland. Forced to avoid the Fenlands on the east and the wild Welsh Marches to the west, armies tended to take this middle route, one later adopted by both canal and railway engineers. As was the case in many other county towns selected as the locations for early Norman castles, Saxon houses were cleared away to create space in Northampton. Built by Simon de Senlis around 1084, Northampton's castle consisted of a small motte with a bailey. De Senlis had become the first Norman earl of Northampton, by taking a wife of important lineage. Her father was the Count of Mortain and, more importantly, her mother was Judith, widow of the last Saxon earl of Northampton, and a niece of William the Conqueror who, himself, held nearly sixty manors in the county. In the early years of the twelfth century, Northampton Castle passed to the crown and underwent an ambitious rebuild under Henry I. The motte was absorbed into the north-eastern rampart of an enormous ringwork, which formed the Inner Bailey, while outer baileys were added to north and south, their moats fed by the adjacent River Nene. The impressive banks of the ringwork were 80 feet (25 metres) wide and 20 feet (6 metres) high, above a ditch 90 feet (28 metres) wide and 30 feet (9 metres) deep. The entire castle with its outer earthworks extended over an area measuring 350 × 250 yards, occupying a larger than usual share of the town's real estate. Reflecting its royal ownership, geographical position and status as one of the largest towns in England, this rebuild provided the Inner Bailey with a curtain wall, mural towers, and two gatehouses, all in stone, as were many of the domestic buildings. Simon Senlis II briefly regained possession of the castle from King Stephen, but when the de Senlis line died out by *c.* 1185, it reverted to the crown as one of Henry II's principal fortresses. One of the defining characteristics of Norman castles was the keep, usually a large square or rectangular stone tower, often built on the motte once the earth had settled. Although Northampton has sometimes been depicted as having such a keep, there is no archaeological evidence of the necessarily massive foundations to support this supposition. The substantial stone tower with three buttresses abutting the western wall of the Inner Bailey would appear to be the nearest Northampton Castle came to having a keep. Speed's map of 1610 shows a strong inner bailey with prominent mural towers. The main entrance into the Inner Bailey was to the north, where a rectangular tower was pierced by a gate passage. The contemporaneous gatehouse between the Inner and the South Baileys was of unusual plan. Contained in an L-shaped tower, which straddled the inner curtain, the entrance passage itself described a dog-leg, a feature often found in ancient hillforts, but less common in the medieval context. The river wall containing the large buttressed tower required shoring up after the inner bailey was levelled and the weight of earth caused it to collapse. The postern gate adjacent to the tower is now repositioned near to the railway station. The royal apartments were located on the eastern side of the Inner Bailey; a large hall built in fine ashlar masonry stood in the western corner; and a stone building has been excavated in the Outer Bailey. An outer gatehouse probably stood in the Outer Bailey's south-east angle. Speed depicts a spur wall and what appears to have been a mill where the southern bailey meets the river.

The motte and bailey castle at Rockingham, built at the express command of William I, appears to have employed a different technique for spreading the load. The motte, 30 feet (9 metres) high and 100 feet (31 metres) across, was topped by a shell keep, where the original palisade encircling the summit of the motte was replaced in stone with pentices built around the inside. This keep measured 80 feet (24 metres) across, with eighteen sides outwardly and a hexagonal inner courtyard corresponding to the six main penthouse chambers. A timber bridge with a drawbridge crossed the moat and stairs ascended to a gatehouse in the shell wall. Other domestic buildings were situated in the baileys, with a simple stone gatehouse, later made much grander, controlling access. A similar arrangement obtained at Fotheringhay, another castle built by Simon de Senlis, where the D-shaped shell keep, in a seventeenth-century description dubbed 'the fetterlock', was served by a well in its circular central courtyard, and accessed by a covered stone stairway with gates at top and bottom. Higham Ferrers castle was built soon after 1066 by William Peverel on a site, north of the church, now occupied by a quadrangle of alms-houses. It originally consisted of earthworks of unknown form, for those impressive banks and 'moats' remaining today are fishponds rather than defences. What was once identified as an L-shaped moat on the east side was, in fact, two separate rectangular ponds connected by narrow channels but with no corresponding feature on the west. Later owners built in stone, but all has long disappeared, save for some limestone slabs, found in the paddock, south of the southern arm of the moat, and a later dovecote.

Other Northamptonshire castles also had their initial earthwork defences rebuilt in stone within a generation or two. At Alderton, standing next to the much later church, is the ringwork known as the Mount, possibly established by Robert, Count of Mortain, in the later eleventh century, and recorded in 1226. Although a *Time Team* excavation revealed little of note in 2000, subsequent work reported in the Castle Studies

Fotheringhay Castle: the massive motte, now bereft of the 'Fetterlock' tower that once crowned its summit.

Little Houghton: the largest motte in the county appears never to have carried any significant structure, probably due to the instability indicated by its partial collapse.

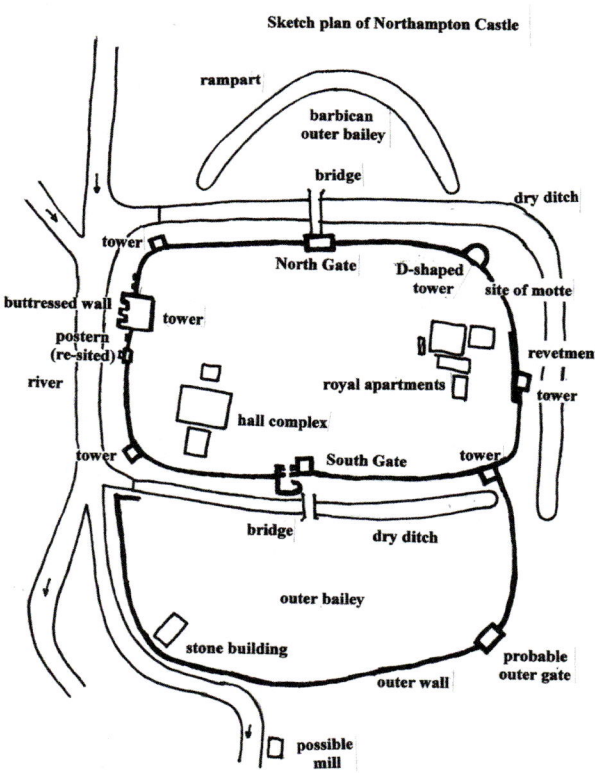

Sketch plan of Northampton Castle

rampart

barbican
outer bailey

bridge

dry ditch

tower

North Gate

D-shaped
tower

site of motte

buttressed wall

tower

postern
(re-sited)

revetment
tower

river

royal apartments

hall complex

tower

South Gate

tower

bridge

dry ditch

outer bailey

stone building

probable
outer gate

outer wall

possible
mill

Above: Culworth: the bank and ditch of this early ringwork.

Left: Northampton Castle: sketch plan of this now mainly vanished fortress.

Bulletin 24 (2010–11) and in Northamptonshire Archaeology 37 (2012) found a platform constructed in the first half of the twelfth century, with a stone building in the southern half that remained in occupation for 200 years. A robbed wall provided evidence for a defensive structure, apparently a stone curtain that may date from the time of the Anarchy. Castle Dykes at Farthingstone has been widely described as a ringwork, but RCHM(E) calls it a motte, attributing its hollowed-out centre to eighteenth-century quarrying. This central feature almost bisects the narrow principal bailey, effectively producing two inner baileys, one to each side. An outer, D-shaped bailey, possibly prehistoric in origin, lies to the north. Evidence for the castle's clear possession of significant, possibly vaulted, stone structures, has been recorded on site.

Towcester may represent an example of a further refinement of the defences of the motte. A few castle builders solved the problem of settlement by mounting the timber tower on posts planted on rocky or otherwise stable ground with the motte piled up around them. Rarer still was a stone basement, embedded in the motte with a stone or timber superstructure rising through the layers of earth. The presence here of a 15-yard-long vaulted stone passage through the base of the mound could represent the entrance to a stone tower encased within the motte. It has also been suggested that the Bury Mount at Towcester was built over the Roman east gate, providing an equally plausible explanation.

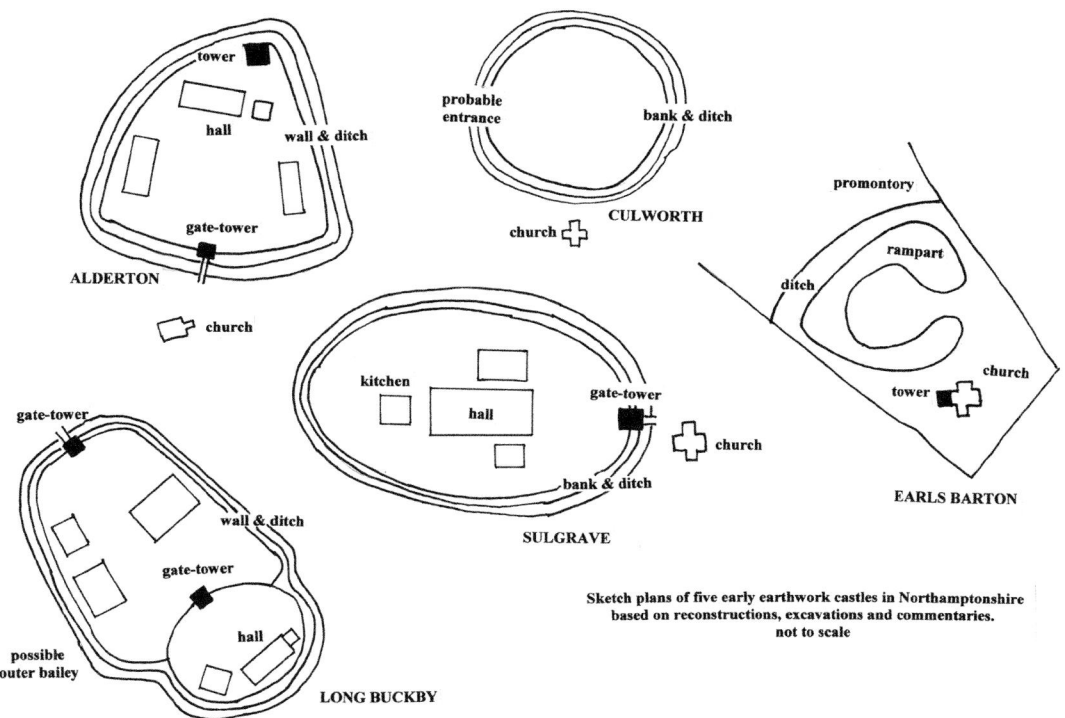

Sketch plans of five early earthwork castles in Northamptonshire based on reconstructions, excavations and commentaries. not to scale

Earthwork castles: sketch plans of five early earthwork castles.

Other motte and bailey castles of the period to 1215 include Lilbourne, Sibbertoft, Little Houghton, and Thrapston. Lilbourne, occupying a site close to where Watling Street crosses the River Avon, has a conical motte, 23 feet (7.25 metres) high, with a ditch and a bailey on the north-east side. A second, much larger bailey lies on the uphill side to the south-east, its ditch 84 feet (25.5 metres) across on the east, forming a raised rectangular platform with a massive bank and ditch on three sides, rising above the motte. Small, raised mounds at two of its corners may indicate the former presence of timber towers. In contrast, Castle Yard, Sibbertoft, occupies a remote site, 500 feet (155 metres) above sea-level, on a spur between two streams over half a mile (1 km) distant from the village. It consists of a motte, and on the flat uphill side, a quadrant-shaped bailey. The motte at Little Houghton is remarkable for its sheer mass. It rises to a height of 60 feet (18 metres) above the ditch, 16 feet (5 metres) deep in places, making it one of the largest mottes in the country. Its surface measures a generous 100 × 70 feet (30 × 20 metres) but there are no traces of structures. Neither is there a discernible bailey, only a counter-scarp bank. Its position on the south bank of the Nene would suggest that it was intended to guard a crossing-point, but signs of a partial structural collapse may point to its failure to thrive. At what may represent the lost castle of Thrapston, indications of a stone building, either on or within the large, artificial mound, once surrounded by a ditch, were identified in the 1970s and reported in RCHM(E)'s Inventory.

At Sulgrave, the Saxon building within its unfinished turf rampart was taken over by a Norman lord, Ghilo of Picquigni, who adapted it to his own requirements, raising the ramparts to such a level that the weight of earth began to destroy the buildings within. The detached stone tower was brought into play briefly as a gatehouse, but was subsequently swallowed up by the massive bank. In addition to the earlier ringworks at Culworth, Sulgrave, Stowe Nine Churches, Earls Barton, and Weedon Lois, there were a number of others in the county. Long Buckby is an oval ringwork inside a triangular bailey, with a rampart 13 feet (4 metres) high and a shallow ditch. It dates from the mid-twelfth century and was possibly built by the de Quincy family, later earls of Winchester. A pre- or immediate post-Conquest enclosure on the west was superseded by first a wall, and then a bank with a deep ditch. A small twelfth-century stone building stood inside the wall, and later, a curtain wall was built around the bailey. There may have been an eastern bailey, now also destroyed. The castle was built to protect an earlier, possibly Saxon settlement on a different site from the present village. At Preston Capes, a ringwork, 23 feet (7 metres) high with a flat top 90 feet (27 metres) in diameter, with ditches on the north marking a probable bailey, was in existence by 1090. Nearby at Little Preston, a site mentioned in 1235 when a chapel existed beside the manor-house of William de Montacute, a ditch of defensive proportions may indicate an earthwork castle, possibly another ringwork rather than a motte. Beside Benefield church is the moated platform of a ringwork licensed before 1208. At some stage, it was walled in stone, the ruins of which were still visible in the early 1700s. There are no traces of buildings on the platform, and it had fallen out of use by 1315, become ruinous by 1378, and then replaced by a later manor-house to the north. The design of the eleventh-century castle at Castle Ashby, or of that at Aynho, each buried under later mansions, remain unknowable. To the north of Moulton church, Castle Hill was held by the Fitz John family in the thirteenth century. The traces of a moat have been found around a circular natural knoll, possibly adapted as a motte, bearing the foundations of a masonry structure.

The Anarchy 1135–54, and the Reigns of Henry II and his Sons

On 8 September 1131, a large gathering of bishops and barons met at Northampton Castle to swear fealty to Matilda, daughter and chosen successor to Henry I, promising to ensure her smooth journey to the throne when her father died. By the time of Henry's death in 1135, however, many of the barons had reneged on their oaths and were supporting Henry's nephew, Stephen. When Matilda landed to claim her throne, the two opposing parties launched into a civil war, known since as the Anarchy. Simon II of Senlis was one of Stephen's most staunch supporters, and Northamptonshire lay on the western fringe of Stephen's territory. It faced Matilda's territory, which would include Oxford until it was captured in 1142, seven years into the conflict. At Eastertide 1138, Stephen held court at Northampton but, returning to celebrate Easter 1141, he was so ill that rumours of his death began to spread. The struggle would last nineteen long years and dominance shifted continually from one side to the other. Its most significant effect, however, lay not in the alternating victories and defeats for the main protagonists in the course of set-piece battles or sieges, but in the misery inflicted on the general population by the breakdown of royal authority. This power vacuum allowed local warlords to terrorise the population through intimidation, extortion, and general banditry. Although leaders negotiated treaties that limited the fighting, few were able, or willing, to exert pressure on those exploiting the prevailing lawlessness. One example of a local agreement was the declaration of a demilitarized zone around Leicester, forbidding the construction of new castles, its south-west corner being anchored on Rockingham. The construction of temporary earth and timber castles was but one manifestation of the collapse of legitimate authority, and it would be one of Henry II's first tasks as new king to ensure that many of these unregulated symbols of chaos were destroyed.

One of the problems of assigning earthwork castles to specific events is the difficulty of dating. Sadly, one castle that can definitively be linked to the Anarchy by documentary evidence has entirely vanished. This was the castle of Gaultney, or Galclint, probably only consisting of earthworks with timber buildings and located to the east of Rushton on land later developed for open-cast mining. It was owned by William d'Albini but taken in 1140 by Alan of Brittany. When Alan was himself captured by the earl of Chester, he was starved until he gave way and ordered his garrison to surrender. Plausible evidence of military activity at a strategic site dominating Watling Street may be found near to Lilbourne. The small, ditched motte, 24 feet (7.5 metres) high and with a flat top some 50 feet (15 metres) across, lying half a mile (800 metres) to the west of the main castle, may represent a siege castle, sheltering the besiegers and helping to enforce a blockade. As well as the work that we have already seen at Alderton, other possible castles of this era include Towcester, Hymel, and Wollaston. At Wollaston, a motte bearing the foundations of a stone building, and with traces of a small bailey, was erected in the twelfth century but had been displaced by a windmill by the turn of the century. Hymel or Hely Castle was built by the Engayne family to control the Stamford–Northampton road but had been abandoned and demolished prior to their establishment, by 1208, of the Augustinian monastery of Fineshade.

The succession question was finally settled when Matilda's son, Henry, became king in 1154 and it was ironic that his attempt to avoid a repeat of the conflict around his mother's disputed succession was itself to be the cause of further civil war. By having his eldest son crowned, Henry produced only frustration when he failed to bestow land or specific responsibilities to go with his crown. Consequently, the young king raised a rebellion involving King William the Lion of Scotland whose brother, David, held land in the counties of the East Midlands. Earl David raided Northampton, the most important royal castle in the area, and although it proved too strong to capture, a sally by the garrison and townsfolk suffered heavy casualties in driving him off. Ultimately, Henry II's forces triumphed and in July 1174, the rebels were summoned to Northampton to surrender, a process that included the public humiliation of the Scottish king. In 1176, at the Assize of Northampton, the demolition of some twenty castles across the country was ordered. The motte and bailey castle at Brackley had already been destroyed on the orders of Henry II in 1173. Excavations have revealed two stone-lined cellars, accessed by steps, and dating from the twelfth or thirteenth centuries. They may, therefore, postdate the castle itself. Additionally, this rebellion caused the defences of Northampton Castle to be repaired. Spurious mottes such as Barby, Canons Ashby, the second earthwork at Little Houghton, and Cransley have sometimes been assigned to the Anarchy but may never have been fortifications at all.

In 1095, the council of Rockingham had attempted, unsuccessfully as it happened, to resolve a problem of conflicting allegiance, concerning the appointment of Anselm as Archbishop of Canterbury and the relative power, in the matter, of William Rufus and Pope Urban II. The resulting stalemate would drag on into another reign and another century, serving to foreshadow an infamous repeat. Henry II spent time at Northampton during every year of his reign that he spent in England, a total of fifteen visits, and in 1164, it was to Northampton Castle that Henry summoned Thomas à Becket, the long-term friend whose appointment as Archbishop of Canterbury he had secured, to appear before the Great Council as the culmination of protracted disputes over the boundaries of secular and ecclesiastical authority. Here, Becket would face charges of feudal disobedience, and be forced to tap into the financial resources of the church in order to mollify Henry, who regarded Becket's intransigence over political issues as personal disloyalty. Despite his colleagues' support in producing the money that Henry purportedly required, it soon became obvious that nothing less than Becket's resignation would appease Henry. Refusing to knuckle under, Becket managed, against the king's orders, to quit the town and escape into temporary exile in France. Only after six years was a fragile reconciliation effected, but since neither party was willing to compromise over deeply held but conflicting principles, fresh disputes soon arose. Henry's intemperate outburst holding his household knights responsible for allowing Becket's defiance to go unchecked was interpreted by four of Henry's knights as a cue to murder this upstart, low-born priest. They crossed the Channel and murdered Becket in the cathedral at Canterbury. One of those knights, Sir Reginald fitzUrse, generally held to be the group's leader, came from Bulwick and held lands in the county.

Northampton hosted a further important meeting of barons and bishops in 1176 when, at the Assizes of Northampton, elements of the regulation of property disputes were laid down and made accessible to litigants through the royal chancery via a regular circuit of visiting royal justices. In 1177, Henry restored the lands of many who had supported the young king in his rebellion of 1173–4. With another such rebellion in full swing in Aquitaine in 1183, Henry ensured that it would not be allowed to spread into England. He strengthened the defences of Northampton Castle and his justices prosecuted some townsfolk who were accused of preparing for war by buying hauberks and communicating with the king's enemies.

In January 1188, Henry II and Philip II of France used their plans to go on crusade together as a basis for their reconciliation. Within a few weeks, Henry had called a council at Geddington to announce the 'Saladin Tithe', which would finance the operation, and recruiting began there and then. Richard of Poitou, later the 'Lionheart', angered his father by signing up, but after Henry's death in 1189, he would be one of the leaders of that Third Crusade. The Geddington Council, as in similar meetings around Europe, both determined the means of raising finance and set down the rules governing the crusaders' conduct on the road and the safeguards for their families and property in their absence. In 1189, on one of his infrequent visits to England, Richard held the very first council of his reign at Pipewell Abbey near Desborough. In 1194, he had been forcibly detained in Austria during his return from crusade, and an enormous ransom was being demanded for his release. A wholly disproportionate amount had been levied on England's Jewish communities, and Northampton, with one of England's five largest Jewish populations, hosted a meeting to work out how to meet this unreasonable demand. After Richard's death in France in 1199, those most suspected of plotting resistance to John's succession were summoned to Northampton to assert their loyalty to the new regime. Northampton was also the scene of a meeting between John and King William of Scotland, who tried, unsuccessfully, to extort Northumbria as his price for supporting John's claim against his nephew, Arthur of Brittany. In 1202, the prisoners taken during one of John's few successful continental campaigns were distributed across a dozen royal castles including Northampton.

In 1205, John brought his army to Northampton, *en route* to Portsmouth for his abortive invasion of France. Disgusted by the king's incompetence, the barons sabotaged this invasion by refusing to fight in John's lost French domains. In 1209, a further meeting with William the Lion was fixed with Northampton as a possible venue, but the Scottish king's health meant that John travelled to Scotland in the end. Later that year, Northampton was proposed as the location for negotiations with the papal delegates seeking a resolution to the perennial dispute, now between John and Innocent III regarding the appointment of an archbishop of Canterbury. In 1210, Northampton joined John's new network of decentralized offices of the Exchequer, designed to make his tax-gathering machinery ever more efficient. In 1211, the dispute with the pope plumbed new depths when the papal legate, Pandulf Verraccio, dictated his master's non-negotiable terms to a full council at Northampton.

Castles in the Thirteenth Century

By the beginning of the century, the three major castles of Northampton, Rockingham, and Fotheringhay had largely assumed their final form, although improvements would be made to their domestic arrangements, along with repairs to damage caused by the sieges of the Barons' Wars. At Rockingham, a survey of 1250 for Henry III revealed defensive weaknesses as there were cracks in the walls, leaking roofs, and rotten gutters, rendering the fortress indefensible. In 1255, the king ordered that the height of the keep's outer wall should be raised by 6 feet (1.85 metres), and parapet walks renewed. From 1276, further improvements were made by Edward I, and these probably included the new gatehouse with its twin D-shaped towers, and the addition of a further tower at the north-west angle. Northampton, too, received urgent attention to its defences. In

Rockingham Castle: the massive gatehouse with its twin drum towers added to the existing gateway of *c.* 1200, in the reign of Edward I, probably *c.* 1283.

Rockingham Castle: the curtain wall adjacent to the gatehouse showing cruciform arrow loops.

1248, the palisade of the outer bailey had been repaired, but it was the western wall of the Inner Bailey, above the river, which gave most cause for concern. Despite a series of repairs, it was only after a major collapse in 1266 that it was rebuilt.

Fotheringhay, in need of renovation, passed to the crown in 1294. Higham Ferrers came into the possession of the House of Lancaster in 1266, and the existing buildings were maintained in good order.

Although it is possible that the Le Moyne family, tenants of Ramsey Abbey, had an earlier moated residence in Barnwell, their new build of 1264–6 was of revolutionary design. Taking advantage of the distractions of the Barons' Wars, Berengar Le Moyne built a quadrangular castle with round corner towers and a twin-towered gatehouse on a new site and without explicit royal approval. The curtain walls, 30 feet (9 metres) high and initially thinner but subsequently thickened to 11¾ feet (3.6 metres), enclose a rectangular courtyard measuring 130 feet × 88 feet (40 metres × 27 metres). Lean-tos against the curtain walls housed the castle's domestic offices. The circular, two-storey corner towers, all furnished with arrow-loops commanding the curtain, were either one storey higher originally or, more likely, unfinished. The south-east tower combines with the two D-shaped gate towers to create a formidable entrance, liberally equipped with cross-shaped loops, and with all three towers having vaulted basements. Both the two northern towers have semi-circular projections containing latrines and spiral staircases. This quadrangular design may be the earliest example in England of a style imported from France, and which would become a common feature of some of

Barnwell Castle: the tri-lobed gatehouse and, to its left, the south-west tower.

Barnwell Castle: the north-east tower with its garderobe projection.

Edward I's Welsh castles. The date evidence for Barnwell comes from an inquiry into legal issues surrounding the castle's construction; Le Moyne may have needed to raise funds, or it is possible that Henry III had taken exception to the construction of a stronghold appearing under the royal radar. For whatever reason, Le Moyne appears only to have been in residence for around ten tears, as the castle soon reverted to Ramsey Abbey for use as a grange.

The First Barons' War, 1215–16

In 1212, as a result of being suspected of plotting against King John, Earl David of Huntingdon, younger brother of William the Lion, King of Scotland, was required to hand over Fotheringhay Castle and to deliver his second son as a hostage against his good behaviour, but appears to have delayed the handover. The next year, as John's relationship with his subjects deteriorated even further, it was at Northampton that Stephen Langton, Archbishop of Canterbury, reminded the king that his sworn commitment to good government would be jeopardized were he to go to war against his subjects. John promised that he would meet with his barons at Northampton at Easter,

1215, but chose instead to remain in London, while the refurbishment of the defences of his royal castles continued apace, supplied with much of the timber for these works by the royal forests of Northamptonshire. Meanwhile, the barons, many of them from England's more northerly counties, gathered together to oppose John, assembling in Stamford before moving south to Brackley to join with their allies from East Anglia. John, who was in Dorset, sent representatives to Brackley to hear the rebels' demands, which related to the laws of the land: inheritance, military service, justice, and the forest laws. John promptly and angrily rejected these, accusing his barons of being faithless and treasonous, which irrational response pushed the barons into renouncing their fealty to him. Their next move was to attempt to retake some of those castles that John had fortified against them, investing Northampton Castle. John had undertaken extensive repairs here, earlier in the year, putting it into a state of defence, and rendering it a much more significant target than many other royal strongholds. Not only had the defences been strengthened, but 10,000 crossbow bolts had been deposited in the castle along with plentiful supplies of wheat and salted pork. Additionally, the garrison was led by an experienced captain, Geoffrey de Martigny, a close relative of John's mercenary leaders, and bought in specifically to safeguard royal power. Not only had John ensured that his castles were well supplied with victuals and munitions, he had also provided catapults and ballistae for their defence. While the rebels enjoyed some success at lesser fortresses, their lack of siege engines prevented them from taking Northampton, which was too strong to storm and too well-provisioned to be starved quickly into submission. After two weeks, the siege was raised, but only after the standard-bearer of one of the rebel leaders, Robert fitzWalter, had been shot through the head by a crossbow bolt. The barons moved on to Bedford, held by a castellan sympathetic to the barons' cause, and thence on to secure London ahead of the king. The signing of Magna Carta in June was an attempt to reconcile John's autocratic kingship and the barons' ambitions. Ironically, this attempt to avoid head-on confrontation leading to civil war actually precipitated conflict that, were John to backslide on his promises, was the barons' sole sanction. Wanting to see property, purloined by the crown, restored to its rightful owners, and simultaneously seeking to limit the king's military power, the barons pushed for the permanent surrender of five prominent royal castles, including Northampton. By July, some of the provisions of the Charter were in process of being implemented. De Martigny, one of those few specifically picked out in Magna Carta as undesirables, was indeed instructed to surrender Northampton Castle, but rather than sending him home with other hated mercenary captains, John summoned him to his side, along with his troops. Rockingham, which John had obtained as part of a forfeit and used as a residence for his chief forester, Hugh de Neville, was returned to William Mauduit's son. Despite their apparent success over the king, there was still distrust. It was decided that John should go to Oxford while the barons gathered in Brackley. The bishops would then mediate between the two parties. However, in the midst of conflicting messages from Rome, John decided to leave the country. In the resultant power vacuum, the barons divvied up the royal lands, Northamptonshire being assigned to Robert fitzWalter. The rebellion quickly escalated into a full civil war with the Dauphin of France, whom the barons had invited to take up the crown of England, bringing an army across the Channel in May 1216. By the autumn, John was clearly losing the war but continued to campaign backwards and forwards across the country, his support steadily eroding. In October, he was in Northamptonshire, marching on Rockingham and burning Oundle on his way eastwards to the Wash. He had just crossed over from King's Lynn (Norfolk), when he was taken ill and died at Newark-upon-Trent (Nottinghamshire).

At the beginning of the reign of John's eldest son, nine-year-old Henry III, Northampton—one of a string of royal castles held by Falkes de Breauté—remained under his control from the time of its relief in 1215 through to 1223. John had also managed to regain Rockingham, which was then held by William de Fortibus (or Forz), Count of Aumale, until he was forced to relinquish it to Henry III in 1220, after a siege by Hubert de Burgh. Fotheringhay was held by rebels but surrendered to John le Scot, Earl of Huntingdon, in 1220, having been attacked by Henry III's regent, William Marshall. One result of his father's troubles was the decision by Henry III and his advisers to ban by royal decree those ten tournaments scheduled for Northampton between 1214 and 1249. This was indicative of both kings' reluctance to countenance informal assemblies of their volatile barons. While the anarchic events of the latter years of John's reign were much reduced, there were still opportunities for baronial misdemeanours. In 1217, the new king celebrated his, or rather William Marshall's, victory over the rebels at the Battle of Lincoln by summoning any recalcitrant barons to his court at Northampton to surrender those castles they held in his name. Falkes de Breauté, one of John's former captains, was one of those who refused. Another who resisted was the notorious William de Fortibus, Earl of Albemarle (or Aumale), who was determined to hang on to Rockingham. The order to lay siege to him there gave de Breauté the opportunity to prove his loyalty. It took a surprise assault to capture the castle but six months later, de Fortibus next seized Fotheringhay Castle by crossing the frozen moat and forcing the gate. He was evicted from there, too, but in 1223, de Fortibus was plotting to seize the Tower of London and Henry III and his officers sought refuge in Northampton Castle. A year later, de Breauté was still defiant, abducting Henry of Braybrooke, one of the king's justices. After this act of overt rebellion, Henry III was given no option but to attack him. Using timber from the royal forests, the king's army had siege engines built in Northampton, and marched on de Breauté's castle of Bedford, then held by his brother, William. After a siege lasting eight weeks, the castle was stormed and William and his eighty defenders were hanged as an example. De Breauté himself finally surrendered at Northampton and was exiled to Normandy by the young king. After this, Albemarle also submitted to the king, staying loyal until his death in 1242.

Further Barons' Wars, 1264

Simon de Montfort led many of the barons in rebellion against Henry III who was accused of reneging on his agreement to implement constitutional reforms. Having won a battle at Lewes (Sussex) in April 1264 and having extracted concessions from the king, de Montfort held a strong position in London, with his main support spread across East Anglia and the Midlands. His son, Simon de Montfort II, currently held the hitherto royal stronghold of Northampton. Henry—at Oxford with many of those barons remaining loyal to him, including the local de la Zouches—perceived Northampton as a target ripe for the taking and knew that the rebels would not willingly relinquish their grip on London until they were more certain of his intentions. He therefore set out for

Northampton hoping for a quick strike before help might arrive. Henry's army, led by his son, The Lord Edward, immediately launched an assault on the town's South Gate, possibly masked by a feint on the north-western sector of the walls, which bounded the priory of St Andrew's. Not only had the walls here been reported as being in a poor state of repair, but the prior facilitated the royalists' entry, resulting in Henry's troops capturing the town without difficulty. The young de Montfort attempted to stem the attack by riding into the breach with some mounted knights but with only temporary success. Edward was soon in control of both town and castle, and the town was sacked by the royalist army. Using this new base as a springboard for regaining ground lost to the rebels, Edward quickly took Nottingham and Lincoln. From 1265, Northampton provided the secure base from which the prolonged siege of Kenilworth Castle (Warwickshire) was conducted, becoming the royal headquarters. In the meantime, under cover of the violent activity in the area caused by the Barons' War, Robert de Ferrers, Earl of Derby, had launched an unsuccessful attack on Fotheringhay in 1264.

After all this disruption, for the nobility at least, normal service was quickly resumed. The king's antipathy to warlike pursuits was overcome by his martial heir, The Lord Edward, and Northampton, previously sanctioned by Richard I as one of only five sites named as tournament venues, got on with organising these pageants of chivalry. Brackley had been added to the list of official venues in 1232, and in 1249, things had got out of hand there, when the two sides in the mêlée, traditionally representing locals *versus* the rest, became disorganised, causing total confusion. However, insecure kings were apt to discourage gatherings of their untrustworthy barons and the Northampton tournament of 1323 was one of only a few held in the reign of Edward II, and in 1328, a proposed tournament was banned to ensure that the magnates had no excuse for not attending parliament. The Northampton tournament of 1330 passed off without incident but that in 1342 saw John of Beaumont, the brother-in-law of Henry of Grosmont, Duke of Lancaster, and one of Edward III's most important captains, killed, aged twenty-four. In the particularly bloody fighting, described as *hastiludes* ('spear-games' perhaps), many other participants were seriously injured. It was not only the nobility at risk of violent death out of a blue sky. Homicide figures for the thirteenth century suggest that one was twenty times more likely to be killed, and probably by a stranger, than nowadays.

The Fortunes of Town and County in the Dangerous Fourteenth Century

Northampton ranked twelfth in wealth at the time of Domesday, rising to sixth a century later. The town's population peaked at just under 4,000 around 1300, having more than trebled in the preceding two centuries. The hundred years between 1240 and 1340 may be considered the summit of Northampton's prosperity, founded largely on the wool trade as abbeys such as Peterborough had begun the process of establishing large flocks from the mid-twelfth century. Northampton, as we have seen, had figured significantly in the affairs of the nation through the preceding two centuries and was to play a part in the troubled reign of Edward II and the regency of his wife, Isabella. Parliament met at Northampton in 1308, and in 1317, Edward's court was at the royal hunting lodge of Kingscliffe, prior to a further parliamentary session in Northampton in 1318. A pretender, named Dreydras, purporting to be the true king himself, was brought before Edward, accusing him of being a changeling. Under torture, he confessed that he had been put up to the scheme by the devil in the guise of a cat. Both the impostor and, somewhat unjustly, the cat were promptly executed. After Edward's own reported death in 1327, and the accession of their son as Edward III, Rockingham Castle was among the many properties assigned to Isabella as compensation for her husband's cruelty. Despite clear offence caused by Isabella's avarice and the undisguised vanity of her unofficial consort, Mortimer, the queen mother was not generally held responsible for her husband's disappearance. In 1328, the Treaty of Northampton brought an end to the expensive and distracting conflict with Robert the Bruce's Scotland, but was held to be shameful and disgraceful, and all the fault of Isabella and Mortimer. By the terms of the treaty, Scotland was granted independence; Edward III's younger sister, Joan, was given in marriage to Bruce's heir; and the restoration of the Stone of Scone to the Scots was promised. At the same time, Isabella and Mortimer sought to strengthen the royal authority eroded throughout the course of Edward II's reign with the Statute of Northampton. Its admirable provisions included preventing defendants attending court accompanied by armed men; placing limits on those pardons and grants issued under the Privy Seal; extending the powers of justices of the peace; and requiring royal officials both to conduct their business fairly and to maintain the king's peace. But all this was happening in a climate of constant violence exemplified in 1328 by the attempt by the earl of Lancaster, at the head of troops from his castle of Higham Ferrers, to abduct the young Edward III on his way from Northampton. Isabella herself was to contravene the Statute when she issued writs under the Privy Seal to protect her supporters from prosecution, a blatant act that undermined the very JPs whose integrity and authority she had been purporting to promote. In the aftermath of Edward III's coup against Mortimer, he and his mother held court at Northampton and Kingscliffe three times in 1329 and 1330. Once Isabella had regained a more secure position from which to settle her affairs, she granted the manor of Brigstock to the advocate, Sir Henry Green, a key member of her household.

After this time, Northampton began a gradual decline, suffering catastrophic losses in the Great Plague of 1348, from which its population would not recover for another 300 years, and losing out in a serious dispute with the king over tolls. During the reign of Richard II (1377–1399), just one parliament, which would be its last, was held in Northampton. Instead of meeting in the castle as was usual, parliament gathered at the church of All Saints and the king lodged outside the town at Moulton. This neutral venue was chosen as an alternative to London where trouble was expected as the main business was the reimposition, for the third year running, of the hated Poll Tax and full-scale rebellion was only a year away. Alongside the general grievances against the king's officers, discontent with the abuses of the clergy was also gaining ground, much of it led by the Lollards, the followers of John Wycliffe, a preacher whose ideas anticipated later protestant movements. Two local knights, Sir Thomas Latimer of Braybrooke (a knight in the household of Joan, the queen mother) and Sir John Trussel of Flore, were especially active in their support for Lollardry. Joan, like her brother-in-law, John of Gaunt, was sympathetic to the Lollard movement attempting to shield its adherents from persecution. In 1389, the Sheriff of Northampton was ordered to arrest nearly fifty people at Latimer's manor of Chipping Warden, as they had ignored the bishop of Lincoln's warnings over their heretical beliefs. Persecution of suspected Lollards continued in 1392 when townspeople were imprisoned in Northampton Castle.

Religious and political tensions were accompanied by social and economic woes. Rural Northamptonshire had traditionally derived much of its wealth from operating the 'Champion' form of agriculture, which had originated in the ninth century. This combined the collective cultivation of arable open fields with the raising of livestock for food and for maintaining the fertilisation of the land. By establishing nucleated settlements, the necessary labour could be mobilised, generally under the auspices of a feudal landowner. But the success of this system was brought to a standstill by climatic change, in the form of the Little Ice Age, causing famines from 1315–22, when the harvest failed in successive years. In 1315, twenty-three prisoners starved to death in Northampton jail. This recession had been followed by a partial recovery, which was brought to a halt by the Great Plague of 1348–9 with further outbreaks in 1361 and 1368–9. Owing to its position straddling major routes, exposed to infection brought by travellers, the county was particularly hard-hit with half the clergy dying, and the death of around a third of the population taking large areas of land out of cultivation as communities directed their depleted energies into only the more productive lands. In addition, markets collapsed and some settlements continued only greatly reduced in size or disappeared altogether, like Hale, a hamlet in the parish of Apethorpe, which had gone by 1356. The effects of such economic and social catastrophe were particularly noticeable in 'Champion' areas, which had been not only self-sufficient but also able to trade a surplus of grain, meat, leather, and wool. The colder, wetter climate also accelerated a move from arable or woodland to pasture, where sheep were raised on large estates and common land began to be enclosed by landowners. Between 1350 and 1500, some eighty villages in the county became shrunken or were depopulated completely in order to increase the number of flocks. Little Oxendon declined from a thriving village with fifty over-fourteens paying the Poll Tax in 1377, only a generation after the Great Plague, to a huddle of eight survivors in 1405. The lands of a village like Church Charwelton, for instance, could yield grazing for 1,500 sheep. Such economic pressure was exacerbated by the flat-rate Poll Tax, which impacted most on the poor, and all these factors together caused peasant unrest, culminating in the Great Rebellion. Although many of the agitators and leaders were nearer to being bourgeoisie, as ever, it was the 'Peasants' who got the blame. A study of homicides in Northamptonshire in the fourteenth century has shown that murders were carried out predominantly by 'middling peasants'—tradesmen, clergy, or servants; mainly as a result of sudden altercations; and in the majority of cases with knives. Unless the alleged murderer was a member of the victim's family, he was unlikely to face justice, let alone be penalised.

The third collection of Poll Tax dues in early 1381 revealed a significant shortfall as large numbers of previous payers, up to 50 per cent in some counties, now disappeared from the rolls. Northamptonshire was one of a *tranche* of nine counties whose sheriffs were instructed to enforce a proper collection of the tax, ensuring that no one might avoid payment. This was despite the fact that much of the *raison d'être* for the revenue had evaporated when failures of leadership caused the latest military expedition to France to be aborted. Trouble flared up initially in Essex and rapidly attracted support from neighbouring counties, leading to a march on London and the famous confrontation between Richard II and Wat Tyler, resulting in the latter's death. In the belief that the king supported their actions, men returned to their villages to raise support for further demonstrations of discontent with the establishment. Within days of the dispersal of the rebels, the king sent out an appeal to his sheriffs and justices to keep the lid on the situation by broadcasting a disclaimer but chose not to order indiscriminate reprisals against the offenders. Mayors were enjoined to ensure that any sign of rebellion was quickly snuffed out. The mayor of Northampton appears to have successfully suppressed the efforts of one William Napton to incite the citizens to riot, but Napton was still regarded as a subversive a year later. Nevertheless, agitators were at work in the villages. John Saint-Peyre, for instance, went recruiting in Harlestone and Church Brampton under cover as a London merchant buying up surplus wool for export. Additionally, the rebellion had provided a golden opportunity for individuals to pursue vendettas and gain personal advantage from the chaos. A year after the excitement had died down, John of Northampton, as Lord Mayor of London, was still trying to pick up the pieces.

A number of factors had coincided to produce this unsettled age: the circumstances of climate change caused crop failure and famine, and the fall in population resulting from the Great Plague caused significant societal dislocation, resulting in lawlessness and criminal opportunities, affecting both trade and day-to-day life. In 1348, Queen Isabella's market at Geddington was disrupted by armed men who assaulted her officers. Much more corrosive were the actions of those in authority who nevertheless regarded themselves as above the law, pursuing feuds and intimidating those around them while seeking wealth and preferment at any cost. Sir Robert Holand, a favourite of the earl of Lancaster, had been rewarded with lands and marriage to an heiress, Maud, the daughter of John, Lord Lovell of Titchmarsh. Under Lancaster's protection, he survived prosecution as one of the murderers of Piers Gaveston, Edward II's hated favourite, and weathered a dispute over his privileged status among Lancaster's other supporters, some of whom were killed. However, in 1322, he declined to come to his patron's aid at the Battle of Boroughbridge, resulting in Lancaster's defeat and subsequent execution by Edward II. Sir Robert was disgraced, imprisoned, and, on his release or, in some versions, his escape from Northampton Castle, murdered by Lancastrian supporters in 1328. His four sons, Robert, Thomas, Alan, and Otho, were fortunate to be taken into the royal household to be trained as squires, with Thomas serving in Scotland and being knighted by Edward III by 1337. To replenish the ranks of a depleted nobility, William, the third son of Elizabeth de Bohun, and hence a grandson of Edward I, serving as a prominent captain in the king's service in the Hundred Years' War, had been created earl of Northampton by Edward III in 1337, and it was in his service that the Holand brothers sought to make their fortunes. Thomas and Otho went with the king to Flanders in 1338, and were with the earl in Hainault in 1339. In 1340, aged about twenty-four, Thomas contrived and consummated a secret marriage to the twelve-year-old Joan, daughter of Edmund of Kent and granddaughter of Edward I. After his elder brother, Robert, inherited what remained of the family estates after their father's disgrace, Thomas was forced to advance his military career. This he did at the sea battle of Sluys, the siege of Tournai, and on crusades in Granada against the Moors and with the Teutonic Knights in Prussia. In 1342, Thomas, Otho, and Alan, with their nephew, Robert Holand III, all served under the earl of Northampton again, sailing from Southampton for Brest. Thomas was promoted and led successful attacks on Morlaix and Vannes in Brittany. Further expeditions for the brothers under Northampton's leadership followed in 1345–6. An episode in March 1347 exemplifies the violence and uncertainties of the times. A body of troops, including sixty knights, was on its way to Southampton, *en route* for France to join the English army fighting there. A small group, under Thomas's elder brother, Robert of Thorpe Waterville, made a detour into Berkshire where the fortified manor house at Beaumes, also Beaumyss or Beams, near Shinfield, licensed to Nicholas de la Beche in 1338, was attacked. The objective of this surprise assault was the abduction of an heiress, Margery Poynings, albeit already married to Sir Gerard Lisle, and her delivery to Sir John Dalton of Apethorpe, who had commissioned this act of terrorism. As it happened, the royal children of Lionel, Duke of Clarence, were staying at Beaumes, and their escort put up a fight, suffering fatalities in the process. Despite this spirited defence, the lady Margery was allegedly 'raped', probably meaning 'abducted', by Holand, seized, and despatched back to Sir John in Northamptonshire, where she became his fourth wife but was dead within two years. While Thomas appears to have got away with his earlier seduction of Joan of Kent, Robert was censured for his action at Beaumyss, more, one infers, for endangering the royal children than for his mistreatment of poor Margery.

In 1346, Thomas had received the manors of Brackley, Halse, and King's Sutton from his mother, and in 1352, the early death of his brother-in-law, John, brought over forty manors to Thomas and Joan. These included Easton, Upton, and Torpel (the latter two, formerly the property of Eleanor of Castile, now in Cambridgeshire) but all suffering from the long-term effects of the Great Plague. A further expectation was that John's earldom of Kent would be granted to Thomas, and both he and his brother, Otho, also knighted by this time, adopted seals and armorials featuring a ducal coronet and the ostrich feathers of the Prince of Wales in anticipation of Thomas's elevation through his wife's inheritance. Both were respected members of the Order of the Garter, but their violent lives caught up with them. Otho had been given custody of the captured Constable of France in 1346, but allowed him to return to France on parole and was heavily criticised for his laxity. He died in Normandy, aged about forty-three, in 1359. Thomas was taken ill in Rouen while in post as the king's lieutenant of Brittany and co-captain-general of English forces in France, and died in his early forties. By 1339, Alan had been severely wounded by a Nottinghamshire squire and died at Brackley. Robert, the eldest brother, however, lived into his sixties and died at Halse in 1373, possibly in the same year as his son, also Robert, who died in his manor of Thorpe Waterville.

As we have seen with Alan Holand, disputes between neighbours quickly escalated. When, in 1413, a lawsuit against him failed, Sir John Mortimer of Grendon was abducted and held prisoner. Thomas Wydeville of Grafton Regis, as sheriff of Northamptonshire, was required to ensure that the offenders were served a medieval ASBO. Wydeville, or Woodville, enjoyed royal favour, becoming the guardian of noble French prisoners, and receiving the income from disputed properties. His granddaughter, Elizabeth, would marry Edward IV. While there were those who benefited from the French Wars by ransoming hostages or returning home with loot, the depredations of marauding bands of discharged soldiers could threaten the security of townsfolk, gentry, and peasants alike, particularly during episodes of weaker royal authority. The depopulation of Charwelton, leaving a vacuum to be filled by sheep, was attributed to attacks by marauding soldiers. Such widespread insecurity generated a need to adopt measures, which would defend against these threats.

Castles of the Fourteenth Century

Several of our castles went out of use while others underwent reconstruction. Despite some minor repairs at Northampton, the story is one of slow deterioration until in 1318, the hall and other domestic buildings burned down, and Edward II thought it not worth proceeding in view of the enormous replacement cost. In the end, the hall was rebuilt in the 1330s for the sessions of the circuit judges, and in 1385, a new prison was built, by which time most military activity had ceased. Under Edmund of Langley, from 1359, the House of York acquired Fotheringhay in 1377, and an ambitious building programme was started, which would continue well into the next century, producing a powerful castle with the keep on its mound, an inner bailey with mural towers and gatehouse, and two outer baileys, both walled in stone, surrounded by deep ditches fed by the River Nene, and accessed by strong gatehouses. Recent (2018) geophysical survey work, carried out by Steve Parry of MOLA for the Castle Studies Trust, has revealed much of the layout of the keep, and the buildings of the inner bailey. While Fotheringhay passed to the Yorkists, with the Lancastrian Henry IV on the throne, Higham Ferrers passed to the crown in 1399. After a fire in 1411, the hall was rebuilt, but the only surviving structure is the dovecote of 1406. At Rockingham, repairs were carried out throughout the century, but the castle had become more of a comfortable hunting lodge in the royal forest than a fortress. It is possible that John of Gaunt's castle outside Daventry belongs to this period. This moated site, which may have been little more than a hunting lodge, was entered over a drawbridge and contained a long rectangular building with three cross walls and the foundations of two free-standing circular towers, revealed by excavation. Another enigmatic site is at Harlestone, where foundations of a building measuring 88 × 36 feet (27 × 11 metres) with walls 6.5 feet (2 metres) in thickness and a circular structure on its north-east corner, 23 feet (7 metres) in diameter, possibly a stair turret, have been excavated. A flanking wall extends nearly 130 feet (40 metres) to the south, and one interpretation of this structure is that it represents a tower house, possibly standing on an earlier, low motte.

Later Castles

Moor End Castle, Yardley Gobion, was licensed in 1347 to Thomas de Ferrers, descendant of a Norman family of long-standing. There was a platform with sides of 160 feet (50 metres) with wide, wet moats crossed by a causeway. In 1363, it passed to the crown and was frequently visited by Edward III, who spent over £850 on its refurbishment. It comprised a hall with, at one end, a chamber, a chapel, at least three towers, and a rectangular building with turrets at the corners, possibly the 'King's Tower', whose foundations were uncovered in the early nineteenth century. The improvements included a completely new chamber, stained-glass windows for the chapel, and fireplaces in the towers. Ancillary buildings were rebuilt or replaced, and a reference to an outer gate would suggest that the castle consisted of two courtyards. Despite this lavish expenditure, after Edward's death, the castle appears to have been little used, passing through various royal hands. Additions to existing castles were mainly domestic. At Fotheringhay, although the palatial accommodation of one of the Yorkists' principal seats had already been expanded into the outer bailey on the north-west, further

Fotheringhay Castle: the archway into the courtyard of the New Inn, lodgings added by Edward IV. It is now known as Garden Farm.

lodgings—one of them the New Inn, entered through a gateway with armorials—were built outside the castle's northern gatehouse in 1460. Opposite a row of stone cottages representing the Old Inn, these survive as Garden Farmhouse, but everything else apart from the earthworks has gone. Richard, Duke of York, and his son, Edmund, Earl of Rutland, had both been killed at the Battle of Wakefield in 1460. In 1476, their bodies were brought to Fotheringhay for reinterment in the church. So great was the crowd of people who attended the service and the feast afterwards that 1,500 tents were said to have supplemented the available accommodation in the castle itself.

Fortified Manors and Licences to Crenellate

The need for defensible structures was apparent among several disparate groups. The established land-owning families such as the Treshams of Rushton, the Ferrers, and the de la Zouches found it advisable in troubled times to find some security behind high walls, as did many prelates. Those soldiers, such as Thomas de Latymer or Simon de Drayton, returning from the French wars loaded with booty and ransom money, sought to secure their wealth and position by building strong houses incorporating defensive elements. Successful merchants such as the Knyvetts of Southwick, with a fortune gained from the wool trade, consolidated their ascent through royal service and demonstrated their importance in the medium of solid battlemented masonry. Other 'new men' in royal service, such as Guy Wolston or the Empsons, reinforced their standing in the traditional way by building sturdy residences. All these people wanted to live in fashionable, comfortable, but, above all, imposing dwellings: houses that would leave their neighbours, of whatever station, in no doubt as to their status. The significance of the licence to crenellate, issued by royal authority, to enable a subject to build a defensible house, has been the subject of much debate. Not all fortified manors were licensed, but that did not apparently make them illegal. It would appear that many licences were simply visible marks of royal approbation, to be valued and flaunted by their recipients in the same way that orders and decorations from the Garter to the MBE always have been. Licences were issued by the crown in England between 1127 and 1622, and in Northamptonshire, twelve licences were granted between 1301 and 1512 (see Appendix II).

John Knyvet was one who opted not to license his fortified house. He had profited from the wool trade but chose the route of royal service to further the family's fortunes, his son, Richard, serving as keeper of the royal forest of (King's) Cliffe. Richard's son, another Sir John, entered on a career in the law. He, too, entered royal service, becoming Chief Justice and Lord Chancellor to Edward III before 1372. By 1352, when Richard died, he and his father had built a stone house with a hall at Southwick. At one corner of the hall, there is an almost detached two-storey tower with a smaller, slightly later, annexe. A circular stair turret, attached to one corner of the tower, gives access to an upper solar chamber over the vaulted ground floor. This tower is clearly meant to suggest a defensive capability, even if only to deter the casual aggressor who might be persuaded to take his criminal intent elsewhere. From a slightly earlier date is Thorpe Waterville, licensed to Bishop Walter Langton of Lichfield in 1301. The surviving barn has medieval windows and may represent the hall of the fortified manor house, with traces of a moat. Investigations in 1976 uncovered the foundations of a rectangular building measuring 55 feet × 33 feet (17 metres × 10 metres) with walls 9 feet (2.7 metres) thick. Further surveys in 2010 appeared to confirm the former presence of a large stone building with corner turrets, with more of the structure to its east. Castle Ashby, in 1306, was one of several further licences granted to Langton, but no evidence survives of this earliest house, reported as ruinous by Leland in 1530, on the site of the later mansion. Bishop Roger, Walter's successor from 1322, built a fortified manor at Northborough, now in Cambridgeshire. There were two manors at Braybrooke, one in the hands of the Knights of St John in 1361, while the other, East Hall, was owned by the Latimers. Licence to crenellate had been granted to Thomas de Latymer in 1304, allowing him to raise a stone wall within the moat. A great chamber was roofed with timber supplied by Pipewell Priory, and other buildings ringed a courtyard. A later Latymer fought alongside Edward III in the expeditions to Gascony and Aquitaine. By the mid-1500s, the house was in poor condition and the current occupiers, the Griffins, moved to their new house at Dingley. Extensive earthworks comprising a central enclosure with bank and double ditches can be seen, but no stone defences remain. The main moat appears difficult to fill as it is higher than the adjacent stream. It is surrounded by other depressions interpreted as possible fishponds and fish-breeding tanks.

Thorpe Waterville: the only significant remnant of the fortified manor house of the bishops of Lichfield; this barn may represent its former great hall.

Southwick: the fourteenth-century tower with its stair turret of the fortified manor house of the Knyvet family who held public office under Edward III.

Titchmarsh was licensed in 1304 to John, 1st Baron Lovel(l), whose son was killed at Bannockburn in 1314. Excavations in the 1880s uncovered the foundations of stone buildings within a roughly circular stone wall. This wall had later been demolished when a rectangular moat was dug, around a new curtain with four pentagonal corner towers. The castle was reported as being moated round and walled in stone at the time of John Lovel(l)'s death in 1346, but as ruinous in 1363 when a new manor house was built on a fresh site. The first phase may align with the original licence, and the rebuild to a time prior to John's death. Barton Seagrave was licensed to Nicholas de Seagrave in 1313 and presents a complex of earthworks. There are two moated enclosures, the more southerly of which is generally accepted as being the manor, occupied until at least 1433, and the other mainly fishponds. The manor house site consists of a rectangular banked enclosure with a 6½-foot-deep (2-metre-deep) ditch. Disturbed ground in the interior may represent stone foundations and surrounding walls, and the recovery from the site of masonry, including recognisable architectural features, has been recorded.

Within the later buildings at Drayton House, some medieval survivals remain. The house was licensed in 1328 to Simon de Drayton, who built a house within a moat and a curtain wall. The much-altered great hall and an undercroft formerly under the great chamber, both dating from the 1300s, survive within the late-sixteenth-century rebuilding, and the battlemented outer walls of the fourteenth-century house survive either side of the later gatehouse. Sir Simon accompanied Edward III's expedition to Gascony in 1336. The military achievements of a later owner—Sir John Germaine, who campaigned alongside Marlborough in 1702—are reflected in a military trophy in the baroque façade of the hall block.

A house was first built on a site at Harringworth in 1272 with a hall, and chamber forming the west range, and a gatehouse. A deer park was licensed to William de Cantelupe in the first half of the fourteenth century. This earlier build was integrated into the manor house of the Zouches, licensed in 1387, and formed the northern inner court, with a second outer one within the moat. All that remains, as Manor Cottages, is a fragment of the north range of the inner court. Here, a fifteenth-century two-light window in the upper floor can be seen. This would have faced into the inner court, but a further contemporary window in the end wall would have afforded only interior views. A house at Collyweston begun soon after 1412 was acquired in 1441 by Ralph Cromwell, Lord Treasurer to Edward IV, who rebuilt it. He died there in 1455 and it eventually passed to Margaret Beaufort, mother of Henry VII, *c.* 1490. She held it until *c.* 1500 when it passed to the crown. The main part of the house consisted of a hall, chapel, and a tower, with private apartments and public spaces where the Queen Mother could try local cases, malefactors being kept in the prison next to the gate of the walled compound.

Boughton House, near Kettering, was licensed to Richard Whetehill, a soldier, on his return from commanding the garrison in Calais in 1473. At the time, it was described as an embattled tower of stone and timber with (gun) 'loupes and other necessary engines'. It was replaced by the house that provides the core of Boughton House today. Bradden Manor, a stone hall with two cross-wings, had been a preceptory of the Hospitallers. It was licensed in 1477 to John Holcot. In 1471, Thomas Lovett exchanged Rushton for Astwell. Here he built a moated courtyard house whose three-storey embattled gate tower with higher stair turret is all that remains of his fifteenth-century fortified manor house.

Drayton: the buttressed walls of the entrance front, resulting from the licence to crenellate granted in 1328, are the only defensive features remaining.

Harringworth: few obvious architectural features of the fortified manor survive—the two-light window on the first floor and, behind the glass in the gable-wall, another medieval window.

Astwell Castle: the gate tower remains from the fortified house of 1471.

Apethorpe: Guy Wolston was a member of the household of the duke of York; between 1470 and 1480, he built a fortified manor house with a gatehouse having symmetrical staircase turrets and retainers' lodgings. Here we see the surviving eastern part.

Apethorpe was built *c.* 1470–80 by Guy Wolston, a member of the household of the duke of York, later Richard III. He was appointed Constable of Fotheringhay Castle in 1464, and served as sheriff of Northamptonshire. Although he had served a Yorkist king, he was knighted in 1487 by the Tudor monarch, suggesting that he had mastered the art of political dexterity. There is a hall range and porch from this period, refaced in 1653, incorporated in the later house. The gatehouse was flanked by lodgings that survive on the eastern side, retaining a stair turret, replicated on the western until alterations were carried out in 1740. There are four-centred archways in the gatehouse and in the entrance porch to the hall range. The house later came into the possession of Sir Thomas Empson, whose father had been one of Henry VII's enforcers. Richard Empson's licence at Easton Neston, granted in 1499, also included parkland. There, the property changed hands in 1530 and a new house was built on a different site.

Other fortified houses from the later Middle Ages include such diverse examples as Warkworth, Muscott, and Grafton Regis. Warkworth Castle was a mansion with a gatehouse and semi-circular towers, which was converted into a Jacobean house and demolished in 1805. At Muscott, the fourteenth-century gatehouse with side walls, a reset cross loop, low buttresses, and a newel stair to an upper chamber survives as the entrance to a farmyard. The house was probably reduced after its acquisition by the Spencers in the sixteenth century. Grafton Regis was a small monastic site around a cloister, which was converted by the Woodvilles into a manor house with a gatehouse in the fifteenth century.

The motifs of the fortified house continued on into the sixteenth century. A very late licence to crenellate was issued to John Spencer at Althorp in 1512, but this may have related more to the deer park of 300 acres (120 ha). At Ashby St Legers, a stone and timber-framed early Elizabethan gatehouse stands at an angle to the church. In the grounds of Clopton Hall, stands a square, two-storey, roofless gatehouse with armorials of the Dudleys, who occupied the house from the fourteenth to the eighteenth centuries. It has been assigned, by Pevsner, to the Elizabethan period. Dingley, a manor held by the Knights Hospitallers, passed to the Griffins who built the present hall around 1560. They retained traditional defensive features such as the surviving gatehouse flanked by polygonal towers, turrets and rounded merlons, possibly incorporating elements of the knights' original buildings. Billing Priory is a possible fortified manor immediately north of the church. The fragment that remains of Henry VIII's palace at Grafton Regis, includes sturdy buttresses and the hint of a gatehouse. The language of feudal military architecture continued to be spoken for some time in order to ensure that ideas of power and dominance were effectively communicated.

As more domestic models took over, then the pure fortress elements declined, new manor houses took their place. These often incorporated earlier fabric as at Boughton House, Castle Ashby, Drayton, and Apethorpe. Northampton Castle became little more than a prison and courthouse; Fotheringhay's hall and domestic ranges survived for a while, but the castle was ruinous by 1635; at Higham Ferrers, demolition began after 1523 when Sir Richard Wingfield received permission to remove stone and lead for his new house at Kimbolton (Cambridgeshire); Moor End was ruinous by the late 1500s and building materials were removed for use at Henry VIII's new palace at Grafton Regis. Not until the civil wars of the 1640s would some of these sturdy structures come into their own once again.

Muscott: the fourteenth-century gatehouse has a room above accessed by a stair in the entrance passage.

Dingley: the Griffins moved from the dilapidated Braybrooke to this former preceptory of the Knights Hospitaler, retaining defensive features for image rather than substance.

Town Defences

Simon de Senlis is assumed to have commenced work on Northampton's town walls close to the time he was building his castle. The Saxon defences are thought to have enclosed an almost circular area about 700 yards across, close up against the river on the west, but some distance away on the south. The Norman castle occupied around 10 per cent of this area in its mid-western sector above the river. The new Norman defences, however, enclosed a greatly enlarged pear-shaped area getting on for a mile (1.6 km) across on each axis, making Northampton, by area enclosed, some 250 acres (100 ha), the third largest walled town in England. The excavation in Green Street, just to the south of the new castle's southern bailey, demonstrated the development of these Norman defences, in this one location where the new coincided with the earlier construction. The timber revetment of the Saxon clay bank was replaced by a dry-stone wall. It has to be assumed that this model was followed along the whole course of the new defences, combined with a ditch of comparable dimensions to the Saxon one it was extending. This preliminary stage was followed in the twelfth century by the construction, on the top of the rampart, of a stone wall, 6 feet (1.85 metres) thick. It consisted of large masonry blocks on both interior and exterior faces, and a rubble fill. The ditch, already wide, was widened still further and the former Saxon West Gate was blocked and a new gate opened nearer to the castle, accessed by the west bridge. On the east and north sides of the town the walls were reported as wide enough for six people to walk abreast, but on the south where there were multiple water defences, the walls were narrower, and much of the western perimeter was taken up by the castle. Gates were constructed to the north and south, with two more on the east across Derngate and St Edmund's End. In the north, a salient contained the walled precinct of St Andrew's Priory. Town walls were in constant need of maintenance, paid for by taxes on trade raised for the purpose through royal permits known as Murage Grants. Northampton received such grants in 1224, in the 1250s, the early 1300s, and 1378. In 1278, the Carmelites of the Whitefriars between Abington and Princes Streets wished to incorporate part of the town wall into their closed precinct. This request provoked complaints from townsfolk not, as one might expect, on grounds of security, but on the basis of a lost recreational amenity. Walking the town walls kept them fit and above the nastier smells of the town. In 1410, the town raised £240 towards expenditure of over £300. By this time, however, the population had shrunk and many plots were derelict, devolving the task of keeping up the town's defences on to a smaller group of merchants with a shrinking tax base.

At Towcester, it would appear that little was added in medieval times to Edward the Elder's ninth-century refurbishment of the Roman stone town walls. Excavations have uncovered evidence that the Roman bank was heightened by 2 feet (61 cm) but, at least at one point on the circuit, there was no evidence for new masonry. At some time in the Middle Ages, stone buildings encroached on the rampart, but there appears to have been no further building activity of a defensive nature until the Civil War (see Chapter 3).

Monastic Defences

The county contained sixty-five monastic houses, including sixteen abbeys/priories and seven secular colleges, and many of these exhibited defensive features. It was normal for monastic establishments to regulate comings and goings by provision of gatehouses, usually with chambers for watchmen or porters. Within the walls of Northampton, St Andrew's Priory (Cluniacs), and both the Whitefriars (Carmelites) and the Greyfriars were surrounded by their own perimeter walls entered through gatehouses. The Augustinian abbey of St James and the Cluniac Delapre both lay outside the town defences within their own walled precincts. Daventry Priory and large monasteries such as that of the Cistercians at Catesby are recorded as having a precinct wall and gatehouse, and the Premonstratensian abbey of Sulby was bounded by a precinct bank. Monasteries functioned as businesses and made themselves unpopular by enclosing land for raising sheep and converting arable land to pasture. The abbots of Peterborough and Pipewell, the prior of Daventry and the prioress of Catesby had all enclosed extensive areas of land totalling many hundreds of acres, obliterating the open fields and dwellings of whole villages.

The military orders were well-represented in the county with, in Northampton, Holy Sepulchre Church, Sheep Street, a circular Templar church founded *c*. 1110 by Simon de Senlis. In 1215, King John made a personal gift to Aymeric, Grand Master of the Templars in England, of all those houses and palaces in Northampton that had been seized from Aaron of Lincoln, one of the country's foremost financiers. Hardwick was a Templar preceptory, dating from 1199, but by 1250, it had been conveyed to Henry

Higham Ferrers: Archbishop Chichele's College of 1422 at Higham Ferrers may have needed a gatehouse to control egress rather than access.

de Seymour. There were preceptories of the Hospitallers at Dingley, Harrington, and Bradden Manor where the house with its hall and two cross wings became the basis for a fortified house licensed in 1477 to John Holcot. At Higham Ferrers, Archbishop Chichele's College of 1422 has a gatehouse and attached lodging. The tower of the college, founded in 1354 at Irthlingborough, is attached by undercrofts and a two-storey building to the church itself. Two fireplaces in the tower point to the insertion of floors for domestic purposes. Nassington Prebendal House, greatly remodelled in the fifteenth century, is an early thirteenth-century house with a hall, a solar wing, a service wing, and a detached kitchen. There was also, once, a gatehouse to the east of the house. A number of monastic granges were built on moated platforms.

Moated Sites

One of the defensive elements of most of those obviously fortified manor houses was the moat, and this became a common feature in the medieval landscape. There are around fifty medieval moats in Northamptonshire, placing it in the lower half of the county league table. The majority of these moats were dug between 1200 and 1325, overlapping with the fifty years up until 1350 when most of the county's medieval manor houses were built. Very few of the county's moats have been excavated, but much has been interpreted through the observation of their remains. Moats were dug for a number of different purposes, in a variety of locations, using a wide range of techniques. The vast majority were designed to be wet, so water sources and geology were important, along with the engineering works necessary to retain the water. Some were fed by streams as at Astwick, Stoke Albany, and Stoke Doyle where an inlet channel diverts water from a stream into the moat, while others relied on adjacent hills to drain into them as at Walgrave, where a dam and massive external banks, with ditches up to 3 metres deep, held the water draining from the adjacent hill. At Pilton, the moat was built on the upward slope of the valley, and it required a substantial outer bank on the downward slope on two sides, acting as a dam to trap the water. Dams feature widely in the county's moats, with examples at Whiston, with its reservoir, and at Higham Park, where a large bank was raised on the outer edge of the ditch to keep the water from draining away too quickly.

Moats were most often dug around houses or farmsteads. They were useful for drainage, keeping a house platform dry; they provided fishponds, at a time when meat was proscribed on nearly half the days of the year; they kept livestock from straying or being poached; and they kept predators, both animal and human, at arm's length. Many moats are still associated with buildings as at Cogenhoe, for instance. Here, probably dating from the twelfth or thirteenth centuries, Whiston is a small moat, around a manor house held by Ramsey Abbey until the fourteenth century. The property then went to the de Whiston family who built a new house, Place House (now Moat House), a little to the north. This preserves remnants of medieval work, with oblong buttresses at the corner. The rectangular moat was fed by an adjacent stream, which then ran into a pond with a massive retaining dam. At Stoke Albany, a small moat and an extensive complex of fishponds were fed by a stream dammed to the north. The manor was held by William d'Aubigny in the thirteenth century, and the moat appears to have been associated with the fourteenth-century stone manor house west of the church, whose solar survives in the later building. An embanked enclosure to the north of these works, suggest an earlier building. Inside some moats, only excavation can provide evidence of former buildings, as at Weldon, a moat excavated in the 1930s, and recorded as containing massive building foundations. At Quinton, a roughly rectangular moat contained the foundations of a stone manor house with walls 2 feet (61 cm) thick. Elsewhere, evidence can be even more tenuous. Weldon's second moat, excavated in the 1970s, is Hall Close, site of the manor house of the Basset family. Here, traces of a building on the platform were dated by pottery to the thirteenth to fourteenth centuries. At Aldwincle, a scatter of building rubble and roof tiles provided evidence of a building within the square moat. Documentary evidence is the key to some moats, exemplified by three conventual sites: the monastic grange at Badby; the Hermitage at Brampton Ash, a grange of Pipewell Abbey, which was rebuilt in 1298, with two conjoined rectangular enclosures, one of which contained a chapel and a house; and Hemington, a manor belonging to Ramsey Abbey. Defence may have been a consideration at some of these sites but a moat would have needed the back-up of a palisade of some sort. Few moats have been excavated at all, and one in particular gives information only of what is not present: when a moat at Yelvertoft was examined prior to its destruction, it was noted as having had no surrounding wall or timber palisade. The very nature of moats themselves, occupying predominantly lower ground, saw many overlooked quite closely by nearby eminences, as at Chadstone, Orlingbury, and Pilton, detracting from their defensive potential. Some moats are known to have enclosed no structure of any sort. Known as 'empty moats', their platforms may have accommodated orchards, or sources of other valuable cash crops, which merited some protection. One other factor that should not be overplayed, but, nevertheless, cannot be ignored, is social mobility. For instance, it has been suggested that the moat at Grendon, around the manor house of the de Harrington family, and in use by 1325, may possibly have been a signal to neighbours that the family was going up in the world. Moats, therefore, may have served as a demonstration of status, of keeping up with the de la Zouches.

Moats came in a variety of shapes and sizes but the majority were square or rectangular—that at Wythmail Farm, Orlingbury, being a rare example of an oval moat. The most common dimensions for the length of sides were in the range of 170–200 feet (50–60 metres). Ditches were seldom more than 7 feet (2 metres) deep but could be up to 40 feet (10 metres) wide. At a number of locations, including Harrington, Hemington, Holdenby, Newton, and Papley, moats were later adapted as garden features. At Papley, this may have been as early as the fifteenth century when the village was consciously depopulated by its landlords. At Hemington, in the sixteenth century, the Montagues enlarged the existing moat into gardens and water features around Beaulieu Hall.

Deer Parks, Royal Forests, and Hunting Lodges

Throughout the Middle Ages, large tracts of Northamptonshire were covered by the Forests of Whittlewood, Salcey, and Rockingham, and these could be dangerous places, and not just for the game. Although the forest laws had been amended around the time of Magna Carta, removing the death penalty for poaching and, by 1225, substituting a scale of fines, there remained strong resentment among the peasants over the king's monopoly of hunting rights. This led to an intensification of poaching, often resulting in violent confrontations with the royal foresters. In 1229, such an affray in Rockingham Forest resulted in a forester being hit by two arrows fired from a longbow. Crossbows were officially banned altogether, and only foresters were allowed to carry bows and arrows in the royal forests, but illegal hunting still went on. In 1272, a dozen poachers are recorded as being pursued by the king's wardens, and Matthew, the king's forester at Brigstock, was mortally wounded when he and some colleagues confronted a group of poachers armed with a crossbow and several longbows. The foresters, as royal agents, responsible for applying the hated forest laws and living in isolated spots in the forest, were constantly vulnerable to attack. In some parts of East Anglia, their two-storied stone lodges resembled fortresses. In the royal forests of Northamptonshire, the solution lay in moated defensible lodges. At least half a dozen of these lodges survive in one form or another. Built before 1232, Harringworth Lodge stands in the deer park licensed to William de Cantelupe. The present lodge was started in the 1400s by William de la Zouche, and currently retains a core from this build with later additions. At Higham Park, Newton Bromshold, near Rushden, lies a moat beside the medieval deer park of 1327. It formerly contained the keeper's lodge with hall, chamber, and chapel. The ditch was 6½ feet (2 metres) deep and 35 feet (10 metres) wide, the water being retained by a dam. Slipton Lodge, the keeper's lodge at Lowick, occupied a trapezoidal moated platform but now retains no trace of entrances or structures. The outer banks on two sides of the moat are formed by the deer park pale itself, placing the lodge snugly in a corner of the park. An earlier farmstead moat inside the deer park of Rockingham Castle, by 1485, held a hunting lodge. A causeway crossed the 25-foot-wide (8-metre-wide) moat to access a platform measuring 180 feet × 210 feet (55 metres × 65 metres). Beanfield Lawn at Corby was a lodge for the keeper of the deer-grazing area. It stood in a moat measuring 130 feet × 145 feet (40 metres × 45 metres), with a wet ditch and a retaining bank on one side, now enclosing a later house. Wakerley Lodge, Oundle, a small moat standing in Park Wood, near Biggin Grange, outside the deer park of Peterborough Abbey first mentioned in 1327, but probably much older, would have housed the keeper.

The whole point of the royal forests was to provide hunting for the king and his court, so a number of hunting lodges were built to accommodate the royal party during their expeditions. Brigstock was the centre of a Saxon estate with a church and was a royal manor in 1086. It was a royal residence and a moated royal hunting lodge operating from *tempus* Henry II until 1319 when it was replaced by Geddington. The earlier manor house was taken down to be replaced by another moated house and a mews next to the church. It had a single-storey hall with a chamber above, and was built in stone with two-light windows. It occupied a platform measuring 160 feet × 100 feet (50 metres × 30 metres). Only three sides of the moat now survive. Excavations in the 1990s uncovered what appeared to be a substantial medieval wall, 4¼ feet (1.3 metres) thick, with a semi-circular buttress measuring over 11 feet (3.5 metres) across. The associated deer park extends over 2,000 acres (800 ha) down to Slipton Lodge, Lowick (see above). Geddington operated as a royal hunting lodge through two and a half centuries, taking over from Brigstock by 1319 and continuing in use until no later than 1374, after which the structure had disappeared leaving a site still known as Castle Close in 1717. The lodge had been built for the king's use by William d'Aubigny in 1129 and consisted of a hall and chambers for King Henry III and his queen, Eleanor of Provence, with the addition of a chapel in 1247. Though timber-framed, the building was richly decorated with paintings that had to be frequently renewed due to rainwater damage. Geddington was a frequent venue for the hunting trips of his daughter-in-law, Eleanor of Castile, who maintained the lodge's luxury. Kingsclffe, or just Cliffe, near Hall Yard, was the centre for the administration of the Forest Laws and a royal residence from the eleventh century. Henry III had the hall repaired and added a stone chapel, two chambers, and a kitchen, but the lodge was ruinous by the 1400s. Three further royal hunting lodges have long ago disappeared. Silverstone, whose site may be represented by fishponds near the church, was in use from the reign of Henry II until the early 1300s, when it passed out of royal ownership. Wakefield Lodge, in Whittlebury Forest, was rebuilt in 1158 and remained in use until at least 1217, when it appeared in a list of royal hunting lodges. The eighteenth-century house, which takes its name, may occupy its site. A lodge at Kingsthorpe, built on land belonging to Northampton Castle and later another of Eleanor of Castile's cluster of acquisitions in the locality, had been in use from 1114.

While features such as stone walls, gatehouses, towers, and moats gave an impression of defensive intent, there were other contemporary houses where the absence of such features did little to dispel suggestions of wealth and power. Stone remained a high-status building material for most of the Middle Ages, and even the passive defensive properties of stone houses were demonstrated in the civil wars of the seventeenth century. At Hardwick—a preceptory of the Knights Templar of 1199, but by 1250 conveyed to Henry de Seymour—there survives a medieval three-storey cross wing of 1320–40, with later windows and buttresses. Harrington was a manor granted to the Knights of St John in 1228, but has disappeared under the later house of 1720. Earthworks on the site probably represent medieval fishponds. A thirteenth-century hall house forms the basis of Loddington Hall, and at Shutlanger, the fourteenth-century hall house, with its two-storey porch, cross passage, service wing, and spiral stair, remain. Also surviving at Yardley Hastings, north of the church, is the two-storied service range over cellars, with the screens passage with its four doors to the services, the cellars, and the upper level of the mansion built in 1320–40. There is evidence in the adjacent replacement manor house for a detached kitchen, and earth banks may indicate the extent of stockyards. Deene was acquired by Robert Brudenell in the reign of Henry VII and built in that of Elizabeth, but contains traces from *c*. 1300 of an earlier house, with a solar over an undercroft and signs of a chapel, possibly in existence by 1215. All these examples were ostensibly unfortified, but would nevertheless have presented as solid, fireproof, secure lordly dwellings.

The Wars of the Roses

While continuing the casual, largely unstructured violence of the preceding century, the struggle between the Houses of Lancaster and York ushered in a period of no-holds-barred civil conflict punctuated by set-piece battles made unpredictable by changing allegiances and shifting loyalties. The Hundred Years' War had preserved elements of chivalry such as the ransoming of important prisoners, but this vicious civil war saw such conventions abandoned in favour of bloody revenge. England's nobility

Yardley Hastings was an unfortified but nevertheless imposing stone manor house; here the two-storied service wing contained doors to the kitchen, pantry, buttery, and hall.

would be decimated as, after a battle, those on the losing side were summarily executed but, for once, the humble foot soldiers were less likely to be massacred. Sir Thomas Tresham, for instance, was beheaded after the Battle of Tewkesbury in 1471. This only echoed the fate of his father, Sir William Tresham. A former attorney-general to Henry V and, as would be his son, Speaker of the House of Commons, he had bought his Rushton estate in 1438 to add to his manor of Sywell. Although blessed with a long record of loyal service to the House of Lancaster, by 1450, he was apparently out of favour with Henry VI. Thought, by contemporary chroniclers, to be riding north to meet with the Yorkist leadership, he was ambushed on the Moulton road and stabbed to death. His son was wounded and his escort arrived late on the scene. It was rumoured that Lord Grey of Ruthin, later himself to betray Henry VI at the Battle of Northampton, was behind the assassination. Although the victim was robbed of jewels and a considerable sum of money, no one believed robbery to be the motive. These two Treshams were just two victims out of many of the unrestrained violence and political chicanery of the time. Jockeying for positions of power during the reign of the weak king Henry VI had brought the duke of York within an ace of armed rebellion in early 1452 when ducal forces were gathered at Fotheringhay while the king was at Northampton. In the event, it would be a further three years before York brought the king to battle at St Albans.

The Battle of Northampton

In July 1460, Henry VI, threatened by the arrival of the earl of Warwick from France with 2,000 men and alarmed by the news that this was stimulating the build-up of Yorkist forces to over 20,000 men, decided to march his army of 10,000–15,000 men from Coventry to Northampton. Led by the duke of Buckingham, the royal army constructed a defensive position outside Delapre Abbey. This '*castrametatio*' armed with '*gonnes*', backed onto the river Nene and was fronted by a water-filled ditch, behind which was a rampart, strengthened with carts and sharpened stakes. The army was composed mainly of foot soldiers, with archers and specialists to service the cannon. On 10 July, his offer of negotiations rejected, Warwick's army advanced in heavy rain, which made the water-logged royal cannon ineffective, although at least one stone cannon-ball was retrieved from the battlefield in 2015. Through a hail of arrows, a division of Warwick's troops under the earl of March, the duke of York's son, and the future Edward IV, attacked the royalist right whose leader, Lord Grey of Ruthin, had already agreed to change sides. March was aware of his intention and warned his men not to harm those wearing Grey's badge of a black, ragged staff. No resistance was offered and Grey's men physically helped the Yorkists over the barriers and together they started rolling up the royalist army from the flank. There was no room in the fortified enclosure for Buckingham to manoeuvre and it was all over in under an hour. Despite efforts to win time for the king to escape, he was captured in his tent and conveyed as a prisoner to Delapre Abbey before being escorted to London, where York, wrongly as it transpired, expected to gain the throne. The duke of Buckingham, the earl of Shrewsbury, and Viscount Beaumont, former Constable and Great Chamberlain, were all killed, and many Lancastrian foot soldiers were drowned in the Nene attempting to flee the defeat. This demonstrated the dilemma imposed on wearers of the heavy 'jack', the leather coat sewn with chain-mail: strip it off and be defenceless, keep it on and drown.

After the Battle of Bosworth and the death of Richard III in 1485, Sir Thomas Lovell, MP for Northampton, was appointed by Henry VII as Chancellor of the Exchequer for life. He had accompanied Henry Tudor from France and fought at Bosworth Field. He was appointed Speaker of the House of Commons, Secretary of the Treasury, and a Knight of the Body, also administering the royal chambers. He is not to be confused with Francis, 1st Viscount Lovell, Richard III's Lord Chamberlain and lord of Titchmarsh Castle. He was deprived of Titchmarsh by Henry VII who bestowed it on Sir Charles Somerset. Lovell, the 'rat' in the famous rhyme, was one of the leaders of the rebels defeated at Stoke in 1487, and last seen after the battle, attempting to swim the river Trent on horseback. William Catesby, the 'cat', had been beheaded after the Battle of Bosworth in 1485. Margaret Beaufort, the Queen Mother, ruled the Midlands for her son through a governing council, based on the palace she had enlarged at Collyweston. The royal court stayed there for three weeks in 1503 while conveying the Princess Margaret to Scotland for her marriage to James IV. This early Tudor period saw the rise of the 'new men', public servants who owed their status entirely to the patronage of the paranoid Henry VII, and were preferred to the unreliable and often self-seeking aristocracy. Stafford, Earl of Wiltshire, had entertained Henry VII at Drayton, but when he died in 1499, aged only twenty-eight, disputed wills, it allowed Sir John Mordaunt, a lawyer at the royal court, to obtain the castle by marrying his son to the heiress whom he held in ward. The Mordaunts became earls of Peterborough in 1610. Another lawyer to benefit from royal service was Robert Brudenell, who accompanied Margaret Beaufort when she deputised for her son in the northern counties. By 1521, he was Lord Chief Justice and adding to his estates in Northamptonshire, including Deene. John Spencer was a Bedfordshire grazier who purchased Althorp in 1508, and was granted one of the last licences to crenellate four years later. The robust approach to his task of Richard Empson, one of Henry VII's tax gatherers, made him extremely unpopular. He was granted a licence to crenellate Easton Neston in 1499 and knighted in 1504, but on the accession of Henry VIII, he was charged with Constructive Treason, tried, convicted, and beheaded in 1510 at Northampton. His son, Thomas, was restored to the family fortunes in 1512 and married a daughter of Sir Guy Wolston, thereby adding Apethorpe to his Easton Neston property. Other Empson siblings also made locally beneficial dynastic marriages, one marrying a Catesby and another a Lovell.

3

Tudor, Stuart, and Hanoverian Northamptonshire 1500–1815

Northamptonshire in the Sixteenth Century

The town of Northampton, in 1524, was larger than Leicester but smaller than Cambridge. It probably had a population of around 3,000 people, in 640 households, producing 480 taxpayers. The rest of the county at the time of Henry VIII comprised twenty Hundreds, including Nassaburgh (Peterborough and the Soke), now part of Cambridgeshire. Typical was the Hundred of Nobottlegrove, consisting of nineteen parishes, including Duston, Flore, and Bugbrooke. The tax assessment of 1524 lists a total of 421 persons liable for tax, but included among them is just one gentleman, at Holdenby, and two esquires, at Upton and the Heyfords. Seventy different trades were practised in Northampton but many of the county's rural inhabitants worked on the land or were involved in the raising of sheep for the wool trade. Northamptonshire was one of those counties in the forefront of the enclosure movement, and by 1600, flocks were being grazed on enclosed pasture in half of the county's parishes. In a process begun by the great Cistercian monasteries, landowners enclosed arable land and followed a deliberate policy of depopulation in order to create more pasture for sheep. Some Hundreds, such as Chipping Warden and King's Sutton, would lose up to a third of their settlements in the process. The Priory of St Andrew's in Northampton had run 1,000 sheep over the depopulated village of Stuchbury right up until the Dissolution, but this was but one flock among the many across the county that combined to a total of over half a million sheep, with prominent families like the Spencers, the Knightleys, and the Catesbys owning significant numbers of them.

The Enemy Within

There had been executions in Northamptonshire following the rising against enclosure in 1549, but more unrest was to follow when the Treshams enclosed common lands. In 1607, a peasant rebellion led by John Reynolds of Raunds, calling himself Captain Pouch, saw around 1,000 men in the neighbourhoods of Rushton and Kettering, identified as the 'Levellers', begin to rip up the offending hedges. The rising was quickly put down by local JPs mobilising armed tenants, as the militia refused to respond to their callout. At Newton, a large crowd was dispersed, with forty to fifty unresisting protestors reportedly being killed. Several of the rebels, including Captain Pouch, were hanged, drawn, and quartered as an example, and their remains displayed at Northampton, Oundle, and Thrapston, but despite official inquiries being held, enclosure for pasture continued, producing eighty-two deserted villages by 1700. While, compared to many counties, this process was relatively advanced, large expanses of open heathland, arable, and unenclosed pasture still, nevertheless, remained.

Besides economic and social disquiet, religion also played its part. The reigns of Henry VIII and his three children all brought about sectarian conflict. John, Lord Latimer, Lord of Bozeat, Corby, and Stowe Nine Churches was one of the leaders of the Pilgrimage of Grace, a rebellion of 1536 protesting against Henry VIII's break with the Roman church. While many of the leaders were convicted of treason and executed, Latimer, a prominent member of the Neville family with estates in Yorkshire where the revolt began, pleaded coercion, joining them against his will. Although he helped secure an amnesty for some of them, he denied commitment to their cause. The Treshams of Rushton had never tried to conceal their Catholic loyalties, but Sir Thomas Tresham I had nevertheless been appointed in 1537 to the inquiry into the Lincolnshire Rising, which had preceded the Pilgrimage of Grace. He had later been created prior of the reconstituted Order of the Knights Hospitaller by Mary I in 1557. Despite the family's recusant status, his grandson, Thomas II, managed to stay onside with Elizabeth I and was knighted in 1575, having been made sheriff of Northamptonshire two years earlier. However, he was reckoned a loose cannon during the plots surrounding Mary, Queen of Scots, which would lead to her trial and execution at Fotheringhay Castle in 1587, precipitating the Armada crisis. Prominent local Catholics, such as Tresham, desperately tried to avoid being implicated in this threat to State security, but he was nevertheless fined heavily and imprisoned. Those underlying sympathies continued to reverberate into the next century, and Sir Thomas Tresham II's later situation cannot have been helped by the involvement of his son, Francis, in the rebellion of the earl of Essex in 1601, but he continually flaunted his religious beliefs by designing local buildings rich in Catholic symbolism at Lyveden, Rushton, and Rothwell. In the meantime, Francis sought support from Spain for English Catholics, a treasonable activity in itself, and was then recruited into the Gunpowder Plot by his cousin Robert Catesby, whose house at Ashby St Legers was, in 1605, the centre of the conspiracy. Francis was imprisoned in the Tower where he died in December 1605, his father having died three months earlier. Francis Tresham was posthumously decapitated and his head displayed, along with that of Catesby, in Northampton. The requirement on gentry to maintain stocks of arms and armour in their houses for local and national defence became a double-edged sword. In 1613, Sir Thomas Brudenell was convicted of recusancy, either as a practising Catholic or for harbouring Catholic priests, and the discovery of a cache of arms at Deene Park was used as evidence to implicate him in Catholic plots against James I.

Ashby St Legers: the house, with its timber-framed gatehouse, home of the Catesby family, was the centre of the Gunpowder Plot.

External Threats

England faced a number of invasion scares emanating from France and Spain in the reigns of Henry VIII and Elizabeth. The responsibility for defending the realm against invasion lay with the constitutional force, the militia. The Statute of Winchester of 1285 had required all men between fifteen and sixty years of age to keep in their homes the arms and armour (harness) appropriate to their station, determined by the value of goods, land, or income. This generally meant that the majority had bills (pikes) or knives, while the better off had a bow and arrows. In each community, the gentry, landowners, or wealthy merchants would hold items of armour. Musters of archers and billmen were carried out in 1539 and 1542, incidentally revealing the extent of the depopulation of dozens of villages since 1450. The Statute was repealed by Mary I in 1553 after the weapons specified were deemed obsolete, but new legislation now required all gentlemen with incomes over £100 *per annum* to keep six horses for demi-lances, heavy cavalry, with at least three sets of harness, as well as ten horses suitable for light horsemen. They had also to store forty pikes, thirty longbows (each with a sheaf of arrows), twenty bills, and thirty steel skulls or helmets. In Northampton, the number of armourers, or 'furbers', whose job it was to maintain and repair arms and armour, had increased from a single practitioner in the previous census to nine in 1525.

The militia assessment was based on population numbers and official data gathered by the tax authorities. The Hundred of Nobottlegrove, with its 421 taxpayers in 1524, was ordered, in the assessment of 1539, to produce 170 men for the militia. It would appear either that Mary's reorganisation lowered the requisite total, or that fewer men were meeting the criteria. In 1531, the county had found a total of at least 781 archers and 2,542 billmen, with an additional 167 sets of harness. Not all Hundreds submitted detailed returns so cannot be included in those totals, while others went so far as to distinguish between trained ('best') and untrained ('mean') men in their returns. Numbers ranged from the generous 754 men raised by the Hundred of Corbye to the meagre eighty-one from Spelloo, but by 1588, the quota had been reduced yet again to less than half that of earlier assessments.

War had broken out again with Spain in 1585, and Sir Christopher Hatton of Kirby Hall and Holdenby House, Lord Lieutenant of Northamptonshire, was commissioned to muster the militia and to organise the construction and manning of five alarm beacons across the county. These were generally set up on church towers such as Titchmarsh, near Thrapston, and Ecton, between Northampton and Wellingborough, with four villagers at each site detailed to attend it in shifts. On sighting neighbouring beacons alight, then all those within sight would be lit, a brazier being kept constantly readied with kindling and a convenient fire source nearby. The motte at Wollaston is known as 'Beacon Hill' so may also have fulfilled that function. All landowners with incomes of more than £10 *per annum* were required to supply a pike, a bow, and a hackbut (a primitive type of firearm), while each parish contributed its armour and weapons at the direction of the squire or lord of the manor. In 1586, the eastern division of the county assembled 300 men under Edward Montagu of Boughton, William Brown of Oundle, and Edward Pickering of Titchmarsh, and the next year, the entire force of Northamptonshire's levies was mobilised for an assessment of their efficiency in Northampton, Culworth, Daventry, and Towcester, the cavalry being reviewed by Hatton at Kettering, with a view to sending them south on anti-invasion duties. Sir Christopher, however, quickly recognised the limitations of these troops. Already greatly reduced from the 1539 totals, the current quota of 1,200 infantry and 190 horse still outstripped the county's capacity to train and equip these numbers. Given that fewer than half the required infantry were trained, he argued that fewer properly equipped men were more use than a larger force with significant deficiencies in equipment and training. He therefore reduced the quota to 600 trained foot and 100 cavalry, comprising twenty armoured lances and eighty light horse, organised in smaller units under captains. In the end, the danger of imminent Spanish invasion saw a force of only 400 men, suitably armed and uniformed, assembling. Following a few days' extra training, it was despatched to London forthwith, covering the distance in an impressive two days and camping outside London for a fortnight. These may have been among those troops famously harangued by Queen Elizabeth at Tilbury. By this time, the Armada, harassed by ships commandeered for national defence, had fortuitously foundered in the worst storms in living memory, and so the immediate danger having passed, the militiamen were sent home.

Those unlucky men balloted to join the militia were understandably reluctant to serve. In 1597, the leader of a forced draft of ninety-four men—enlisted in Kettering, with each one being paid 6d and ordered on pain of death to gather at Northampton—described himself as at his wits' end as so many of them had hired alternates, bribed their way out, or simply disappeared. These particular troops had been bound for Ireland, an especially unpopular assignment, but were representative of a prevailing aversion among townsfolk and countrymen alike to becoming soldiers. Both the breakdown of feudal service and governmental refusal to maintain a paid, professional standing army meant that new recruit and discharged veteran alike would contribute to public disorder and personal beggary. Problems with funding the arms and equipment of local levies had often left commanders with rag-tag forces, but despite the clergy of the county refusing to fund militia training up until 1614, the numbers of trained men still increased from 600 in 1612 to nearly 1,300 fourteen years later. If the army provided social problems for Northampton by discharging the maimed and the misfit into the community, then it also provided a solution, as few public officials could resist the temptation to unload vagrants, sturdy beggars, and convicts into the muster. This came to be seen as a legitimate way of counterbalancing the demands made on local authorities to produce fit and healthy, trained men for the crown's, usually unpopular, adventures. Until the army could cease its practice of effectively creating rogues and vagabonds, those would continue to be the men it was sent. It would be a long time before soldiering might come to represent an even part-way respectable occupation.

The Lead-Up to Civil War

In the early 1600s, there were around 350 families of gentry in Northamptonshire, only a very few of whom had ancient roots, as many had filled the vacuum caused by the extinctions of the Wars of the Roses. Country houses abounded as men gained social status by investing the profits from sheep farming or by securing government posts or royal patronage. Many of these gentry were followers of the puritan movement, which had gained a strong foothold in the county from the 1570s and enjoyed some measure of official approval as an antidote to the perceived dangers of Catholicism. These men generally disapproved of the Stuart kings' Catholic tendencies, or were vocal supporters of a parliament, actively resisting attempts to establish a royal autocracy. Between 1629 and 1640, when Charles I had dispensed with the services of parliament altogether, the local gentry were hit with unjustified levels of taxation and faced with fines for falling foul of ancient, long-forgotten forest laws. John Pickering, married to a Dryden, was imprisoned in 1626 for refusing to pay forced loans to Charles I, who was constantly seeking new ways to avoid having to gain parliamentary approval for royal expenditure. Additionally, parliament won the support of many who had been turned off their land and commons by the enclosures of their landlords. Quarrels over religious affinities between, for instance, the Vaux of Harrowden and the Pickerings of Titchmarsh had already become violent and may have exacerbated political differences on a wider scale. Sir Richard Knightley of Fawsley Hall withheld his payment of 'Ship Money' following Charles I's failed expedition to Spain. Along with Sir Henry Dryden of Canons Ashby, he met with parliamentary leaders, including Hampden and Pym, to discuss resistance to the king's unconstitutional demands. These men, characterised by their social status, religious affiliations, local influence, and political principles, naturally favoured parliament over the king. With the exception of Oxfordshire, Northamptonshire at this time was more densely populated than all those counties around and it has been estimated that up to four-fifths of the leading families were newcomers to the county establishment. Having made their fortunes through trade, the law, or service to the crown, and acquired their estates through their own efforts, they felt able to challenge representatives of the old aristocracy such as the Compton earls of Northampton, or the Montagu family of Boughton. So when civil war broke out in 1642, the county, with its puritan MPs and aggrieved gentry, declared for parliament. Many of the nobility, whose natural home remained the royal court, decamped to join the king.

As in most shire towns, the outbreak of war saw a scramble by the representatives of the two protagonists to secure the manpower of the militia, along with the firepower of its armoury. In Northampton in September 1642, Baron Montagu of Boughton, a local MP and former High Sheriff, attempted to implement the royal Commission of Array, which would mobilise the militia for the king. Although he had 100 men with him to escort their two cartloads of arms, he was captured by Lord Brooke. A large amount of royal plate and treasure was seized from Sir John Byron *en route* from the king at Nottingham to his future base at Oxford. He lost fifty men taken prisoner by the men of Brackley before he fled to Oxford with two troops of horse. From the safety of that royalist stronghold, he despatched 'menacing letters' to those Brackley men he considered 'Traytors and Rebels', threatening to obtain satisfaction for his injuries. Defiantly, they invited him to return and 'receive his desires'. In Northampton, Colonel Whetham, the military governor, was to be supported by a county committee, which included representatives of local parliamentarian gentry and committed borough councillors. Throughout the wars, this mechanism kept a firm check on the town, which did well out of supplying the parliamentarian army with—particularly, boots and horses—Cromwell ordering 4,000 pairs of shoes for the New Model Army in 1648. The town lay at the centre of the frontier zone, acting as a buffer zone between the royalist territories to its north and west, and the Eastern Association heartland. Thus the main task of parliamentarian forces in the county was to keep the road to London open with garrisons in Northampton and in Buckinghamshire, at Newport Pagnell and Aylesbury. Northamptonshire was a member, with Buckinghamshire, Derbyshire, Leicestershire, Nottinghamshire, Rutland, and Bedfordshire of the parliamentarian Midland Association. As with the Eastern Association of East Anglian counties, the intention was to ensure a network of united fronts against the royalists, but local interests and rivalries often led to a lack of co-operation. The county was taxed by parliament in order to keep fortifications in good repair and armies in the field. After 1644, John Claypole, senior of Northborough Manor, was parliamentarian tax assessor for the county, as would be John junior, Cromwell's son-in-law and Master of Horse, later on during the Commonwealth.

Raids, Battles, Skirmishes, Sieges, and Garrisons

The first major, but indecisive, battle of the war was Edgehill, fought in October 1642. The king had spent the night before the battle at Edgecote House, his troops spread among surrounding villages, including Culworth. The parliamentarians, under the earl of Essex, assembled at Northampton but had garrisoned Banbury. The two armies stumbled across each other, and although the incompetent Essex actually got the better of the fighting, he left Oxford undefended for the king to occupy and the road to London wide open for the royalist army, which would be only narrowly repulsed on the capital's very doorstep. The king now established his headquarters in Oxford, where it would stay for the duration. William Compton, the second earl of Northampton's younger son, occupied Banbury, establishing an outpost there that he would hold for the king throughout the war. Much of the king's support still came from the northern counties, so it was vital that lines of communication were maintained. Strong royalist garrisons were established at Newark-upon-Trent in Nottinghamshire and Ashby-de-la-Zouch and Belvoir in Leicestershire. In June 1643, Queen Henrietta Maria was able to travel unmolested from the Yorkshire port of Bridlington to Oxford via Daventry and Weedon. She was conducting a convoy of munitions, secured by the sale of the crown jewels on the continent, demonstrating just how difficult the different commands found co-ordinating an effective blockade, even in the parliament-dominated areas through which she passed. As well as fending off raids from Banbury then, Northamptonshire's parliamentarian garrisons needed to guard against royalist sorties from the north, aimed at penetrating the north-western defences of the Eastern Association. In July 1643, such an incursion temporarily took Stamford, but was quickly defeated at Burghley House, where three counties all meet on the Great North Road. In March 1643, a parliamentarian force under Lord Grey of Groby in Leicestershire, the commander of the Midlands Association, ordered a garrison into Rockingham Castle, aiming to protect the crossing of the river Welland. A royalist force took Newport Pagnell in October 1643 and began to fortify the town. Three weeks later, a disastrous misunderstanding caused the garrison to evacuate the town, and a parliamentarian force marched in, completed the defences, and stayed there until the end of the war, maintained by funds from the war chest in Northampton. The retreating royalists were pursued by Skippon, Sergeant-Major General of the London trained bands, but managed to establish a garrison in Henry VIII's palace of Grafton Regis. This strong point controlled the Northampton road to

Old Stratford on Watling Street, thus severing one of the county's routes to London, and could not be allowed to remain in royalist hands. The royalist tenure was, therefore, brief, as Skippon, with a force of 3,000 men from Newport Pagnell, quickly attacked. The royalist garrison had, in the short time available, thrown up a bank enclosing both the palace and the adjacent church. Henry VIII's palace had been partly demolished by 1628, so the ruins may have provided effective defensive positions, but the sheer weight of Skippon's numbers proved decisive and the garrison had been overrun by the end of December. Surveys have revealed the spread of musket balls on all sides except the north, which would have necessitated an uphill assault. Other houses were pressed into service as temporary fortresses by both sides. Castle Ashby, home of the staunchly royalist earl of Northampton, was occupied by a parliamentarian force of sixty musketeers and a troop of horse in February 1644, while Holdenby House underwent occupation by a force of 500 royalist musketeers and Fawsley hosted a parliamentarian garrison for a short while in 1645, as would Thorpe Mandeville a year later.

Banbury was a thorn in the side of parliamentarian forces throughout much of the war. A royalist sally won a minor skirmish at Middleton Cheney early in 1643, and in October, a more successful raid led by Prince Rupert advanced on Northampton via Daventry, Long Buckby, Holdenby, and Chapel Brampton, and was only repulsed at the north gate of the town. The royalist force headed for Olney (Buckinghamshire),

Grafton Regis was one of Henry VIII's seventy-odd palaces, and served as a garrison controlling the road to Old Stratford for a brief while in the Civil War; it fell to parliamentarian forces after a short siege and assault.

intending to cut the main road by occupying Towcester, which could control Watling Street and provide a springboard for further attacks on Northampton. From his headquarters at Easton Neston, Rupert directed Towcester's refortification as a base for cavalry raids. He mounted artillery to defend the town itself, but is also reported, possibly fancifully, to have emplaced guns in the old hillfort of Hunsbury Hill, in a very much more threatening position to Northampton. However, following a number of skirmishes with troops from Northampton, after only a very short occupation, the garrison had slighted the fortifications and moved on by the end of January 1644. In February 1644, a parliamentarian force from Northampton established a garrison at the Drydens' house at Canons Ashby, occupied the church, and began to collect taxes. In response, a troop of eighty cavalry under the third earl of Northampton sallied out from Banbury to eject the trespassers. Unseen by the defenders, a petard, a hollow explosive device, was fixed to the door of the church, forcing a retreat to the steeple. On seeing their colleagues smoked out of the church, those in the house itself surrendered. The survivors were taken back to Banbury along with captured weapons and provisions. In March 1644, a party of horse from Banbury carried out an attack on Major Mole's house at Kingsthorpe, but Mole's twenty men, armed with firelocks, held them off for three hours until relieved by troops from Northampton. This targeted assault may have been in retaliation for Mole's rough treatment of royalist sympathisers in Wellingborough well over a year previously, but whose memory was kept alive by royalist propaganda.

Towcester: the Norman castle mound was adapted to carry cannon during Prince Rupert's brief tenure during the Civil War.

In May 1644, the parliamentarian leadership had had enough and decided to put an end to the nuisance caused by the Banbury garrison, but an initial move by a force of 200 cavalry achieved little. In July, it was realised that a greater commitment was necessary and a strong force under Colonel Fiennes occupied the town in August, establishing its headquarters in St Mary's church, within range of the castle, which was a powerful fortress manned by a determined garrison. Although Fiennes had 3,500 men under command, along with a 32-pounder cannon, two other guns, and three 9- and 6-inch mortars firing grenades into different parts of the castle, they could make little impact. Musketeers and a light cannon were lodged on top of the church tower to fire down on the defenders, but the nineteen-year-old Compton refused to surrender. The besiegers then resorted to traditional siege techniques, digging mines under the walls, but these became flooded by underground streams. News that Rupert was on his way to relieve the castle was met by the deployment of Colonel Cromwell with 2,000 horse as a protective screen. At the end of September, a breach had finally been opened in the western wall, promising the possibility of storming the castle. Faggots and bundles of hay were assembled to fill the ditch and ladders were collected from all around the town. Even though simultaneous assaults were mounted at four other points, as well as in the area of the breach, the defenders' fire was so effective that not even in the breach itself could the attack be driven home. The advantage was very much with the defenders who admitted to only nine casualties to the attackers' 300. Now soldiers were released for what Fiennes hoped would be a final assault by impressing labourers from towns up to 10 miles away to extend the saps. However, time was running out, and a royalist army from Oxford, under Compton's elder brother, the third earl of Northampton, set out in the late autumn to relieve the besieged garrisons of Donnington, Basing House, and Banbury. Hearing of the imminent arrival of this relief expedition, Fiennes dispersed his force to fight another day, and Northampton encountered minimal opposition when he cleared the town of besiegers. The siege had lasted over three months, and had taken a lot out of his men, but Compton would now be free to regroup and resume his activities raiding deep into parliamentarian territory. It would be another eight months before Compton and his 400 defenders were again besieged, and outnumbered by the 3,000-strong army of Colonel Whalley. However, Sir William, knighted in the December, held on, and only after a siege lasting five months did hunger force him to surrender in January 1646. Compton's resistance may have been courageous, but the cost to the civilian population of the town was immense. The combination of bombardment, privation, and plague caused the civilian death rate to more than treble. The interval between the two sieges also saw the royalist horse resume their pillaging expeditions within a 20-mile (32-km) radius of Banbury. In return for a promise not to bear arms against the king, extracted from the villagers of Kilsby, for instance, who had been robbed of 300 cattle and sixty horses, Compton was forced to make reparations. He hung on to the horses, however. The Banbury garrison was described at the time of its surrender as the 'most pestilent, pernicious and vexatious den of Theeves and Royall Robbers … especially to the Inhabitants of Northamptonshire'.

One of its last acts, in September 1645, had been to convey large amounts of combustibles to Aynhoe Park, home of parliamentarian John Cartwright. In order to prevent it becoming a parliamentarian garrison, they burnt the house to the ground, along with all the buildings around it. Cartwright sued the earl of Northampton for

£10,000, but it was not paid until 1680, four years after Cartwright's death. The citizens of Northampton and its hinterlands must have been relieved to have been spared the prolonged miseries of a siege. However, they could not avoid the tax burden, and for many, by the end of the war, their community's liability had increased tenfold. The area suffered less material damage than many, but instances included Kingscliffe Church, which was used as stables by parliamentarian troops who set fire to it on leaving.

Unsurprisingly in a civil war and in a county straddling the territories of divergent allegiances, men fought and died on both sides. The second earl of Northampton led a royalist force to victory at Hopton Heath in March 1643, but was hacked down in the course of the battle, and disputes over the possession of his body did little honour to either side. His leadership duties were assumed by his elder son, who led the royalist cavalry at the Battle of Newbury, survived the wars, but then went into exile. After the return of Charles II, he served as Lord Lieutenant of Warwickshire and Constable of the Tower of London, dying in 1681. His younger brother, Sir William Compton, after finally surrendering Banbury, travelled abroad for two years. John Dolben of Finedon, born at Stanwick and in later life Archbishop of York, was one of the county's gentry who fought for the king. Another was Monckton of Fineshade, whose sword arm was shattered at Naseby. Sir Edward Montagu of Boughton House was interned at the outbreak of the war, and spent much of the war incarcerated in the Tower of London until ill health forced a move to the Savoy Hospital where he died in 1644. He had been removed from his ancestral lands in order to stifle his influential royalist sympathies. Henry Spencer of Althorp, lately created first earl of Sunderland, was killed at the Battle of Newbury in 1643. Sir Lewis Watson of Rockingham Castle was a covert Catholic but nevertheless was sheriff of Northamptonshire in 1632 and sat as an MP. His family was connected to the royalist Montagues of Boughton; to the parliamentary-leaning Manners of Belvoir, whose castle was seized by royalist troops and held as an important outpost of Newark-upon-Trent; and having royalist commander Lord Willoughby d'Eresby, son of the earl of Lindsey, as a son-in-law, to the Berties as well. These affinities produced conflicting loyalties, which encouraged him to opt for neutrality, a stance that was to prove untenable. When Rockingham Castle was seized by parliamentarian troops, Sir Lewis and his brother got away and joined the king in Oxford. Charged with dereliction of duty for failing in his duties as a Commissioner of Array in 1642, and for meekly surrendering the royal castle of Rockingham, he was imprisoned. His evident rehabilitation and subsequent loyal service to Charles I were rewarded with a barony in 1645. He died in 1653 at the age of sixty-nine.

The forces of the Midland Association had been commanded by Lord Grey, but 1644 saw a radical reorganisation of the parliamentarian armies to form the New Model Army. This necessitated the raising of new regiments to be trained and equipped as a permanent, professional force. Colonel John Pickering of Titchmarsh raised and commanded a regiment of foot in the army of the second earl of Manchester, and was present at a number of actions including the Battles of Marston Moor and Naseby, and the sieges of Bristol and Basing House. He died of fever in Devon, as the war was drawing to a close in 1645. His elder brother, Sir Gilbert Pickering, sat on the Midland Association committee, raising funds to support the parliamentarian army, and then became Cromwell's Lord Chamberlain. Sir John Norwich of Brampton, created baronet in 1641, had raised a troop of dragoons in 1642 in order to arrest Montagu of Boughton and to secure the county armoury. He occupied Rockingham Castle in 1643 and held it for parliament throughout the war. He became High Sheriff of Northamptonshire for 1645 and was elected to parliament in 1654 and again in 1660, but he died a year later. Colonel John Butler had commanded Oundle's parliamentarian garrison, but like the parliamentarian General Monck and many others, he was quite comfortable supporting the return to Monarchy, becoming quartermaster-general of the post-Restoration army of Monck, now made earl of Albemarle. Another senior officer to adopt the royalist cause in 1660 was Sir Thomas Myddleton, the parliamentarian sergeant-major general in North Wales, responsible for a decisive defeat of the Welsh royalists at Montgomery in 1644, and a frequent visitor to his niece at Courteenhall.

The Battle of Naseby

After Edgehill in October 1642, the area had witnessed no real battles until June 1644. An attempt by the king to head off a parliamentarian force seeking to link up with Waller's army on the eastern, or Northamptonshire, side of the river Cherwell caused a confrontation at Cropredy Bridge, north of Banbury. Having crossed over the river to exploit a dislocation in the royalist army, Waller found himself outnumbered and isolated. Although he managed successfully to regain the eastern bank and get his troops to Northampton to regroup, it was at the cost of his artillery and his pride, and it could have easily been much worse. As it happened, a month later, the royalists would suffer a catastrophic defeat at Marston Moor near York, and that autumn, scramble an indecisive outcome at Newbury, but it would be another year before the war would reach its climax at Naseby. The spring of 1645 found the royalist army in the Midlands torn three ways: Charles and Rupert could commit their resources to a resurgence in the north by marching on Chester; they could ensure that Oxford, currently under siege, was relieved and thoroughly secured; or they could join forces with their army in the South West. Given that, realistically, only one of these three alternatives would be viable, the king, following his normal practice of avoiding any discussion of strategy, declined to select a single, achievable option and split his forces to attempt all three objectives. At the end of May, Leicester fell to royalist troops under Prince Rupert, prompting a swift parliamentarian response. The siege of Oxford was temporarily abandoned with troops being returned to their garrisons. Some 400 men were sent back to Northampton to prepare to defend what was seen as the royalists' likely next target, while on 4 June, the garrison of Rockingham was preparing for the royalist assault, which was anticipated as a prelude to the investment of Northampton. Instead, the royalist army followed the main road through Market Harborough, plundering villages along the way and making for Daventry. On 7 June, the main royalist army camped on Borough Hill while the king lodged in the Wheat-sheaf Inn. Meanwhile, the parliamentarian New Model Army was converging on Northampton: Fairfax and Skippon coming from the abandoned siege of Oxford via Newport Pagnell; Cromwell from the Fens via Olney; and Vermuyden's cavalry from Stamford. The troops were quartered in the villages around Northampton, including Wootton, Rothersthorpe, Harpole, and Kislingbury. While Fairfax had made arrangements through the County Committee for supplies to be bought and paid for, these villages still all suffered grave financial loss from the presence of so many troops and animals. Once Fairfax felt confident that sufficient forces were gathered, he sought to bring the king's army to battle. The royalists meanwhile remained at Borough Hill, which they had refortified, but the few patrols they had deployed were subjected to unexpected harassment by squadrons of parliamentarian cavalry, which had approached unobserved. The king, let down by his scouts, hoped to break off the action and ordered a withdrawal towards Melton Mowbray and Newark-upon-Trent, there to await reinforcements. Both armies were attempting to conceal their intentions while they manoeuvred across the countryside, with the parliamentarians closely shadowing the royalists. Having reached Market Harborough on 13 June, the king realised that he could not avoid a full-scale battle. Tradition holds that Cromwell spent the night before Naseby at the late sixteenth-century Hazelrigg House in Northampton's Marefair, but the formerly Elizabethan Thornby Hall also stakes a claim. Charles, having spent the day hunting at Fawsley Park, may have passed the night at the Old Hall in Stanford-on-Avon, while Rupert's HQ was in Market Harborough, and that of Fairfax was in Guilsborough.

Thus the royalist army next day found itself drawn up along a ridge, a few miles to the south of Market Harborough, facing a parliamentarian army composed of well-trained and well-led troops, drawn up opposite them on a suitably elevated position. Estimates of the relative strengths of the two armies cover a wide range, based on everything from hearsay to precise documentation. Not all units of the field armies were up to establishment and some, such as detachments from the garrisons of Northampton or Rockingham, only arrived after the main action was over. Taking all these factors into consideration, a reasonable estimate of the parliamentarian numbers lies somewhere around 15,000–17,000 men, with a ratio of cavalry to infantry of roughly 7:10. The smaller size of the royalist army has never been in question, but estimates of the precise shortfall vary considerably. Again, a reasonable estimate would seem to be an absolute maximum of 12,000, with a horse to foot ratio of 5:7. The battlefield itself was largely devoid of cover, being mainly a mix of open fields and pasture, set in a landscape of rising ground interspersed with deep coombes. While both the composition and disposition of the two armies are well established, there is still doubt as to the width of their frontages between the natural features of the battlefield. Glen Foard has researched the battle in great detail using archaeological and documentary evidence, and has produced a detailed and critical synthesis of the numerous narratives of the battle, so no more than a brief summary will suffice here.

One significant factor in the parliamentarian deployment was the positioning of Okey's 500 dragoons, mounted infantry armed with matchlocks, along the hedge line that flanked the western edge of the battlefield. This position served both to protect the left flank of the parliamentarian army and to impact on the royalist advance by inhibiting the introduction of their reserves. The archaeological evidence would suggest that these dragoons were more proactive in the battle by advancing to threaten the royalist right, which was seen to be stronger than those forces opposing it. As was his habit, Prince Rupert, seeing that the parliamentarian right was the stronger flank, led a cavalry charge on their left, breaking through at least two of Ireton's regiments but not completely routing them. However, the impetus of the charge, morphing into the pursuit of those of Ireton's troopers who fled the field as far south as Naseby village, lost Rupert the initiative. Meanwhile, in the centre, the infantry were locked together and

Haselrigg House in Northampton is one of those places where Cromwell reputedly passed the night before the Battle of Naseby.

the royalist foot, supported by cavalry, which included some of Rupert's men, gained the advantage, breaking the parliamentarian first line. Skippon's regiment appears to have borne the brunt of this assault, taking heavy casualties, with officers among them. However, casualty figures from the other parliamentarian infantry units suggest that the damage was confined to only two or three regiments. Though wounded, by friendly fire as it happened, Skippon brought the parliamentarian reserves into the action to check the royalist advance. Then the numerically superior and fearsomely intense Ironsides of the New Model charged Langdale's Northern Horse on the royalist left. Cromwell, recently appointed lieutenant-general in command of the New Model cavalry, had trained his troopers to advance at a measured trot to get within the correct range before firing their pistols, and to bulldoze their opponents, the complete antithesis of Rupert's tactic of the headlong charge, the icebreaker model. Despite the unevenness of the ground, nothing could possibly have withstood their inexorable advance downhill, and despite putting up a spirited fight, Langdale's heavily outnumbered horse were inevitably forced to withdraw. This allowed Cromwell's cavalry reserves to be sent in to roll up the royalist centre, putting the entire royalist army to flight. Archaeological evidence, musket balls, and coins to the north of the battlefield east of Sibbertoft suggests that royalist resistance was centred briefly on the area around the baggage train. Further concentrations of musket balls were found at Wadborough, scene of another stand by the fleeing royalists. Refusing to accept the defeat of his army, Charles gathered the remnants of his cavalry around him to make a last stand, but his troops felt that enough had been asked of them already and took off towards Leicester. As it was, royalist dead extended several miles back from the battlefield.

The training and discipline shown by the parliamentarian troops allowed their commanders to capitalise on their superiority in numbers. The battle had lasted some three hours, during which time the royalist army had been destroyed. No more than 4,000, around a third of the army, escaped the field, and a further 4,000 were captured, being taken initially to Northampton and then to London. Some of those who had made it to Leicester were captured when the town was retaken by Fairfax a couple of days after the battle. Estimates of the dead and wounded are confused, but weighing all the evidence, it would appear that around 400 royalists died on the battlefield; a further 300 were killed in the flight; and perhaps as many as 200, out of the thousand or so seriously wounded, subsequently died. Parliamentarian losses were around 300 killed on the battlefield and those forty-four of the 535 seriously wounded who died later as a result. The Battle of Naseby is generally regarded as the decisive action of the Civil War, and royalist fortunes went downhill thereafter.

Civil War Fortifications

Much of continental Europe had existed in a state of almost continuous warfare right through from the early medieval period to the Thirty Years' War (1618–48), so the art of fortification had, of necessity, kept pace with the demands of military strategy and tactics. Hence, the majority of towns and cities across Europe were defended by circuits of walls designed to both mount and resist artillery. The art of fortification had evolved into a highly sophisticated science based on geometry, topography, ballistics, and construction, with national traditions, or schools, being developed in Italy, Spain, France, and the Netherlands. In England, for the most part a relatively peaceful island throughout the medieval period, most cities had outgrown their medieval cores and had allowed their walls to deteriorate or, in some cases, had even demolished them. With the exception of Henry VIII's chain of coastal forts erected around 1540, few modern fortifications existed. Both sides in the Civil War employed experienced engineers, but there was generally neither the time nor the resources to produce anything to rival continental achievements, with only Bernard de Gomme's work at Oxford coming anywhere remotely close to emulating the defences of the cities of continental Europe. Nevertheless, there were still some basic principles that would apply in England. In order to lessen the effect of artillery bombardment, stone walls could be strengthened with earth ramparts but, above all, earthwork defences should be extended outwards to keep the enemy at as great a distance as possible, lessening the destructive effect of cannon shot. Although sieges would figure significantly in the campaigns of the Civil War, they were merely the means to the end of securing and holding territory. Thus the war was essentially one of movement, of manoeuvring armies around in order to gain dominance in a particular area, and then securing it with garrisons. Most of the important battles came about as the result of such tactics, as armies collided with each other, sometimes unexpectedly. Marston Moor (1644), for instance, was the result of an attempt to relieve the siege of York, and Naseby (1645) came after the siege of Leicester and the king's attempt to relieve pressure on Oxford. The need to control territory would tie up large numbers of troops in garrisons, often conveniently situated manor houses, not necessarily displaying many of the attributes of fortifications. A stone house, preferably within a moat, could present a significant obstacle, especially to an attacker denied the use of cannon by the effect of weather on the already appalling roads. In any case, cannon were scarce and expensive, and required inordinate numbers of men and horses to move them. Therefore, by adding a circuit of earthworks, blocking doorways and windows with wool sacks, hay bales, or sandbags, and punching a few loopholes in inner and outer walls, any isolated manor house or church could be prepared for defence and, with a committed garrison, would often prove a hard nut to crack. At Weedon Lois, the vicar resisted an attempt by parliamentarian troops to arrest him by barricading himself in the crossing tower of his church, accessed by a narrow and easily blocked stair. In some instances, earthwork redoubts might be raised for a particular purpose, such as to guard the approaches to an especially vulnerable position, or to control movement along a strategic highway, but Civil War fortifications were, for the most part, a case of improvisation or make do and mend.

Northampton was seen as a particularly important obstacle to royalist ambitions beyond those Oxfordshire heartlands protected by Banbury and its outliers. Consequently, its garrison was strong, ranging from the local militia of several thousand men and the dragoon regiment of Colonel Norwich in the early days to some 1,500 trained horse and foot later on. Local volunteers were always available to supplement the trained troops of the garrison in an emergency. The town's medieval defences, enclosing a generous 250 acres (100 ha), easily contained the shrunken town, with significant suburbs only on the south, extending from the south gate to the river Nene. Much of the actual circuit, including the gates, still survived in 1642, but was ruinous in the north by St Andrew's Priory, and had largely disappeared on the south and west river frontages. Supplemented by refurbished gates and chains across the bridges, what was left would form the basis of perfectly viable new defences. The refortification of the town was managed by a committee, which raised money to pay for work delegated to individuals including experienced military engineers. One of these was Cornelius Vanden Boon, who designed the defences of Newport Pagnell and had aided Colonel Fiennes at the siege of Banbury. Another was David Papillon, grandson of a Huguenot martyr of the St Bartholomew's Day massacre in Paris in 1572, who had worked in Gloucester and elsewhere. His design for defences at Northampton might have been appropriate for a flat, Greenfield site, but for a built-up town with irregular topographical features, his symmetrical circuit of nineteen bastions with three flanked redoubts not only could not easily have been superimposed on the existing layout, but would also have been extremely costly. An added problem was his intention to include the suburb of Cotton End outside the south gate. He argued that if not taken into the defences, it would have to be demolished in order to ensure clear fields of fire, thereby alienating a large number of the town's citizens, just those people who worked on the defences and looked to the garrison to defend them. His trace, somewhat appropriately, is best described as pear-shaped, although, to be fair to Papillon, he did recognise that he and his fellow engineers could, realistically, replicate neither the scale nor the precision of those works they had studied in continental Europe. In 1645/6, he would publish *A Practicall Abstract of the Arts of Fortification and Assailing* in London, but although some of his schemes were implemented in Northampton, possibly the earthwork defences in Cow Meadow, his overall plans were rejected and he was succeeded by an engineer from Nottingham.

Captain John Hooper was highly thought of and consequently in such demand that he had to combine his work in Northampton with advising his old governor in Nottingham, and serving as a senior, 'Extraordinary' member of the New Model Army's engineer corps. Hooper carried out a thorough survey of the town's defences in October 1645, soon after his arrival in Northampton. Using the medieval circuit of defences as a basis, the walls were reinforced with earthworks constructed largely by the townsfolk. In August 1642, 500 men and 100 women were labouring on the walls and ensuring that the gates and other weak points were protected by new breastworks. There were artillery present from the beginning and platforms may well have been constructed at this time to mount them. The road still called 'The Mounts' refers to such provision of batteries for cannon. The town walls and castle were refurbished in stone, and some buildings outside the walls were demolished, both to create clearer fields of fire and to deny attackers cover. The threat of siege never went away so work to improve the defences was continuous throughout the war, extending over four years and concentrating particularly on areas of possible weakness. In their final form, the 1.8-mile (3-km) circuit consisted of the original stone walls reinforced with turf and timber revetments. In some places, possibly the new bulwarks outside each gate, there may have been some facing of earthworks in stone, and some of the new earthworks were built on foundations of stone and timber. The optimum dimensions of the bank itself were laid down, but this specification was not achieved everywhere. The bank was to be 35 feet (11 metres) thick at the base and 20 feet (6 metres) on the top, where breastworks of turf, strengthened by courses of brushwood, with any loose earth rammed hard, would be built. The fighting platform would lie behind a 6-foot-high (1.8-metre-high) breastwork, with loopholes cut through as firing ports. Where batteries were constructed for cannon, a platform of planking was laid on top of the bank, and embrasures, strengthened with gabions, were cut through the turf breastwork. On the outer face of the bank, near to its top, there were *frises*, or storm poles, 6-foot-long (1.8-metre-long) sharpened stakes, projecting at an upward angle over the ditch to impede climbers. The ditch itself, which encircled the whole town, was recommended as being 20 feet (6 metres) deep and 30 feet (9 metres) across, with a gradient of 1:3. There were no counterscarps on the outside lip of the ditch, so the ground would slope away as a *glacis*, allowing the defenders to fire directly down onto attacking infantry. Some of the medieval ditches were recut and some held water, while the river itself provided an added layer of defence on the south and west. The castle ditch was still formidable, measuring up to 80 feet (25 metres) across and 25 feet (8 metres) deep. The castle, though ruinous to some extent, retained the curtain wall and towers of its inner bailey, providing an inner core or citadel. It thus constituted an integral part of the defences, especially in view of the weakness of the defences in the north of the town. Rechristened 'The Fort', the castle's triangular earthwork northern barbican was transformed into an imposing bulwark, with a stone or timber revetment, for mounting cannon or ranks of musketeers, and commanding the north-west flank of the new walls. To its east, and lying outside the castle's original perimeter rose 'Castle Hill', a half-moon battery, higher than the adjacent fortifications, and dominating that corner of the town. It was constructed of alternating layers of rubble, sand, and loam with a high charcoal content, and may have been terraced, providing tiers of defences for mounting cannon, for which design precedents can be found at Great Yarmouth and elsewhere. The rubble may have come from properties demolished to make room for this battery and earth came from the recutting of the castle ditch. It is likely that, at this northern end of town, there was a contraction of the defence line, abandoning the salient previously occupied by St Andrew's Priory, and reverting to the line of an earlier wall. An artillery platform or 'mount' was built west of the north gate to command the northern approaches. These mounts, technically 'cavaliers', may have been built forward of the old medieval wall rather than astride or against it. On the south side of the town, the problem of inserting artillery into bulwarks, flankers, or mounts without having to build ramps over the existing town wall was to put a roadway, like the Roman *pomerium*, in-between the old and new defences. The other problem with the mounts paradoxically lay in their height. They were designed to command a wide field of fire and to achieve a maximum range, but their very openness rendered them vulnerable to incoming shot, and their cannon could not be depressed sufficiently to fire on attackers who had fought their way to the base of the rampart. The solution lay in flankers, which projected from the rampart and allowed lighter cannon to fire from protected positions in order to enfilade the curtain. Providing they were close enough together, Papillon suggests intervals of 600 feet (185 metres) an effective coverage could be achieved, but this did not always obtain at Northampton. The ditches surrounding the town appear to have been dug in a piecemeal fashion responding to the availability of labour and to competing priorities. In the south-west corner, a double Civil War-period ditch has been found consisting of an inner, flat-bottomed one, 20 feet (6 metres) wide and 39 inches (1 metre) deep; and an outer, V-shaped ditch, 9 feet (2.7 metres) wide. Where the castle ditch survived, a V-shaped ditch was inserted, in places, between the medieval ditch and the wall. Elsewhere, improvements were made to the silted up mediaeval ditches on which Papillon had poured scorn. Some of the medieval ditches were recut, but some appear to have retained their strength. The medieval ditch on the north side of the fort, for instance, was found to have been 30 feet (9 metres) wide, and 19 feet (6 metres) deep, but had a narrower and shallower V-shaped ditch cut on its inside in the 1640s. As in the case of the northern defences, the opportunity was taken elsewhere to shorten the circuit, and this will have necessitated the digging of fresh ditches. Both the West and South Bridges had drawbridges inserted.

At Towcester, the remains of the Roman and Saxon walls provided a basis for the new royalist defences in 1643. The earthworks were strengthened along the line of the *burh* walls to produce a rampart around 6 feet (1.8 metres) wide and 10–12 feet (3–3.5 metres) in height. The rampart was raised on a foundation trench 8 feet (2.4 metres) wide with dry-stone walls forming both inner and outer faces to produce a sandwich with a filling of stones and earth containing quantities of Roman and medieval pottery and tile. Outside this curtain was an 18-foot-wide (5.5-metre-wide) and 6-foot-deep (1.8-metre-deep) ditch. It was the fill in this ditch that furnished clues to the make-up of the rampart, because Rupert's exit from the town in January 1644 was marked by the toppling of the curtain into the ditch as he deliberately slighted the defences. Contemporary descriptions suggested that they had consisted simply of the ramparts topped with a fighting platform behind a breastwork, and that there were no

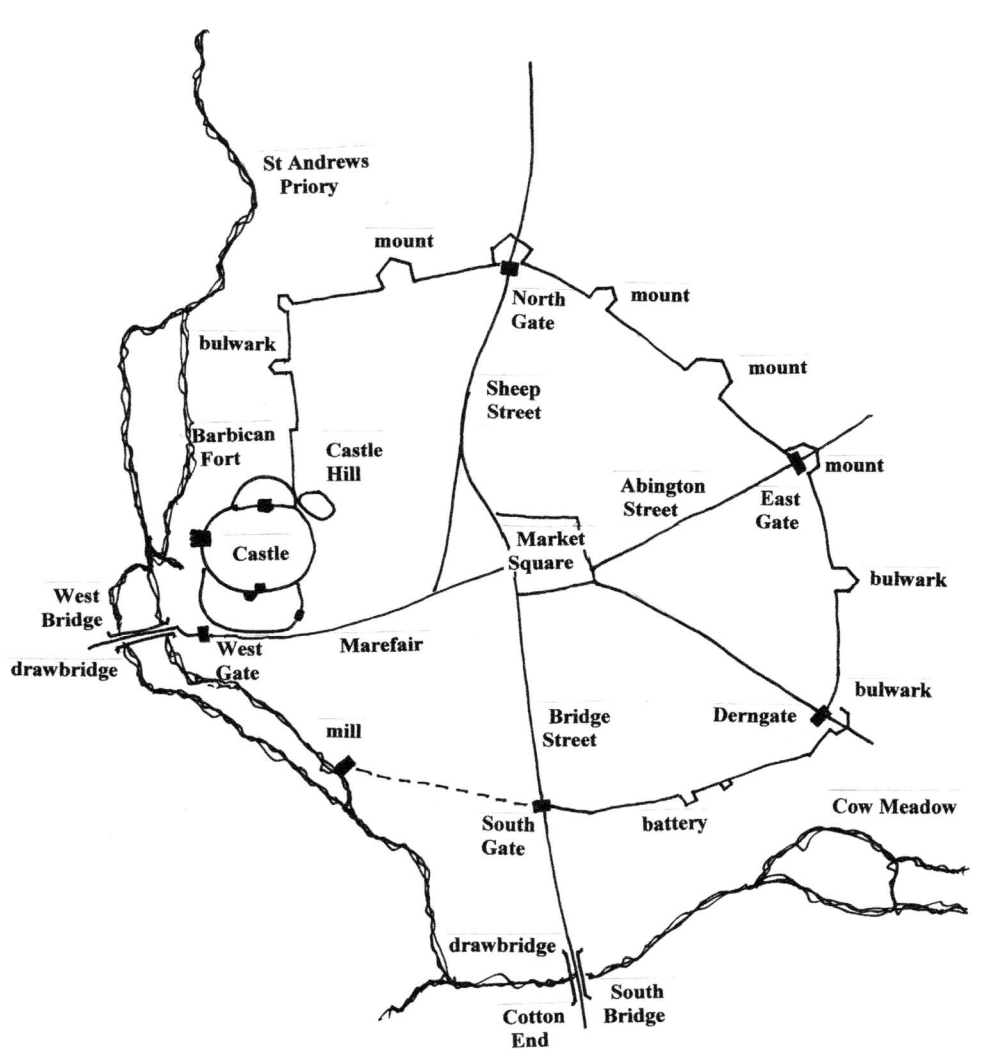

Sketch plan of Northampton's Civil War defences

Northampton Civil War defences: sketch plan.

bulwarks, mounts, or flankers. It would appear that the Bury Mount was adapted to take, possibly two, cannon, as anything up to a dozen guns were reported as present in the town, though some may have been mounted elsewhere to threaten the approaches to Northampton and to protect this base for Rupert's cavalry against pre-emptive strikes.

In 1534, Henry VIII had allowed one of his courtiers to remove building materials from Rockingham Castle for a house nearby in Leicestershire, and within a short time, the buildings inside the walls were ruinous. Although the Watsons rebuilt much of the domestic accommodation, the fortifications were not in good repair at the beginning of the war. However, the castle occupied a key position in the defences of the Eastern Association's northern borders so it was vital that its defensibility beyond the surviving gatehouse and eastern curtain was restored. The motte with its hexagonal shell keep was transformed into an artillery platform with cannon mounted on the keep's roof, and on five flankers, three built at the base of the motte, and two more, of timber, at a slightly higher level. The base of the motte was surrounded by an earthen rampart surmounted by a palisade, inside which a passage provided a covered way permitting safe movement for the defenders. Above this passage, a further breastwork joined up with the two wooden flankers and defined a terraced platform below the keep itself for storehouses. These concentric circuits of new defences significantly enhanced the strength of an already impressive position, and it may have been the presence of cannon that allowed Colonel Norwich to repulse several determined attacks by strong royalist forces. A further, drastic measure was the demolition of the church and eleven cottages in the village, in order to establish clear fields of fire.

Schematic reconstruction of Rockingham Castle's Civil War defences

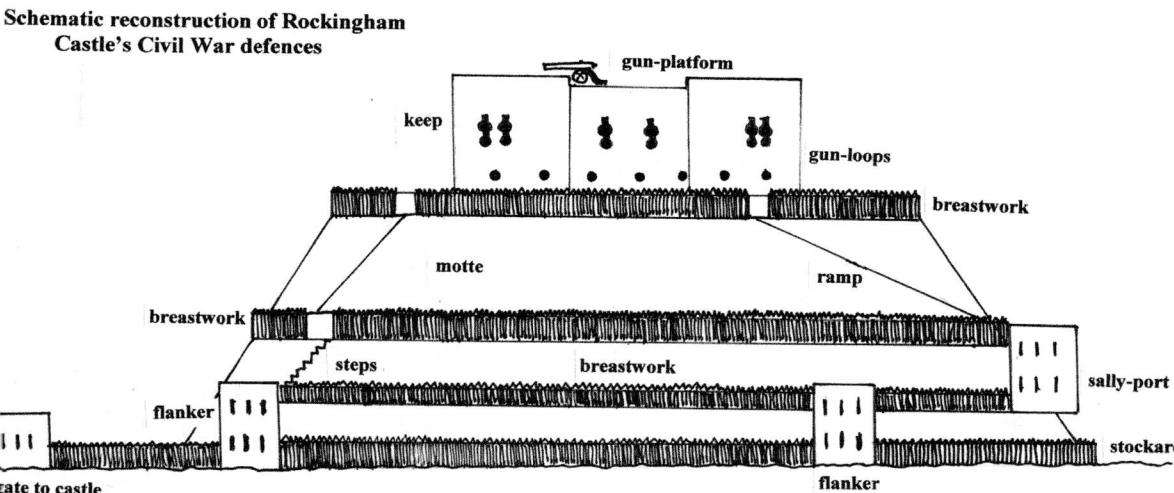

Rockingham Castle: cross-section of the motte showing the Civil War defences, reconstructed from a contemporary plan.

Many of the temporary garrisons held for only short periods of time were not occupied for long enough to warrant the construction of defensive works. Some were naturally strong. At Grafton Regis, for instance, work was carried out for Henry VIII on a palace between 1528 and 1548, on a site some distance from the Woodville's manor house. This palace was enclosed by 14-foot-high (4.3-metre-high) stone walls and a gatehouse. To these, the royalist defenders added a rampart, palisade, and ditch, which encircled the palace and took in the adjacent parish church of St Mary.

A number of earthworks have, over the years, been identified as defensive works from the Civil War period but have subsequently been rejected. These include Hall Close at East Farndon, where supposed entrenchments with cannon emplacements have been reinterpreted as old tracks within medieval settlement remains, and dismissed by RCHM(E). Similarly at Kelmarsh, a reputed Civil War sconce has been seen as more likely to have been a medieval fishpond. At Walgrave, however, a possible Civil War-period battery at the junction of the minor road to Walgrave and the main Kettering–Northampton road (A43) is more plausible (SP82439734). A formerly trapezoidal mound with sides of 25 yards, but now reduced to a mound, 100 feet (30 metres) across, and just over 3 feet (1 metre) high, could be a barrow or a gibbet hill, but if its reported shape is, in fact, authentic, the likelihood of a Civil War origin is increased.

The Second Civil War and After

Following the king's surrender to the Scots in Nottinghamshire in April 1646, he was held by them before being handed over to parliament in January 1647. He was held for a short while at the Hattons' house at Holdenby, riding over to Harrowden and Althorp to play bowls, prior to being taken to a more secure lodging at Army HQ in Cambridge. Captain Baynes, MP, bought Holdenby House in 1650 and demolished most of it. In the spring of 1648, a second Civil War broke out. Sir William Compton returned as a royalist major-general and served at the siege of Colchester in Essex. Unlike some of his royalist co-commanders who were breaking parole and, having been captured, were summarily shot, he was fortunate to survive the siege. After the Restoration, he was appointed master of the ordnance and served as an MP, but died aged thirty-eight in 1663. As a result of this ill-conceived insurrection, following the king's execution in early 1649, parliament appointed the snappily named Commissioners for Militia to Suppress Insurrections and Preserve the Peace for the Counties of Northamptonshire and Rutland. Many of these commissioners were former officers and minor gentry and their job was to keep the peace. Later that year, incited to mutiny by the pamphlets and speeches of the leveller John Lilburne, soldiers from Banbury and Northampton were intercepted at Walgrave and routed by troops loyal to parliament. Conscious of ongoing discontent, parliament opted to ensure that numerous fortresses should be rendered indefensible and the defences of Rockingham Castle were slighted. In 1650, a parliamentarian army under the command of Zouch Tate was quartered around Wellingborough, and was visited by Cromwell who may have stayed at the recently built Hind Inn. After the Restoration, an early act of Charles II in July 1662 was to signal his extreme disapproval of the town's steadfast opposition to his father by ordering the swift demolition of Northampton's town walls, recorded in great detail in the surviving accounts (*Northamptonshire Past and Present*; Volume VI, Number 2, 1979). Labourers were recruited from each parish by constables and paid for eight days' work with half a hogshead of beer thrown in for doing overtime. The work, which chiefly involved toppling the ramparts and palisades into the ditches, was carried out under the eye of the trained bands, which had been mobilised by way of asserting royal authority and issued with powder and match to dissuade any dissenting townsfolk from obstructing the operation. Waggoners were paid to carry away armaments from the parish church to the earl of Westmorland's house at Apethorpe, and drums and halberds to Major Pemberton's house at Higham Ferrers. The whole operation cost £135—almost £300,000 at modern labour prices.

A New Army Develops: Regulars, Militia, and Volunteers

The restoration of the monarchy in 1660 saw the continuation of the struggle between king and parliament to obtain funds. Although the existence of a standing army remained anathema to much of the population, Charles II, abetted by the earl of Albemarle, formerly the parliamentarian General Monck, saw the benefits to be had from retaining a cadre of trained troops. The third earl of Northampton was one of the commanders of the troops at Barham Down, Dover, reviewed by Charles on landing. One of the king's financial requests was for the militia, and legislation was finally passed in 1684 to fund this constitutional force. At the same time, regular regiments were being raised, and George Holman of the vanished Warkworth Castle near Banbury raised a cavalry regiment for Charles's brother, James II. The fourth earl of Northampton was among those of the nobility who deserted James II and gave their support to William of Orange. He carried the king's sceptre and cross at the coronation, and became Lord Lieutenant of Warwickshire, and Constable of the Tower of London. In 1688, the county militia declared for William III, and a mob ransacked Drayton, the earl of Peterborough's seat, in search of weapons and provoking alarm among the establishment who feared a breakdown in central authority following the flight of James II. However, life went on and the troops of William III who trod the banks of the Boyne were shod in Raunds-made boots. The reigns of William and Mary and also of Anne saw further legislation regarding the militia, but it was only embodied in 1715 to counter a Jacobite threat in Northamptonshire under the duke of Montagu. A second Jacobite rebellion evinced a stronger reaction. In 1744, as a response to the threat of this combined French and Jacobite invasion, the government authorised the establishment of volunteer associations. Northamptonshire was the first county to take action, raising a number of units across the county under the command of John, 2nd Duke of Montagu of Boughton House. Many of the 530 men in his force were freeholders and yeomen, people with property worth protecting. Worryingly, the Jacobites came as far south as Derby and the militia were called out again. In 1756, at the start of the Seven Years' War, the Northamptonshire militia, with an establishment of 1,280 men, was embodied under Lord Halifax. The Militia Act of 1757 laid down the establishment and terms of service for the county militias. Under the control of the Lord Lieutenant, officers were required to meet wealth criteria—a captain, for instance, needing an income of £200 *per annum*. The Northamptonshire militia had become fully established by 1763, producing an establishment of 640 men with twenty-four officers, meeting the official ratio of 3:80. The Northamptonshire Militia Returns of 1777 comprise a list of able-bodied eight to forty-five year olds eligible for ballot. It records 13,741 men, representing 70 per cent of the age group, of whom some 40 per cent were either agricultural labourers or farm servants. In 1764, there was a riot over enclosure in West Haddon, but order was restored without recourse to military force. In 1780, however, the Northamptonshire militia were called on to serve in London at the time of the Gordon Riots and were stationed at Lambeth Palace, opposite the Palace of Westminster. In addition to internal security, another of the functions of the militia was to provide cover in times of war for the regiments of the regular army to be deployed abroad where the fighting was and, it was hoped, would remain. So the Northamptonshire militia was embodied during the American War of Independence in 1778, with further volunteer units being raised in 1779.

The 48th Foot was one of six new regiments raised in 1741 to fight the War of the Austrian Succession. In 1755, the 48th fought against the French and their Native American allies in the Seven Years' War. The 58th Foot was one of twenty new regiments raised in 1755, which would remain in being after the end of the war. Along with the 48th, it served in Wolfe's army at Quebec. The 58th was part of the garrison of Gibraltar during the siege of 1780–3, and part of the force that fought Napoleon in Egypt in 1801. In 1810, the 48th, under Lord Fitzroy, was awaiting deployment to join Wellington in the Peninsula, enjoying Northampton's society until eventually transport was found for them at the very end of November. During the campaign of 1812–13, the 48th were credited with a major part in the victories at Talavera and Albuera. Its 2nd Battalion was on garrison duties in Portsmouth in 1804 to defend this vital naval base against yet another threatened French invasion.

In Britain, the French Revolution of 1789 had caused palpitations among aristocracy and bourgeoisie alike. Part of their joint reaction was to form citizens' defence forces, known generically as 'Volunteers', to counter the possibility of internal upheaval. A further safeguard was the building of cavalry barracks, a revolutionary construct in itself, in industrial towns perceived by the government as prone to disturbances. Leicester Parade on Northampton's Barrack Road is one such location. The War Office had built a group of what were essentially police barracks in 1792 in seven places, such as Manchester, Nottingham, and Norwich. In 1794, a further twenty-five were planned mainly on the invasion coast, with others inland as backup. That scheduled for Leicester never materialised, but Northampton's duly appeared. It was designed to accommodate two troops of cavalry: each of fifty-eight troopers with an officer. The ashlar-built, white-painted building fronting Barrack Road, next to St Sepulchre's Parochial School, represents a small section of the oldest part of this barracks. It probably held the officers' quarters and mess at one end with tack rooms and stables on the ground floor, and rooms for the troopers above. It would have been set in a walled compound with hay barns, sickbays for horses and men, armoury, stores, and the forge set around the edge. The whole idea of barracks was new at this time and would have been welcomed as an alternative to the hated practice of billeting soldiers on houses both public and private. One of the country's provincial Ordnance Depots was built *c.* 1806 in Northampton, to the standard design of James Wyatt, architect to the Board of Ordnance, whose prototype armoury still stands in London's Hyde Park.

Northampton: the cavalry barracks built during the French Wars.

In 1794, a public meeting was convened by Richard Booth, the county's High Sheriff, at Northampton County Hall, to discuss a plan already circulated in response to a request from the Secretary of State for War regarding the raising of voluntary cavalry, closely followed by the Militia Act. The proposal was for troops of from fifty to eighty men to be available for local defence and for suppressing riots and tumult. A subscription fund, headed by Earl Spencer, was started to raise funds for harness and to meet the cost of kitting out the troopers, whose uniforms were reckoned to come to over £6 apiece. Troops were recruited in Northampton, Peterborough, Daventry, Brackley, Kettering, Oundle, and Towcester. Thomas Pickering, having spent twenty years in the Household Cavalry, was appointed as riding master to drill new recruits and accomplished horsemen alike, in the unfamiliar equine choreography of the military. Cavalry manoeuvres were complicated, but it was only in 1798 that the regiment would receive its first drill book of a full twenty-six pages. Arms were acquired; the king graciously allowed his Hanover horse to be incorporated in the cap badge; and a standard, or guidon, was designed by Earl Spencer. His terms of engagement were clearly well thought of as they served as a model for other similar bodies such as the East Riding Gentlemen and Yeomanry Cavalry recruited in Yorkshire in 1794. By October 1795, the regiment, now the Northamptonshire Yeomanry, was ready to assemble on Northampton racecourse prior to parading through the town. Before this, however, Northampton-based yeomen had been called out to deal with a riot when townspeople had stormed a food convoy in protest at the soaring prices. A few years later and the Northampton and Althorp troops were called to Wilbarton, where the protests were against enclosure of the commons. The Riot Act was read and the troopers stood by until the crowd of 300 villagers had dispersed. Although the Peace of Amiens had provided a brief lull in the wars, hostilities were soon resumed and invasion was once more seen as possible. By late 1805, more formal and regular inspections were instituted, and the regiment was regarded more as an entity than a collection of dispersed troops, and instructions were issued to assemble at Northampton's Market Hall in the event of an emergency callout. Despite falling short of its required establishment, by 1804, there were sixteen troops of yeomanry cavalry in the county, and in 1805, a total of nearly 600 men under the command of Lieutenant-Colonel Corbett were ready for whatever Boney might throw at them. Training continued apace, and while expert horsemen, many of them accomplished huntsmen, might quickly learn the riding drills, mastering the skill of firing carbines from the saddle was particularly difficult. Not only were there eleven discrete operations to carry out in loading and firing, but it was felt to be desirable that maximum effect might be gained by all the troopers firing a volley in unison. Similar skills were needed to fire the pistol, and all this had to be achieved without frightening the horses. Sword-fighting drills were also practised, at first on foot and then on horseback. By the time that the yeomen were approaching fitness for purpose, the wars were over and many volunteer cavalry regiments had been disbanded by 1815. Some, including the Northamptonshire Yeomanry, were retained, at least for a further decade, as much for their usefulness in support of the Civil Power as for their place in any scheme of national defence.

During the French Wars of 1793–1815, the militia served mainly at home, being stationed at Dover Castle in 1805, but also in Ireland and France. In 1798, the 2nd Northamptonshire Supplementary Militia was raised specifically for home defence, but was disembodied a year later. In June 1797, a meeting had been convened at Daventry's Wheat-sheaf Inn to form a company of volunteer infantry. An initial subscription of 5/- was levied and members were expected to equip themselves and parade with their hair properly powdered. Mondays were used for field days, when members were fined for non-attendance. By 1804, there were forty such companies in the county, with a total membership of nearly 1,800 men under Lieutenant-Colonel Delaval, based in the towns and also on stately homes such as Boughton House and Castle Ashby. Many of these units drew up their own terms and conditions and those accepted by Northamptonshire's volunteers were adopted in other counties but often with modifications—one unit in Berkshire cutting out Sunday drills. In 1808, an attempt was made with the Local Militia Act to tidy up the chaotic state of the armed forces. Across the country, the 13,000 volunteer corps that had been formed, equipped, and uniformed haphazardly were reorganised into 270 units of local militia, much to the disappointment of many who had revelled in the glory of local command. The volunteers of Castle Ashby and Northampton were among those who resigned *en masse*. Local militiamen were now permitted to join the Regular Army and this provision proved a useful recruiting tool, producing 10,000 recruits to the regulars each year. On the ground, it made little difference to the individual. Poet John Clare describes signing up along with a rabble of lawless fellows, collecting his £2 bounty, and spending three weeks drilling and drinking in Oundle, and then going home. Clare may have been less than charitable in his assessment of his colleagues as they were predominantly artisans, shopkeepers, and servants with only a minority of unskilled labourers. In Northamptonshire, there were two regiments of local militia, the East and the West Regiments, but a couple of volunteer units like those of Kettering contrived to continue with unaltered status, refusing to join, and maintaining their independence until all local militias were disbanded in 1814.

An Act of 1793 had sanctioned the construction of a canal from Braunston on the Oxford Canal to the Thames at Brentford. By the end of the century, the stretches from Braunston to Blisworth and from Blisworth to Brentford had been completed and the Blisworth Tunnel was under construction. Until it could be opened, a road linked the Grand Junction Canal to the Northampton turnpike and, later on, a temporary tramway was laid over Blisworth Hill to Stoke Bruerne. The first attempt at tunnelling ended in a collapse, but a fresh tunnel on a different alignment eventually opened in 1805. From mid-1798, troops were transported by road to Blisworth where they transferred 100 men to each boat equipped with length-wise plank seats to complete their journeys to Liverpool and onwards to Ireland on internal security duties. These operations were supervised by Messrs Pickfords from their Blisworth depot and paid for by the Commissary General. By the end of 1799, over 8,000 militiamen had travelled this route. By 1803, the country was anticipating invasion, and Pickfords' wharfingers were instructed to override commercial traffic if required to move troops southwards. It was found that not only was the journey by canalboat less gruelling for the troops, but by avoiding a proportion of cart hire and subsistence payments, it was around 30 per cent cheaper for the Commissariat Department. However, in 1807, the thousand men of the 48th Foot marched from Essex to Liverpool as Messrs Pickfords' quotation was evidently too steep. Although the Royal Navy's success at Trafalgar in 1805 had forced Napoleon to abandon his immediate invasion plans, by 1811, fears of a French invasion had been renewed. Consequently, plans were made for militia regiments from Staffordshire to be carried by canal to Blisworth for onward transport to the south if required to repel a French invasion force.

The conjunction of this developing canal route with its proximity to Watling Street and its remoteness from the invasion coast made Weedon Bec a suitable location for the Board of Ordnance to choose for a barracks and arsenal in the invasion scare of 1798, considering it less vulnerable than competing sites, but still easily accessed. As well as the storage of munitions, there was also a need for the manufacture of muskets under government control. Weedon Bec was served by the Northampton turnpike but, more usefully in terms of heavy haulage, by the new length of canal through the Braunston Tunnel, which could access the Oxford Canal, and hence the whole Midlands' network, by 1796. Transport by barge would, anyway, be a far safer way of conveying both heavy loads and volatile materials such as gunpowder. In order to avoid any sudden escalation of land values, the board's representative, Major-General Ross, made discreet enquiries followed by the opening of negotiations with the principal landowner, Eton College, who proved amenable to the sale. After some reluctance on the part of tenants, the deal was made and compensation paid. Work to construct the depot began early in 1804 under Captain Pilkington, RE.

The depot would contain spacious two-storey buildings for storing 100,000 muskets upstairs, and field guns and iron-framed ammunition wagons downstairs behind securely barred windows; gunpowder magazines each holding 10,000 barrels; a small-arms

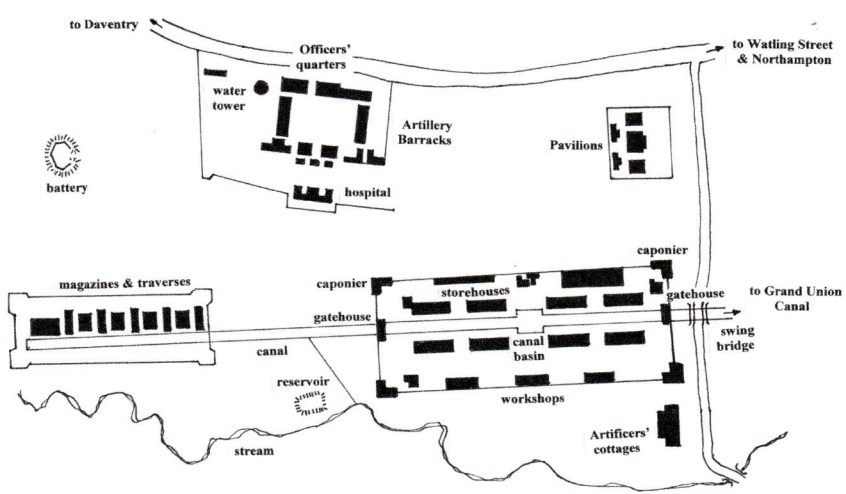

Sketch plan of Weedon Bec Barracks and Depot

Weedon Bec: sketch plan of the barracks and depot.

Weedon Bec Depot: the western gatehouse.

Weedon Bec Depot: Storehouses Nos 4, 6, and 8, and the canal.

factory and offices; a barracks and stables for a brigade of artillery; a hospital; and workshops. The whole site was defended by high walls, loopholed for musketry and with flanking bastions at the corners. Linking the site to the Grand Junction Canal was a 1,100-yard-long canal, running down the middle of the site, entering and exiting through imposing gatehouses, one of which was surmounted by a clock tower. By early 1805, the depot was in operation, and gathering in the products of the nation's largest ordnance factories, its smallest cottage industries, and everything in-between. A typical barge-load would be 10,000 muskets in 500 wooden chests. By 1814, the depot was running down, a process only temporarily interrupted by Napoleon's hundred days. The Pavilion, actually a trio of grand three-storey houses, was built to house the depot's governor and his two principal assistants. It is this group of imposing residences that have prompted the probably spurious explanation that they were intended to provide a safe bolthole for George III and his family were the French to land and threaten London. To the west of the barracks, at a height of 100 feet (30 metres) is a small earthwork (SP622598) described by RCHM(E) as a redoubt. It appears to be an earthen, ditched bastion, some 5 feet (1.5 metres) high, facing north-west, and measuring, overall, 195 feet × 160 feet (60 metres × 50 metres). It could have been raised as an outlying defence of the new barracks and depot or as a practice exercise for the artillery unit based there.

4

Victorian Northamptonshire 1815–1914

The end of the French wars, which had seen over twenty years of fighting with consequent widespread social and economic disruption, brought an immediate reduction in the strength of the various volunteer and regular forces. The regular regiments of foot lost any second battalions they might have raised; the volunteers were disbanded; and the militia almost faded away completely. The yeomanry managed to hang on but was finally disbanded in 1828, after which eight independent troops existed at various times. These included the Kettering Troop (1830–73) and the Deene Troop, raised in 1819 by Lord Brudenell, later to gain notoriety as the earl of Cardigan of Charge of the Light Brigade fame. Some of these yeomanry units' duties were purely ceremonial. In 1844, for instance, the Kettering Troop escorted Queen Victoria and Prince Albert during their journey from the railway at Weedon to Burghley House, meeting them on Market Hill as they changed their horses at the White Hart.

The main reason for the continued existence of such units was as a counter to civil unrest and public disorder. Northampton had seen violent election riots in 1768 when 500 men armed with clubs invaded Northampton in support of Lords Norton and Halifax. Their target, Lord Spencer, was forced to pay out the enormous sum of 1,000 guineas (£1,050) to appease his political opponents. The activities of the Luddites and those campaigning for parliamentary reform, often exacerbated by government spies and *agent provocateurs*, came to a peak in 1817–18. Widespread plans for a general uprising included threats to Weedon Barracks where arms might be seized for distribution to the masses. In 1819, the Kettering Troop was called out to deal with a bread riot. In 1830, as the reform legislation failed to clear a smooth path through parliament, serious rioting broke out once more. The Riot Act was read and regular cavalry were summoned from Weedon to restore order. Soldiers were called out during further disturbances over the next two years, with further violence, associated with the Swing Riots, causing local vigilante groups to be mobilised against the arsonists. At Elmington, near Oundle, 300 armed locals turned out to guard hayricks in the area between Aldwincle and Warmington. In one serious incident, a convoy of prisoners being conducted from Stamford to Northampton and guarded by mounted constables was attacked at Wellingborough. Order was only restored by the timely arrival of local

JPs: Stafford O'Brien Esq., with armed horsemen, and John Smith, commanding a company of volunteers and special constables.

Only in 1836 was a Northamptonshire police force established. Northampton Borough exchanged its five constables, most of whom had spent at least five years in the job, for two shifts, each of a dozen constables, but by 1848, the constabulary had expanded to thirty-seven men. A rural force was organised in 1840 with just twenty-nine constables to cover the county's 306 parishes with a total population of 180,000 people, which had formerly been policed by 396 village constables. Within a year, the force had doubled in size. Echoing previous generations' objections to a standing army, some conservative landowners regarded this new constabulary as yet another unconstitutional military force.

The Grand Junction Canal remained in use as a primary route for transporting troops from London to the Midlands and Liverpool. The branch from Gayton, south of Blisworth, linking the Grand Junction to the River Nene, opened in 1815, replacing the tramway, which had formerly run over Blisworth Hill. In 1820, Norton Junction brought about a connection along the Grand Union Canal to the River Trent via Leicester. Weedon Barracks lay on this main trooping line from London to Ireland using the canal system, and in 1824, a convoy of twenty-eight boats had passed through with troops returning from garrison duty. This was a time of peak movement, and in 1826, a battalion of some 700 officers and men of the Coldstream Guards travelled the route to Manchester. They were being deployed as a response to riotous behaviour by the cotton weavers who were engaged in a struggle to prevent the loss of their livelihoods to the new machines. In 1828, the 50th Foot arrived by canal as Weedon's latest garrison, but from then on, the railways gradually took over the majority of troop movements in Northamptonshire. Canal journeys had numbered in the hundreds between 1834 and 1839, but they had quickly dwindled to single figures by 1843. Reluctant as politicians were to allow the rude and licentious soldiery to mix with innocent civilians on trains, preferring to keep them out of sight and mind on canal boats, the advantages of both speed and cost offered by the railways prevailed.

Weedon Depot retained its importance into the nineteenth century, providing a base in the barracks on the top of the hill for a brigade of artillery, with 420 men and 160 draught horses. In 1830, a time of political unrest, plans were laid by the ordnance board to strengthen the fortifications of the depot. Temporary batteries were constructed on the surrounding heights in order to mount cannon to control the approaches; earthen redoubts were prepared for defending infantry; and musketry embrasures were cut into the bastions of the surrounding walls. In 1831, the standing garrison was increased to 800 men, causing uncomfortable overcrowding in the barrack accommodation, and much of the ordnance stores to be removed, possibly to the Tower of London, and some of the emptied storehouses converted to barracks. By 1844, there were nearly 600 officers and men in four storehouse conversions, and a further 500 in the barracks. Further buildings within the depot were converted for use as barracks, and another was converted as a military prison on three floors containing 120 separate cells. In 1854, the infantry housed in the converted storehouses departed for the Crimea, and by 1858, the depot was again taking in general stores and clothing, particularly boots from the local footwear factories. In 1868, the prison closed as most military prisoners were sent to the new panopticon at Millbank, now the site of Tate Britain. With both infantry and prisoners gone, all the storehouses reverted to their original purpose. In 1884, the facility was redesignated as a small-arms depot, which necessitated redesigned storage for new weapons, plus additional storage for clothing, a new wagon shed, and a tramway linking to the nearby railway line, all in place by 1885. New offices were built inside the east gate, and new workshops added. Outside the inner enclosure, more storage continued to be added into the twentieth century.

In 1843–4, the ordnance office was in the process of carrying out a comprehensive survey of the country in order to produce standardised maps to a uniform scale of 1 inch to 1 mile (1:63,360). A detachment of sappers and miners, later Royal Engineers, under Lt Da Costa, found that the most prominent high point in the north of the county was the church tower at Easton on the Hill. They erected a timber platform as an observatory on the tower and using the heliostat method of reflecting the sun's rays off a mirror enabled bearings to be taken from distant viewpoints. Some 50–60 miles (80–96 km) was the normal range, reaching Lincoln, Boston, and Ely, but it was possible, on occasion, to increase that range up to 125 miles (200 km). After two months' work, the observatory was dismantled and the survey party moved on.

During the Crimean War, two Tryons from Bulwick served at Sebastopol, and the infamous Lord Cardigan from the Brudenells' Deene Park led his 'Cherry-pickers' to death or glory at Balaclava. A Cartwright, from Aynho, the son of a general, was killed at Inkerman. The Northamptonshire militia was embodied and volunteered to carry out garrison duties in the Mediterranean, in Gibraltar in 1855, in order to release regular units for service in the Crimea. The militia had stagnated in the years following the end of the French Wars, but new legislation in 1852 reinvigorated the force with a national strength of 80,000 men. The intention was to recruit volunteers, only resorting to the unpopular system of balloting if unavoidable. In 1853, an act required the construction of armouries or stores for each militia regiment. The Northampton militia armoury in Clare Street dates from 1859, and is built as a toy fort. A loosely castellated style was fairly typical of militia armouries across the country, but Northampton's takes the model to the extreme, resembling a medieval castle with big drum towers and crenellated walls. Behind the show front, which housed an armoury and magazine, was an open courtyard for drilling, enclosed by ranges accommodating messes, stores, and living accommodation for the permanent staff. In 1860, the Northamptonshire and Rutland militias were amalgamated as a two-battalion regiment.

Public perceptions that the musketry skills of the British Army in both the Crimean War and the Indian Mutiny of the preceding few years had been somehow deficient and had caused a certain amount of disquiet. To this concern was added the impression that French bellicosity was once again rampant. These two factors brought about calls for opportunities for civilians to acquire and practise military skills in general and marksmanship in particular. In May 1859, the War Office gave permission for the raising of volunteer corps under the terms of legislation passed in 1804 in a previous time of French belligerency. In August 1859, Earl Spencer established the Althorp Rifles as one of the very earliest of the Rifle Volunteer Corps (RVC), composed mainly of his tenants and friends, and that October, he chaired a meeting at his London residence setting up the National Rifle Association (NRA). In the next year, five further RVCs were formed in the county as well as one of the earliest branches of the NRA. Through the patronage of local aristocrats such as Earl Spencer and the duke of Montagu, and

Weedon Bec Depot: Building No. 14, the rifle store.

Weedon Bec Depot: the powder stores in their separate compound.

Northampton Militia Armoury: the façade of the armoury built in 1859 in the form of a toy fort, accentuating the details of a medieval castle.

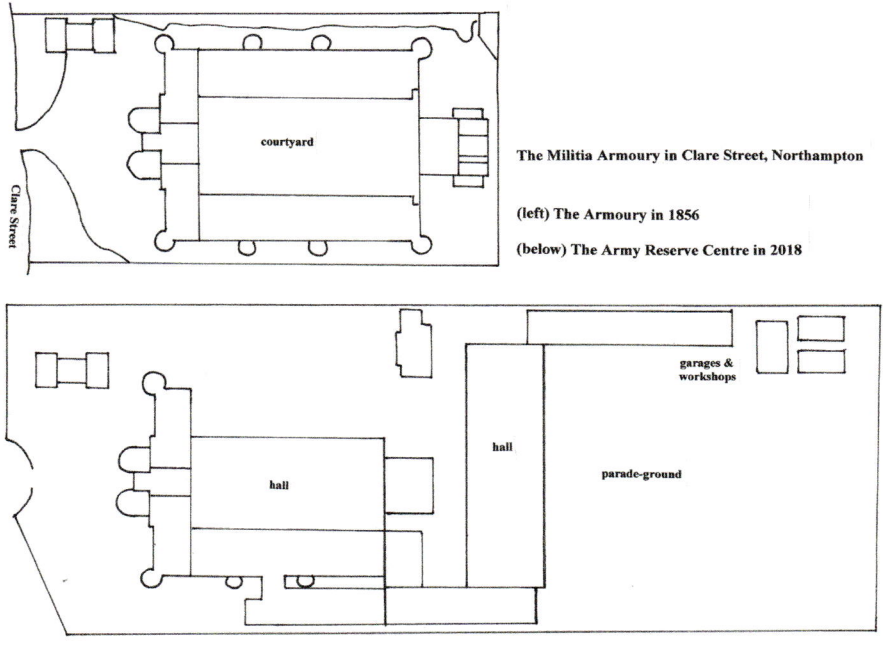

The Militia Armoury in Clare Street, Northampton

(left) The Armoury in 1856

(below) The Army Reserve Centre in 2018

Northampton Militia Armoury: sketch plans showing the extent and layout of the original armoury and the later adaptations and additions.

the burghers of the county's industrial centres, supplemented by subscriptions from the volunteers themselves, these units were intended to be self-sufficient. However, the War Office soon realised that what amounted to a collection of private armies outside their control might lead to future problems of recruitment to the regulars or to the militia, and could even promote internal unrest. A committee, including Earl Spencer and other early adopters of the rifle volunteer principle, was convened to establish ground rules for this new force. Each corps would be assessed on the number of men it could field, trained and practised in drill and rifle shooting, and who had turned out regularly for drill nights and field days. This assessment would determine the level of grant paid to each corps. The Althorp Rifles consisted of countrymen of some social standing, but many of the eager recruits to the town-based 5th Corps were artisans, often from the footwear industry, and the opinion was freely expressed that their social origins might exclude them from the ranks of the RVC, unlike the 4th Corps, which attracted professional men and tradesmen. The chief local proponent of this prejudice was Lord Exeter, who would at least have been gratified to see an earl as the Northamptonshire Corps' commander, with two more earls as his seconds-in-command, and a fourth earl serving in the 2nd Corps in Towcester. This issue of class might be justified by the high costs of uniform and annual subscription in the context of the working man's low wages, but the initiators of the movement saw it as largely feudal in the countryside and bourgeois in the towns, while many of the volunteers saw it as a more democratic movement. However, while many of the early officers of town-based RVC were professional men, as at Wellingborough where the 7th RVC was raised by two solicitors, such men soon found themselves either unable or unwilling to maintain the level of commitment demanded by the job. Some of their successors raised the even thornier question of whether it was necessary to be a gentleman in order to be an officer. The 1st Northamptonshire RVC was fortunate to secure the services of Captain Landon, a former regular, as adjutant from 1860–1886, but the rest of its officers had to come from somewhere.

By 1864, the county's several RVC had been gathered into an administrative battalion in order to facilitate the co-ordination of those War Office handouts of cash grants, weapons, and equipment, which recognised a unit's level of efficiency. A first annual camp was held at Althorp Park to give the county's several scattered corps the opportunity to manoeuvre as a larger unit. There was a decidedly festival atmosphere to this gathering, which provided sports and entertainment alongside military pursuits and would have been seen as a welcome break from the daily grind at a time when holidays for the working man were a far-off dream. Although the present Estate Office at Althorp has been unable to provide confirmation, it would appear likely that the early HQ of the Rifle Volunteers would have been in the monumental stables, since one condition for the receipt of weapons and ammunition, set by the War Office, was the provision by each unit of a secure store. It also soon became necessary for corps to provide an orderly room to accommodate the inevitable paperwork, a covered space for drill during the dark winter evenings, and a range for shooting practice. The invention of the Morris Tube, an insert in the rifle barrel enabling smaller bore ammunition to be fired, allowed 25-yard indoor ranges to be used, as an alternative to the standard 600-yard (550-metre) outdoor ones. In the early days, it would appear that in Northamptonshire, as in many counties, public buildings doubled as drill halls. Northampton's Corn Exchange, built in 1850 and later to become the Gaumont Cinema, provided a base for the 4th and 5th RVC, formed in February and March 1860, and amalgamated in 1872. In 1885, it was still the HQ of the 1st Volunteer Battalion of the Northamptonshire Regiment, the successor to the RVC Administrative Battalion, and served as the unit's drill hall up to the First World War. It is probable that the Corn Exchange of 1853 in Kettering performed the same function for the 9th Corps, formed in 1867, until the purpose-built drill hall in York Road had opened by 1899. Daventry's Assembly Hall in New Street provided a base throughout the time that volunteer units were based in the town. It is possible that Wellingborough's 7th Corps may initially have used the Exchange Hall of 1861, but a converted Methodist chapel in Church Street was to provide a dedicated drill hall and armoury for the 1st Volunteer Battalion's 'K' and 'L' Companies by 1877.

While the Northamptonshire Yeomanry had been disbanded in 1828, a number of independent troops continued to exist unofficially. However, in 1861, Robert Loyd-Lindsay (later Lord Wantage), a winner of the VC in the Crimea, raised a light horse volunteer unit based on the members of the Pytchley Hunt, consisting mainly of farmers. In fact, Loyd-Lindsay, a champion of marksmanship, intended not to replicate yeomanry cavalry units but to promote the use of mounted infantry—riding on to the field of battle, but fighting on foot as riflemen, as Okey's dragoons had done at Naseby. The 1st Northamptonshire Mounted Rifle Volunteers, like similar units across the country, lasted only until 1869. Cheaper to equip and maintain than the generally socially superior yeomanry, costs were nevertheless often beyond their members'

Northampton Corn Exchange was built in 1850 and served as a drill hall for the Rifle Volunteer Corps from 1859, and then the Northampton-based volunteer battalion of the Northamptonshire Regiment until 1918. By 1921, it was a cinema and, more recently, a night club.

Northampton Corn Exchange: its cavernous size is revealed by this rear view.

Wellingborough's first dedicated drill hall was this converted Methodist chapel on Church Street, in operation by 1877.

resources. Consequently, numbers were low, and units would never become viable. While the hunting fraternity had initially been drawn to the idea, they soon found that soldiering proved an unconscionable distraction from chasing foxes.

In 1881, the reorganisation of the army, remembered as the Cardwell reforms, saw the amalgamation of the 48th and 58th Foot as the Northamptonshire Regiment. This reorganisation, aimed at formally linking regiments to localities, also brought into the regimental fold the Rutlandshire and Northamptonshire Militia, which was now absorbed into the 48th Regimental District in Northampton, based on Gibraltar Barracks, as the regiment's 3rd and 4th Battalions. At the same time, the county's RVC Administrative Battalion was brought in as the 1st Volunteer Battalion of the Northamptonshire Regiment, organised into thirteen companies. One would be lost in 1885, but four more were added during the Boer War. In 1899, the two militia battalions were reduced to one, later to become the 3rd (Special Reserve) Battalion when the Territorial Force was forming in 1907–8.

One of the prime purposes of the reforms was to introduce the localisation principle that tied regiments to a geographical area for recruiting and identity. Each regiment would now have a local regimental depot providing a psychological home for the regimental family. Built to a common plan, these depots consisted of a castellated keep with reinforced floors to hold stands of rifles and barrels of powder and shot; three-storey barrack blocks ranged around a parade ground; a grand house for the colonel; officers' and sergeants' messes; a hospital; a chapel; and workshops, stables, and stores, all surrounded by a high wall, loopholed for musketry, with corner bastions. In Northampton, the new Gibraltar Barracks was built on the same site as the earlier cavalry barracks that it incorporated.

The two regiments of foot had fought in campaigns across the Empire from the Maori Wars of 1845, to the Zulu Wars of 1880–1, while, as the Northamptonshire Regiment, they fought on the North-West Frontier of India in 1897. The 3rd (Militia) Battalion contributed a detachment of twenty-five officers and 653 NCOs and men for service in South Africa in 1902. They manned blockhouses along 88 miles of the lines designed to impede the Boer *Kommandos* who, thus deprived of their vital mobility, could more easily be mopped up by the field force.

Yeomanry regiments were not officially eligible for foreign service, but the Army needed large numbers of cavalry and mounted infantry to counter the tactics of the Boers, so recruited a wholly new formation. This was the Imperial Yeomanry (IY), drawn from existing regiments, but reshuffled into numbered companies. Unlike Northamptonshire, some counties had retained a yeomanry regiment throughout the nineteenth century, one of which, neighbouring Buckinghamshire, recruited Northamptonshire men into its Towcester-based troop, and it was from the Royal Buckinghamshire Hussars Yeomanry that the 37th, 38th, 56th, and 57th Companies of the Imperial Yeomanry were drawn. Meanwhile, Lord Annaly, current Master of the Pytchley Hunt, formed a company in Northampton that appears not to have been formally adopted into the IY, but whose members may have been absorbed wholesale into one of the Buckinghamshire companies, as men from the Pytchley are known to have served in South Africa.

In 1902, nearly seventy-five years after it had been disbanded, the fifth earl Spencer set about reforming the Northamptonshire Yeomanry. It would retain its cap badge but lose its seniority. Under the command of Lord Annaly, there would be four

Gibraltar Barracks: the depot of the Northamptonshire Regiment following the reorganisations and reforms of the 1870s and 1880s.

squadrons based at the Northampton HQ, Peterborough, Kettering, and Daventry. The full establishment would be 600 men, and those 120 men previously seconded to the Royal Buckinghamshire Hussars would be reclaimed. The regiment most likely retained officers from the hunting aristocracy who entertained their men at country houses such as Lamport or Cottesbrooke, and held summer camps at Boughton or Althorp, but not all their recruits were from the traditional yeomanry constituency of farmers and hunt servants. Consequently, there were some for whom a mount as well as riding lessons had to be provided. While many of the Yeomanry's drills were held in the rolling parkland of the big country houses, it was still necessary to maintain administrative centres and armouries. The HQ in Northampton was at 53 Sheep Street in a large stone coaching-inn-type building with an archway through to the courtyard, presumably housing tack rooms and stabling; in Kettering, the early yeomanry base was the Old White Horse Hotel in the High Street, and the Peterborough squadron was based at the drill hall in Queen Street. Although the Buckinghamshire Hussars had previously maintained an armoury in Towcester's Town Hall and Corn Exchange on Watling Street, holding weapons and equipment for 100 men there, the newly-formed Northamptonshire Yeomanry's fourth squadron would be based at Daventry's Assembly Hall.

Concerns over the small size of the British Army relative to the demands of Empire raised the problem of home defence. While continental armies were predominantly composed of conscripts and could be counted in millions, Britain's all-volunteer,

Northampton, 53 Sheep Street: in 1906 and 1914, HQ of the Northamptonshire Yeomanry and a base for its 'A' Squadron.

professional troops numbered no more than a quarter of a million. The Boer War had clearly demonstrated the inadequacies of this army, but it was the ongoing imperial commitments—which demanded the permanent presence of large and scattered garrisons across the globe, both in pockets such as Hong Kong, Singapore, Malta, or Gibraltar, or in larger numbers in India or Egypt—that strained the Army's resources to breaking point, with even the home posting of Ireland making a significant demand on troop deployment. The fear was that if a European war were to break out, half the army would be safeguarding the Empire, the other half would be forming a British Expeditionary Force for confining the fighting to the continent of Europe, leaving few troops to defend the homeland. Therefore, Secretary of State for War Richard, later Viscount, Haldane proposed a Territorial Force (TF) of trained volunteers specifically and exclusively for home defence. This force was set up in 1907–8 by recruiting as many of the existing volunteer infantry, artillery, and engineer units as wished to join; militiamen could join the TF or go into the Special Reserve, or, in certain regiments, Extra Special Reserve battalions; and the yeomanry would form new TF cavalry regiments. At the end of this exercise, by 1913, the Regular Army numbered 247,432, with 145,347 reservists, and just short of 270,000 TF volunteers.

The Northamptonshire Regiment retained its two regular battalions, one on foreign service and the other at home, on alternating deployments: a 3rd (Militia/Reserve) Battalion at the regimental depot, and the 4th TF Battalion, with its HQ in the Corn Exchange and four of its companies based in the old militia barracks in Clare Street,

Northampton, with the other four at Wellingborough, Kettering, Desborough, and Higham Ferrers/Rushden. The two Peterborough-based companies were converted to artillery, becoming the Northamptonshire Battery of the 4th East Anglian Brigade, RFA, based in Hertford. A detachment of 'C' Company of the Banbury-based 4th Battalion, Oxfordshire and Buckinghamshire Light Infantry, was based at Brackley from 1908 to 1914. A 600-yard range at Rifle Range Road, Nobottle, opened in 1903 for the Rifle Volunteers, continued in use with the TF. Camps were held annually, with that held in June 1914 being at Milton Park outside Peterborough, while Kettering's Boughton Park had been the venue for the Norfolk Regiment's 6th (Cyclist) Battalion (TF) in 1913.

There were also a significant number of cadet companies, intended to feed recruits into units of the TF to which they were often affiliated. Despite being a church-based organisation, the Boys' Brigade was a paramilitary force, which drilled and shot on the rifle range. Its 1st Northampton Battalion, in existence by 1902, and comprising eight companies, was only, however, recognised by the Territorial Force Association in July 1918. Northampton School on Billing Road had established a cadet corps in 1909 with a strength of 180 by 1914; Wellingborough GS also fielded an infantry company; and Oundle School maintained three such companies. All these corps of the Junior OTC, established by early 1914, expected to provide a supply of young officers to both regular and volunteer forces. Elmington Lodge was a 100–500-yard, full-bore, four-lane range for Oundle School with modern Hythe-style butts. The shooting team from Northampton GS competed with the best at Bisley.

The TF was organised into fourteen self-contained divisions, each with a brigade of cavalry with an attendant battery of the Royal Horse Artillery; three infantry brigades each comprising four infantry battalions; field and siege artillery batteries; and army service corps, engineer, signals, and medical units. The Northamptonshire Yeomanry was attached for training purposes to the Eastern Mounted Brigade; the 4th Battalion Northamptonshire Regiment was part of the East Midland Infantry Brigade; both these formations, along with the East Midland Brigade Company of the ASC, based in Northampton, and the RFA battery and its ammunition column in Peterborough were all part of the East Anglian Division whose HQ was at Warley in Essex. Summer Camps offered opportunities for all these units to work together, but weekly drills were necessarily fragmented and dependent on the experience and enthusiasm of local leaders. While Haldane talked up the valuable contribution to national security of the TF, it was recognised that it was very much a work in progress, and would require a great deal of training before it could be expected to function effectively on a modern battlefield.

The constituent units of the TF were of necessity scattered across the county. Weekly drills were held in public halls, redundant chapels, purpose-built drill halls, and public houses. Adding to those drill halls already established in Northampton and Kettering, the early years of the twentieth century saw new builds at Oundle, Rushden, and Desborough; a purpose-built replacement for the converted chapel in Wellingborough; and the use of public houses in Thrapston, Long Buckby, and Raunds. Use of the Old Chapel in Well Lane, Rothwell, may date from this time. Appropriate facilities included an armoury; an orderly room; an indoor drill space capable of accommodating fifty men or more; an indoor 25-yard rifle range; stores for uniforms and equipment; and a canteen. Often, as at Oundle, a house for the permanent staff instructor was built

Kettering: the York Road drill hall, opened by 1899 with an addition for the local Freemasons of 1901; from 1928, it was run by the Masonic and Drill Hall Co. Ltd, until at least 1940, a new drill hall having opened in Station Road in 1936.

The Nobottle 600-yard rifle range was acquired in 1904 for the use of the Rifle Volunteers and continued in use well into the latter years of the century.

Dating from the early 1900s, the Oundle drill hall in Benefield Road consisted of a house for the resident instructor (on the left) and on the right offices, messes, and armoury, etc., behind which was the hall. The front block and house have now been converted into apartments, with the 25-yard range to the rear.

Wellingborough's Great Park Street drill hall was in operation by 1906, replacing the hall in Church Street. It was only sold in 1957.

Long Buckby, High Street: there was a drill hall recorded here in 1910; the Admiral Rodney PH was in existence in 1864 and was used by the Home Guard during the Second World War. In the absence of other likely candidates, it is possible that this inn, with ample accommodation, represents the Victorian drill hall.

Rothwell: the Old Chapel in Well Lane, with what appears to be an extension to its right, still functions as an ACF centre, and is the most likely venue for the TF detachment based on the town in 1914.

adjoining the hall. Premises used by yeomanry units often needed stables and tack rooms, such as coaching inns might provide, although the majority of troopers would have supplied their own horses.

Military Flight

The first balloon flights in the county had taken place in 1824, but it was not until 1910 that a viable aircraft flew in the skies above Northamptonshire, and another year before a local pilot, whose first cross-country flight brought him from Huntingdon to a safe landing on Northampton Racecourse, received his Royal Aero Club Certificate. Despite only lukewarm interest, attention was beginning to be paid to the possibilities offered to the military by powered flight. The annual military manoeuvres of 1913 saw the 'White' Army, with its HQ at Daventry, defending against the 'Brown' Army. Flying out of Lilbourne airfield, each army had the services of a squadron of the newly-formed Royal Flying Corps (RFC), with a flight of seven Royal Naval Air Service (RNAS) aircraft attached, altogether amassing an impressive twenty-seven aircraft of twelve different models. Useful reconnaissance work was carried out, but the point was made by one of the squadron commanders that airmen risked their lives every time they took off, and would like to feel that their information was used and appreciated by leaders and their staffs on the ground. As well as Lilbourne, landing grounds (LG) were established at Badby, Upper Stowe, Litchborough, and Towcester. Despite the proven effectiveness of aerial reconnaissance, and warnings regarding the clear visibility of cavalry from the air, generals taking part in concurrent manoeuvres elsewhere refused to relinquish totally the notion that scouting was best carried out on horseback. King George V, riding a black horse and entertained at Eydon Hall, was an interested spectator of these 1913 Army Manoeuvres.

Munitions and Strategic Industry

Northamptonshire's footwear industry supplied boots and shoes to a number of armies. In 1871, the French government ordered large quantities of army boots, but the War Office remained the biggest customer. Following complaints about boots supplied to troops during the Boer War, the War Office set new quality standards for contracts for boots, and appropriate piecework rates were established and accepted by the War Office. However, unrest mounted in the industry when the employers repudiated this agreement and refused to modify their position. There were a dozen factories in Raunds fulfilling War Office contracts for the supply of boots, and in 1905, their 300 workers came out on strike as a protest against low wages and their employers' intransigence. Sensing support for their cause at the War Office they set off to fight their case in London. Led by James Gribble, their 'General', and marching in six companies accompanied by a marching band with cyclists riding on ahead, the 115 fittest men, many of them ex-servicemen, completed the journey, being feted all the way. Intent on exploiting the official support they perceived to be behind their case, they moved on Westminster, expecting to hear their case debated. Those who attended parliament, however, were to be disappointed, as the topic was deliberately talked out, and their subsequent show of frustration and anger had caused their ejection from the chamber. A rally in Trafalgar Square, addressed by Keir Hardie, further bolstered public support, which would, indeed, lead to a government inquiry and some improvement in their pay. Having raised realistic expectations of an acceptable outcome to their demonstrations, they enjoyed a triumphant return to Northampton.

In 1880, Samuel Lloyd leased land at Corby from the Brudenells of Deene Park to mine iron ore for smelting at established forges elsewhere in the country. In 1907, furnaces were set up at Corby, and by 1910, pig iron was being produced in small quantities. In 1908, the Kettering Iron and Coal Company was producing 1,000 tons of iron per week. The iron stone quarries and the production of iron were beginning to contribute a welcome addition to the munitions industry as the outbreak of the First World War approached.

Mulliners was famed as a coach-building firm and had been founded by a pioneer of the automobile who also co-founded the Royal Automobile Club. While its works at Battersea in south-west London had dabbled with the production of aeroplanes, their premises at 73–83 Bridge Street and in Victoria Gardens, Northampton, would focus on the production of vehicles for the military once the imminent war broke out.

5

The First World War and the Interwar Years 1914–39

On the eve of war, the British strategy for the deployment of its armed forces had to be fairly simple given the small numbers of troops available. The nucleus of the regular army at home, six infantry and two cavalry divisions, would form the British Expeditionary Force (BEF), the left flank of the Allied defence of the French border with Belgium. The majority of those regular units serving across the Empire would be brought home to reinforce the BEF and be replaced by reserve battalions and those TF units that opted for overseas service. The major part of the TF would assume responsibility for home defence. However, it immediately became apparent to Field Marshal Lord Kitchener who had been appointed minister of war that many more troops would be needed, and he therefore looked for 100,000 volunteers to form the basis of his 'New Armies' (K1-6). Even though the numbers coming forward to join up exceeded his wildest dreams, there would never be enough men to meet the demands of a world war. In fact, the BEF's immediate losses meant that it became necessary for much of the TF to be deployed abroad, devolving the defence of the homeland on to older, less fit men, those in training, and the under-nineteens who were too young to fight overseas. As the supply of willing volunteers was exhausted, then, in the face of public opposition and political instincts, conscription was introduced. Additionally, local units of Volunteer Training Corps, the First World War equivalent of the Home Guard, were sanctioned by a reluctant War Office, and old soldiers, some claiming service as far back as the Crimea, served in the National Reserve or were formed into the Royal Defence Corps.

The Deployment of Local Units During the First World War

The Northamptonshire Regiment raised a total of thirteen battalions, was awarded six VCs, won fifty-eight battle honours, and lost over 6,000 dead in the course of the First World War. The outbreak of war in early August 1914 found the 1st Battalion, at Blackdown Camp, Aldershot, forming part of the 1st Division's 2nd Infantry Brigade, and thus in the front ranks of the BEF. Within ten days of the declaration of war, it had sailed for France, landing at Le Havre to remain on the Western Front until November 1918, fighting and sustaining devastating losses right from the early months of 1915 in such battles as Ypres, Neuve Chapelle, and Aubers Ridge. In the November, an officer related how the battalion 'as constituted at the outbreak of war, ceased to exist.… So ended the old 48th, holding the line doggedly, notwithstanding terrific casualties against appalling odds'.

The 2nd Battalion was at Alexandria but was shipped back to Britain from Egypt and mobilised at Hursley Park near Winchester prior to sailing for France on 5 November. It also spent its entire war on the Western Front. The 3rd Battalion was deployed to Portland, Dorset, to defend the naval base, leaving a cadre at Gibraltar Barracks to receive new recruits and to provide basic training. It was redeployed to Gillingham, Kent, in May 1915, where it remained as part of the Thames and Medway Garrison for the duration. The eight companies of the 4th Battalion (TF) were recalled to Northampton from their summer camp at Ashridge Park in Hertfordshire, sent home, and told to report to their local drill halls for mobilisation. They then reassembled at HQ in Northampton from whence they marched to Bury St Edmunds in Suffolk to join the 54th (East Anglian) Division (TF). After six months training in the St Albans area, they were sent to the Dardanelles, fighting in the ill-conceived and poorly conducted Gallipoli campaign. After their slick evacuation, the only successful element of the whole operation, they spent the rest of the war in Palestine and Lebanon. The 2/4th Battalion formed at Northampton as a second-line TF unit, joining the 69th (2nd East Anglian) Division, providing drafts for other battalions, training recruits, and on home defence duties in Yorkshire and Nottinghamshire. The 3/4th Battalion, formed at Northampton in May 1915, as a third-line TF unit, spent the war in the East Anglian Reserve Brigade in Sussex, training recruits and sending drafts to the 54th Division. The 5th Battalion was formed in August 1914 as part of Kitchener's first New Army (K1). It landed in France in May 1915 and served there as a pioneer battalion for the duration. The 6th Battalion was raised in September 1914, as part of K2, trained in one of the vast camps on Salisbury Plain, and then served in France from July 1915 until the end of the war. Its personnel, including those attached from other regiments, won four VCs. The 7th Battalion was raised in September 1914, as part of K3, largely through the efforts of Edgar Mobbs, a well-known local rugby player, who gathered together a company of sportsmen for the battalion. Dubbed 'Mobbs' Own', it trained on the south coast then served in France from September 1915 for the duration. Mobbs (1882–1917) enlisted as a private soldier but had risen to the rank of lieutenant-colonel by the time he was killed in action at Ypres in July 1917. The battalion fought in a number of famous actions including Loos, Cambrai, and Vimy Ridge, suffering large numbers of casualties, particularly during the German Michael offensive of 1918. Another famous local sportsman was the footballer Walter Tull, who played for Northampton Town. He joined a sportsmen's battalion of the Middlesex Regiment and, unusually for a man of mixed race, was commissioned; he was killed in 1918. A meeting at the Rushden recruiting office was addressed by Captain Stocken of the Northamptonshire Regiment who lamented the fact that local men had joined the RAMC and the RGA when it was infantry that were needed. He asked for recruits in batches of ten to join up together making the 8th Battalion into a 'pals' battalion, being criticised by the infamous Horatio Bottomley for attempting to play on the latent snobbery of potential recruits by suggesting a socially superior 'clerks' company'. The 8th Battalion was eventually formed at Weymouth in October 1914 and served at home as a training reserve battalion. Those TF soldiers who opted not to serve abroad were grouped in Provisional Battalions such as the 9th Battalion, which took in members of the 2/4th Battalion who invoked their right to remain in Britain. It formed at Cley in January 1917 in the 223rd Brigade and stayed in Norfolk on home defence duties. The 1st Garrison Battalion, composed of mainly older volunteers, formed in Surrey and served in Egypt, Palestine, and Salonika. Formed at Sheerness, Kent, in 1915, from older men in low medical categories, the 2nd (Home Service) Garrison Battalion was renumbered as the 13th Battalion of the Royal Defence Corps, for employment in guarding POW camps and militarily sensitive sites at home.

The Northamptonshire Yeomanry was not part of a TF Mounted Brigade, only being attached to the Eastern Brigade for training. It was therefore immediately available for deployment when the war started. It landed at Le Havre and was attached to the BEF's 8th Infantry Division for reconnaissance work, patrols, laying signal wires, and trench digging. By the spring of 1915, the regiment had been split up with individual squadrons being attached to different formations, only being reunited a year later as the cavalry regiment allocated to VI Corps. It was one of the few cavalry units to take part in a battle operating as horsed cavalry when it fought at Arras, losing the CO and sustaining heavy casualties. At the end of 1917, still horsed, it was sent to Italy to help shore up the deteriorating situation there. Operating in the traditional role of reconnaissance troops, there were adventures and narrow escapes in penetrating the Austrian lines. An added complication was the attachment of the Prince of Wales (the future Edward VIII), serving as a staff officer, but nevertheless anxious to see action. The 2nd Northamptonshire Yeomanry formed in 1914, and its 'A' and 'B' Squadrons were using Tiffield Old Brickworks as a training ground the next year. The squadrons were scattered between home defence divisions in Yorkshire and Kent, training recruits to be drafted to the first-line unit. One squadron, however, was detached in 1916 for service in France and was absorbed into the new Tank Corps. The remaining squadrons were incorporated into reserve cavalry regiments. Reinforcements and replacements for the first-line unit were latterly provided by the 3rd Northamptonshire Yeomanry, formed in Towcester in January 1916 and attached to a reserve cavalry regiment based in Canterbury. One such draft included the actor Leslie Howard, who must have been the first ever Northamptonshire Yeomanry officer who had to be taught to ride before taking up his regimental duties. They were latterly absorbed into another reserve cavalry unit at Tidworth.

The initial deluge of volunteers in August 1914 had caused immense logistical problems at the time, but the insatiable demand for manpower lasted throughout the entire war. From the very start, meetings were held in town halls such as Higham Ferrers to explore the implications of joining up, one of the major concerns related to their terms of service and whether employers would keep their jobs open for them. Sadly, not only would the volunteers not be back by Christmas, but many would never return. After the initial surge, the momentum continued, with forty recruits being sworn in at Oundle, in the middle of September 1914, and five more from Benefield two months later. The TF was taking seventeen year olds to be given training in order to release experienced men for service overseas. Recruiting offices, like that in Rushden, along with dozens of others across the country, were overwhelmed, and in January 1915, the recruiting office in Rushden moved from the Church Street drill hall to 87 High Street, formerly the Labour Exchange, and again, by November 1915, to 100 High Street. In September 1915, the Recruiting Office in Oundle was specifically looking for men to join the 3rd Battalion of the Northamptonshire Regiment that, since August 1914, had been expected to provide drafts for the 1st and

2nd Battalions in France. Giving some indication of the impact of recruiting, by the end of 1916, 335 men from Oundle, 12.5 per cent of the total population of 2,700, had joined up. In some villages, the entire eligible male population enlisted, but across the country only 5 per cent of those eligible actually volunteered.

In an attempt to maintain the flow of recruits, special marches were organised. In April 1915, a company of the Northamptonshire Regiment visited towns between Oundle and Northampton, calling men to the colours. This march, bagging over 100 recruits, was a success, as was another in June, but ever more men were needed. As the momentum inevitably slowed, in an attempt to avoid imposing outright conscription, the government introduced the Derby Scheme. Commencing in August 1915, men in the eighteen to forty-one age group, and eligible for military service, would attend a recruiting office to attest their willingness to serve and to have their names recorded in a National Register, placing them in age groups in the army reserve, and then awaiting their call-up. By November 1915, new recruiting depots had opened at Higham Ferrers, Irthlingborough, and elsewhere across the county. Such was the rush to attest that in December 1915, Rushden's Alfred Street Schools were requisitioned to deal with the numbers coming forward, displacing over 600 pupils. Unfortunately, many of those attesting would be unable to serve, so conscription was introduced in 1916. Appeals

The Elmington Lodge four-lane range was created for the use of Oundle School's OTC, and was made available to the Oundle VTC in the autumn of 1914. More recently, the old Hythe-style targets were replaced by Bisley ones, as can be seen here.

against call-up orders were heard at Northampton County Hall, but those whose appeals were unsuccessful found themselves in the forces. A few such men, citing moral principles or religious beliefs as a reason for their refusal to serve, were subject to court-martial, some of which were conducted in the church institute in Kingsthorpe. Many young lads, not content to wait until they were seventeen to join the Territorials, joined alternative uniformed cadet organisations such as the Boys' Brigade, the Church Lads' Brigade, or the Boy Scouts, all of which were involved in keeping watch, carrying messages, and a range of other useful duties. Boys from Northampton GS served as orderlies at Duston War Hospital. These activities both took pressure off the police and military and prepared youngsters for life in uniform. As well as the established units at Oundle and Wellingborough and Northampton Grammar Schools, both Brackley's Magdalen College School and Kettering Grammar School initiated new junior OTCs in 1915 and 1916 respectively. The Oundle OTC trained by carrying out route marches and tactical exercises on Bailey Hill, shooting on their range at Elmington Top Lodge and, starting in 1915, engaging in joint field days with Oakham and Uppingham alongside cadets from schools from Birmingham.

Billeting and Troop Movements

From the very start of the war, Northampton became a place where large numbers of troops were concentrated, some in camps but many billeted on the local population. Over 1,000 troops were billeted in Raunds by the end of August 1914, when the army took over Northampton Castle railway station and prepared to receive 20,000 troops into the town and the surrounding area. The major part of the 53rd (Welsh) Division (TF), from September to December 1914, was based for training around Northampton. Four battalions of the Royal Welsh Fusiliers, four more of the Cheshire Regiment, and the three battalions of the Monmouthshire Regiment, with their attendant RFA, RE, and RAMC units, needed to be accommodated. Some of these units would be detached and deployed to France, but the majority would go with the division to the Dardanelles. The 5th Battalion of the Fusiliers was billeted on the Billing Road with use of a miniature range at the mill; the RFA were put up near the racecourse; and the 5th Battalion, Cheshire Regiment, went to Abington Park. The Fusiliers' 6th and 7th Battalions were placed in Rushden, where medical checks were conducted in the Mission Chapel. The 1st Battalion of the Herefordshire Regiment, like the Monmouths, an all-territorial unit, was based in Irchester at the same time. Even without the Welsh Division's 4th Brigade, which was deployed elsewhere, this still placed over 12,000 men in and around Northampton, all requiring billets. In a repeat performance of the 53rd Division's sojourn in Northampton prior to their joining the Dardanelles expedition, the second-line territorial battalions from those same regiments gathered in Northampton in 1915 to form the 68th (2nd Welsh) Division (TF). Two further second-line TF divisions, the 61st (2nd South Midland) in January 1915 and the 62nd (2nd West Riding) two years later, used Northampton and the villages around as their assembly point *en route* to their Salisbury Plain training camps prior to setting sail for France. While the reassuring presence of troops was generally welcomed as being good for trade, and the government was urged to impose an element of centralised control on such things as food prices, the use at the end of February 1915 of ASC personnel as strike breakers in Northampton was seen as a threat to organised labour.

As a response to the ever-present threatened German invasion, those TF divisions held in the UK prior to deployment overseas, such as the 53rd (1st Welsh) Division, were grouped into a Central Force comprising three armies, occupying an area with Bedford, Cambridge, Northampton, and Peterborough at the corners. In 1915, First Army had its HQ in Bedford and included the 68th (2nd Welsh) Division with its HQ at the George Hotel, George Row, Northampton. As divisions were posted overseas and the number of trained troops available for home defence diminished, the strategy changed. The new C-in-C Home Forces, Field Marshal Lord French, broke up the bulk of the reserves in order to establish a stronger first line of defence nearer the invasion coast. The 68th Division was therefore subsequently moved out of Northampton and deployed in East Anglia.

As well as billets, the War Office provided hutted camps at Kingsley Park and Kingsthorpe, and another on Northampton Racecourse, where the last race had been run in 1910. There were other camps at Wellingborough and Kettering, where huts were erected in the Victoria Pleasure Gardens. In April 1915, billets for 1,000 soldiers had to be found within 2 miles of Oundle marketplace, and in the autumn of 1915, 25,000 men were billeted around Northampton for the winter. In January 1916, there were 12,000 troops billeted in Northampton and a further 5,000 in Wellingborough. For the winter of 1916–17, these numbers had increased to 20,000 in Northampton, and 4,000–5,000 in Wellingborough. In 1916, the 23rd Reserve Brigade, including four battalions of the Middlesex Regiment, was stationed in Northampton prior to a move to Aldershot, while the 26th Reserve Brigade was at Banbury, and in 1917, the 4th Reserve Brigade was in Northampton. All of these reserve formations contained Young Soldier battalions. Kingsley Park provided a base for 51 Reserve Park (HT) ASC from 1916–20. Some units, like the Northamptonshire Battery RFA (TF), which in October 1915, following training, marched into Oundle from Kettering and stayed overnight on its way to France, were simply passing through.

As more and more troops were posted abroad, then it became necessary to organise new formations for home defence. In November 1916, scattered battalions, of mainly either younger, untrained recruits, or older home service men, were collected together to form three new divisions. One, the 72nd Division (Home Forces), comprising 215th, 216th and 217th Infantry Brigades, was based in the south Midlands. Formed in Bath, the division was then centred on Bedford as a strategic reserve for the anti-invasion divisions centred on East Anglia. Throughout the war, there was always a fear of a German invasion centred on the Suffolk coast, and large numbers of, albeit ineffective, troops were stationed in defensive positions. At least two units of 72nd Division were based in Northamptonshire, and Kingsley Park accommodated their accompanying ASC unit: No. 1 (HQ) Company (HT) ASC Train, with No. 4 Company at Wellingborough. The 72nd Division was broken up in March 1918, with those now old enough to serve abroad being sent to France to help withstand the German offensive made possible by Russia's exit from the war and the rest being spread between other home defence divisions. Also at Wellingborough Camp, probably in the grounds of Wellingborough School, was the RE Motorcycle training unit in 1918. The RFA Cadet School, training field artillery officers, occupied Weedon Barracks.

The Volunteer Training Corps (VTC)

Many of those men who were too old or unfit for military service, or who were in reserved occupations, nevertheless wished to play their part in the defence of their country against a possible invasion, or by releasing younger men to fight overseas. One town that was quick off the mark was Oundle. On 17 August, barely a fortnight into the war, a meeting at Oundle's Victoria Hall was called by Mr Brassey, MP, of Apethorpe Hall, to explore the formation of a town guard. This was in response to an open letter from the writer Sir Arthur Conan Doyle, who saw a need to tap the patriotism of men who could not otherwise serve. They would drill, train with rifles, and co-operate with the authorities, consciously complementing the TF rather than competing with them. In Oundle, Mr Sanderson, the school's headmaster, had already promised the use of the OTC rifle range at Elmington Lodge Farm and placed the magazine near the pits under guard. The qualification criteria for town guard membership had been set at the seventeen to sixty age group, with the ability to march a distance of 10 miles; some sixty men enrolled on the night. On the basis of channelling their enthusiasm before it faded, guards for local railway bridges were quickly organised. True to form, the War Office, suspicious of what they saw as unregulated vigilante groups, immediately vetoed the idea. Volunteers were directed to be sworn in as special constables instead, remaining under the control of the civil authorities. From early October, therefore, the Oundle volunteers, now special constables, drilled as a company every Wednesday on the cricket field near the Cross Keys Inn under the supervision of Sgt Leverton from the school OTC. Many of these men were farmers and would be well-qualified to assist with carrying out emergency procedures, such as evacuation, in the event of an invasion. Across the country, however, there grew up enormous pressure for the creation of a body with a more military orientation, and the War Office, it was said with Lord Kitchener's unlikely approval, began to relax its views. Chaired by the mayor, a meeting at Northampton town hall on 10 November determined to set up a citizens' corps. With 300 names already recorded and the approval of the County Territorial Association, granted on condition that instruction in military drill and musketry skills would be given, the new corps could go ahead. Permission to use the Clare Street drill hall had also been granted, and the meeting agreed that the town council would meet the cost of rifles. Soon 1,200 men had enrolled in Northampton. In Rothwell, the Rifle Club and Band may have provided the nucleus of a VTC. The War Office was still withholding full military status, allowing only 'GR' armbands to be worn. Eventually, as wiser counsels prevailed, there would be a county volunteer regiment wearing military style uniform and the Northamptonshire Regiment's cap badge, one component of a nationwide organisation through which would eventually pass a million members. Rushden VTC drilled at the Church Street drill hall on Tuesday and Friday evenings and on Sunday mornings on the town cricket ground. By October 1916, legitimacy had been achieved, marked in Northampton by an inspection of 5,000 Volunteers by Lord French, C-in-C Home Forces. VTC membership fluctuated as health or employment circumstances changed or as youngsters were called up. In Oundle, where the initial enthusiasm had been diverted into the special constabulary, only in May 1917 was a VTC inaugurated with twenty-five members, growing to seventy within a month. They met for two hours' drill on three evenings per week and on Sunday afternoons. In

Above: Oundle's Victoria Hall in the First World War was the venue for a meeting called to set up the VTC, as well as a weekly Red Cross work party, producing bandages and other medical supplies; in the Second World War, it served as a servicemen's social club, and as a venue for agricultural courses.

Right: Raunds Temperance Hall was a recruitment centre for the VTC in the First World War and a Home Guard base in the Second World War.

March 1918, the seventy-strong Oundle Platoon went by train to Bedford to join 7,000 other volunteers being inspected by Lord French. Oundle's parent battalion was based in Peterborough and its surrounding villages, and was one of three battalions forming the Northamptonshire Volunteer Regiment, and in 1918 being recognised as numbered Volunteer Battalions of the Northamptonshire Regiment.

Defence Against Aerial Assault

Throughout the war, right up to the very end, there hung over the country the fear of invasion. The pre-war literature of H. G. Wells, Erskine Childers, and John Buchan had all raised the spectre of foreign invasion, and this had been bolstered by the chauvinism of German politicians, admirals, generals, and journalists, and confused by the behaviour of an anglophile but delusional Kaiser Wilhelm II. This obsession with the fear of invasion led both the army and the navy to concentrate their forces on the eastern side of Britain from Scapa Flow in the Orkney Islands to Dover, and to keep them there throughout the war. There was probably never any real chance of the German army undertaking such a hazardous operation, but when it came to attacking Britain, their preferred option was aerial warfare, using Zeppelin airships and later four-engined biplanes, the Gothas and Giants, to bomb military and civilian targets alike. Home security, even some distance away from the invasion coast, was taken seriously, with measures being taken to guard military installations, munitions factories, utilities, and communications against sabotage or espionage. This was one of the tasks of the local VTC, alongside other bodies such as the National Reserve. This consisted of old soldiers, in the fifty to sixty-plus age group, who had re-enlisted, a thirty-strong platoon of whom arrived in Oundle in March 1916 to guard railway bridges and the like. In July 1915, Lord Lieutenant Earl Spencer had issued a four-page leaflet of detailed instructions as to what to do in the event of an 'actual or imminent hostile landing'. This called on all able-bodied men to enrol in an official organisation such as the VTC in order to help in the implementation of a scorched-earth policy. However, it was made very clear that anyone who stayed out of uniform was a non-combatant and must observe the conventions that governed that status and follow the orders of the emergency committees or their representatives. By this time, the British authorities were aware of the treatment dealt out to *franc tireurs* or, indeed, anyone so branded by the German troops in Belgium.

In January 1916, Northamptonshire saw its first Zeppelin as L19 flew an erratic course, crossing the coast in Norfolk, passing south of Stamford, dropping bombs on Birmingham, and returning over Rugby, Desborough, and Oundle. Although she regained the coast, she then perished off neutral Netherlands. Her companion, L21, took a similar route but dropped some of her bombs, fortunately without success, on the Islip Iron Works, before flying home. From the time of these first air raids, AA defences had become a new and urgent focus. Surprisingly, it was the RNAS that had responsibility for the nation's air defences until early in 1916. During the preceding year, the firepower of the AA gunners was gradually increased, using an astonishing range of available weapons from 6-inch naval guns to 1-pounder pom-poms. Some of the lighter weapons were initially mounted on armoured cars, and it is interesting to note that the Oundle diarist reports Zeppelin activity over Oundle in June 1915, and the presence in the neighbourhood of an armoured car, probably armed with a Maxim machine gun. The main AA effort was understandably confined to the London area, naval ports, selected communications installations, and industrial centres. The shell Filling Factory at Warkworth, generally listed as at Banbury but lying within the borders of Northamptonshire, was defended by AA guns early in 1916, but only later in the year did guns and searchlights, now under army control, reach the iron ore workings in Corby. In the meantime, against local opposition, a number of measures were taken in Northampton and across the county to limit the impact of air raids. In February 1916, churches were required to reschedule Sunday evening services to the afternoon to reduce the impact of non-essential lights. Within a few days, these official lighting restrictions included a compulsory blackout for all buildings and the use of obscured lights on vehicles. On 31 January 1916, Zeppelins had bombed their way across the East Midlands, but had spared Northamptonshire, and throughout February and March, there were constant air-raid alarms. On 25 September 1916, the Corby searchlights were lit and special constables were called out. There was a further alert on 24 May 1917, when the specials were again called out, but no Zeppelins appeared over the county. On the night of the 1–2 October 1917, Zeppelin L34 was passing over the Corby area. Possibly as a result of coming under AA fire, it dropped seventeen HE bombs, including one of 300-kg (660-lb) bomb on to the railway line between Kirby Hall and the southern entrance of the Corby tunnel. It then dropped thirteen incendiary bombs east of the road from Rockingham to Gretton without causing any structural damage or casualties. Several of the bombs failed to explode and two HE bombs were made safe by an Army Ordnance Corps officer, Major Montanaro, although the Oundle diarist has them being disposed of by REs from Chatham. The incendiaries were exhibited to raise money for the Red Cross. L34 was shot down a month later on another sally over the Midlands. On 9 October 1917, there was another Zeppelin alert, but they approached no nearer than several miles away. The next week, on the evening of 20 October 1917, L52, one of a fleet of eleven Zeppelins aiming for the steel works of Sheffield, was blown over Northamptonshire and was seen above Towcester but dropped no bombs. However, one of its partners, L45, was also off course. Finding itself over Northampton, it dropped twenty-two, some reports say sixty-six, bombs on several areas of Northampton from Kingsthorpe to Wootton. One fell on 46 Parkwood Street, killing a mother and her thirteen-year-old twin daughters. L45 later crashed in France and her crew was taken prisoner. The next month, Zeppelins were again heard to fly over but no bombs were dropped. By this time, the Zeppelin effort was largely spent, but desultory activity continued right to the end. It was known on the ground that Zeppelins used the beams of searchlights and the sound of AA gunfire to locate likely targets, and in April 1918, L62 aimed a 50-kg (110-lb) bomb at a searchlight near Nassington, only for it to fall harmlessly in a field.

As more AA weapons were developed and manufactured, their provision was extended to airfields and then to inland industrial sites. The National Filling Factory No. 9 at Warkworth had received two 18-pounder guns on separate sites by February 1916. The 18-pounder, basically a field gun on a high-angle mounting, was an improvised weapon fitted with a 3-inch sleeve that allowed a 13-pounder shell to be fired using a more powerful cartridge, increasing the guns' ceiling. Warkworth's two sites, Overthorpe

Lodge and Bodicote, over the county boundary in Oxfordshire, were administered by Birmingham AA Command. The AA site at Shire Lodge in Corby was equipped with two 6-pounder Nordenfeldt guns, which worked in conjunction with closely located searchlights. On the night of 1–2 October 1917, the Corby guns fired six rounds at L34 without registering any hits.

Although unsustainable losses of machines and crews had brought the Zeppelin attacks on London to an end in early 1916, the aircraft that replaced them did not have the range to reach the industrial targets in the Midlands. This occasioned an increasing number of Zeppelin sorties over the Midlands, throughout 1916–17 and into 1918, and the RFC, who had taken over the responsibility for home defence from the RNAS in early 1916, was forced to station fighter aircraft in the region. These were based predominantly further to the east, on the Leicestershire–Lincolnshire border, but the Midland counties provided a suitable environment for training. Lilbourne was brought up to standard as an aerodrome with permanent hangars and a hutted camp, and No. 55 Squadron from Castle Bromwich took up residence there in June 1916. A succession of other training squadrons followed until the end of the war, preparing pilots for service above the Western Front.

The operation of fighter aircraft in the skies over Northamptonshire necessitated the establishment of a network of additional landing grounds (LGs). These enabled patrolling aircraft to spend the maximum length of time in the sky without having to return to base to refuel too often. Several sites had been used pre-war, and Clipston was added to these. Such LGs normally had minimal facilities beyond a hut for the ground crew, often local volunteers, who maintained a fuel tank and, in the case of a night LG, kept the braziers alight to mark the landing strip.

The RFC and RNAS, combining as the RAF on 1 April 1918, had begun the war with fewer than 200 aircraft, but would finish it with 22,000 and nearly 290,000 personnel. The demands for pilot training were enormous, exacerbated by the need to train hundreds of Americans to fly the new de Havilland long-range bombers, and so around seventy Training Depot Stations (TDS) were set up across the British Isles to meet this need. They were often built paired on adjacent airfields, as were Easton on the Hill (No. 5 TDS), and Stamford (No. 1 TDS), the two airfields that would later combine as RAF Wittering. Each TDS was built to a common plan with three GS Hangars with spacious interiors spanned by timber Belfast Trusses, giving them a distinctive bow-string roof profile. Alongside and similar in appearance, but smaller, was the Aircraft Repair Shed (ARS). Workshops, messes, offices, canteens, sick-bay, armoury, and accommodation were all in sectional hutting, and flying was off a grass field. Lilbourne was given a new role as the Midland Flying Instructors' School. Its task was to produce instructors in large numbers as each TDS required thirty-six of them in order to turn out the forty-five qualified pilots expected monthly. The Wansford LG, used by Avro 504s of the Central Flying School at Wittering and other FTS aircraft, was the predecessor to the Kingscliffe airfield of the Second World War, but how much overlap there was on the ground is unknown. A LG at Clipston, now a playing field, was in use *c.* 1917. The place of communications in modern warfare was developing steadily throughout the war, and the new radio/telegraphy station at Greatworth came on line towards the end of the war.

Hospitals

In the autumn of 1914, no one could possibly have imagined how the war that was expected to be over by Christmas might produce hundreds of thousands of casualties needing surgery, treatment, therapy, convalescence, and rehabilitation. At the start of the war, Northamptonshire was no better prepared for the flood of wounded that quickly appeared than were other counties, and only Northampton General Hospital, Weston Favell, and Kettering were able to take wounded soldiers. Cottesbrooke Hall was offered as a convalescent home, but it was soon realised that it would need to become a hospital proper. Blakesley Hall also served in that same capacity as an auxiliary military hospital from early on in the war. But between them, they could barely muster 200 beds. Before long, it was necessary to convert nearly all existing medical facilities such as the asylums at Berrywood (from 1948, St Crispin's) and Abington Road in Northampton, and the Kettering Sanatorium into fully-fledged military hospitals, and to convert as many suitable premises as could be found, such as the Workhouse at Yardley Gobion, into auxiliary military hospitals and convalescent homes. The Red Cross and the St John Ambulance Associations worked together to recruit both male and female Voluntary Aid Detachments (VADs), taking over public buildings and country houses. Berrywood Asylum's inmates were evacuated and the building converted into a 1,000–1,100-bed hospital, and the St John's Ambulance Brigade HQ in King Street, Northampton, was turned into an emergency hospital. Even the municipal swimming pool in Northampton's Barry Road was boarded over to get as many beds in as possible. Groups across the county, like that which turned Oundle's Victoria Hall into a workroom every Wednesday, were set up to produce bandages and other medical supplies to be stockpiled at the Red Cross Depot in Northampton. From June 1915, convalescent soldiers were taken in at Barnwell Castle, and others were entertained at Deene Park on a daily basis.

War Supplies: Munitions, Clothing, Footwear, and Food

Weedon Bec, long established as the country's premier Royal Ordnance Depot, continued its work throughout the war, maintaining and repairing small arms, collecting and storing everything from boots to ammunition, and providing advice and expertise to the new depots that were mushrooming across the land. The capacity of the storehouses and magazines was increased with some new building. A Browning Shop (Building 78) for finishing the barrels of rifles was built and the arrangements in the workshops/stores (Building 14) were rejigged. A new Fitters' Shop (Building 79) was also built along with shipping sheds and a locomotive shed to serve an extension to the narrow-gauge tramway. The depot was the obvious collection point for the millions of pairs of boots being produced by local factories, and new corrugated-iron Nissen huts were erected to hold these and the enormous quantities of clothing needed to equip Kitchener's New Armies in 1915 and the conscript army of the next year. Two new standard-gauge railway lines breached the east wall to run through the storehouse enclosure and out through the west wall to serve these new clothing stores and the walled magazine enclosure beyond.

Weedon Bec Central Ordnance Store's Building No. 79 was opened in 1914 as a fitters' shop.

Weedon Bec Central Ordnance Store's Building No. 78 was built in 1914 as a new Browning shop.

The great shell scandal, which brought Lloyd-George to prominence in the newly created post of Minister of Munitions, prompted both a drive to industrialise the production of munitions and a proliferation of the centres of production. Thus the developing network could include the workshops at Oundle School at one extreme and, from April 1916, the National Filling Factory (NFF) No. 9 at Warkworth. This consisted of nearly 400 separate structures covering 250 acres (100 ha) and would eventually employ 1,500 people, one-third of them women. It was commissioned late in 1915 as a shell-filling plant. Explosives, mainly Lyddite, would arrive on site by rail to be put into shell cases at a rate of 100 tons per week, which would then be fitted with detonators and stored in filled-shell magazines for removal, initially to ordnance stores on site, and then to gathering points for shipment to the front from either Richborough Military Port in Kent or Southampton. The site was served by nearly 30 miles (48 km) of rail track and surrounded by 9 miles (14 km) of guarded security fencing. For safety, buildings were deliberately spaced the appropriate distance apart and those most combustible surrounded by earth traverses. A year into production, a second unit was added so that production was doubled to a peak of 70,000 shells per week. As TNT replaced Lyddite, production was diversified into mines for the navy and shrapnel shells. From 1918, the design of the site made it suitable for filling shells with mustard gas. The site is now cut by the M40 motorway, whose construction phase revealed buried remains of the factory requiring a high level of decontamination. To avoid danger from sparks, most buildings were of wood, and internal railways used timber wagons running on copper wheels and rails. All floors were built at the same level to enable the whole process to be carried out without the need for unnecessary shifting. Operations were broken down into discrete, repetitive tasks that could be carried out by unskilled labour. The factory ceased production in December 1918 but remained in use for a further six years, making safe and breaking up munitions.

Typifying much of the small-scale effort in the production of munitions was that conducted at Oundle School. Here, the school's carpentry workshop was cleared in order to accommodate £600 worth (£12,000 in current values) of specialist machinery paid for by the headmaster. From May 1915, schoolboys gave up their free time to work in two shifts of five to six hours each day. When the school broke up for the summer holidays in July, many boys stayed on to keep up the production of small quantities of shell cases.

The unsettled nature of industrial relations in the footwear factories, which had begun to find a resolution with the march of the men of Raunds in 1905, lasted a further decade. Fortuitously, in May 1914, the manufacturers' association and the operatives' union had agreed new arrangements for pay and working conditions across the boot and shoe industry, which would set them up for the coming demands of the military when war broke out three months later. Boots lasted for an average of only six weeks in the trenches, so the demand was continuous. The Raunds factories, of which many of the sixteen listed in the 1910 Directory from Adams Brothers to H. W. & E. Wright had held government contracts for boots and leggings for many years, now saw these contracts rolled out across the industry. Contracts for footwear went to, among others, Sears, Collier's, and Crick's in Northampton and to Cave's and John White's in Rushden. In Kettering, Allen & Caswell made boots for the British, Italian, and Russian forces, and in April 1916, an order for 3 million pairs of army boots from Northamptonshire factories was placed by the Russians. By the end of the war, factories in Northampton had supplied a total of 23 million pairs of boots to the armed forces of Britain and her allies. Mulliners was an old established firm

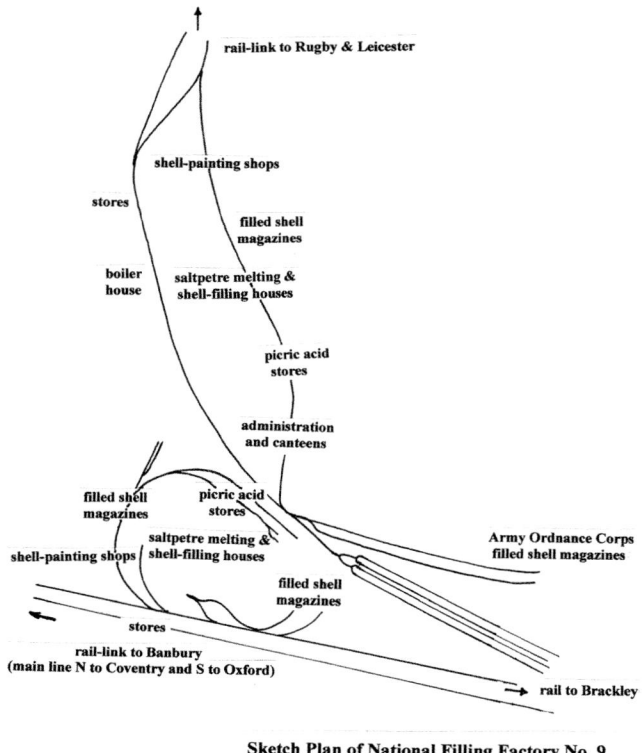

rail-link to Rugby & Leicester

shell-painting shops

stores

filled shell
magazines

boiler
house

saltpetre melting &
shell-filling houses

picric acid
stores

administration
and canteens

filled shell
magazines

picric acid
stores

saltpetre melting &
shell-painting shops   shell-filling houses

Army Ordnance Corps
filled shell magazines

filled shell
magazines

stores

rail-link to Banbury
(main line N to Coventry and S to Oxford)

rail to Brackley

**Sketch Plan of National Filling Factory No. 9
Warkworth (Banbury)**

Plan of National Filling
Factory No. 9 Warkworth
(Banbury).

of carriage makers based in Bridge Street, Northampton. Through their other offshoot companies, family members had strong connections to ordnance manufacturers such as the Coventry Ordnance Works and Cammell-Laird in Birkenhead. The Northampton firm converted from building automobile bodies to meeting the requirements of the military for vehicles. To fend off the attentions of the white-feather sorority, war workers across the munitions industry were eventually issued with a badge that showed them to be contributing to essential elements of the war effort.

In a nation dependent on food imports, the loss of thousands of tons of merchant ships to German U-boats forced a concerted effort to produce home-grown food in large quantities. Farmers had lost a significant proportion of their labour to the armed services but resisted using female labour, seeking to be allowed to employ twelve-year-old boys in preference. Northampton cattle market became a centre for servicing the needs for military horses, many of which had been purchased locally by army veterinary officers, and there was an Army Remount Depot in Kettering from 1915. With hindsight, it appears amazing that female labour continued to be rejected by the farming community until well into the war. Eventually, the Women's Land Army (WLA) was set up along with the Women's Forage Corps and the Women's Timber Corps, its members, unsurprisingly known as 'lumberjills'. Moulton Agricultural College was the location of the County Experimental Farm, training members of the WLA. Once reconciled to the idea of women doing 'men's work' on the farm, many farmers were unstinting with their praise, but others treated their unwelcome labourers appallingly, much preferring schoolboys or prisoners of war (POWs).

POWs and Internees in Northamptonshire

On the outbreak of war, hundreds of German and Austrian merchant seamen, many of them crewing British ships, were interned as enemy aliens, and the National Sailors' and Firemen's Union (NSFU) offered to provide premises and supervision for these men. Once properties in London and the major seaports filled up, accommodation had to be found for the increasing numbers of stranded and interned sailors elsewhere. Land at Eastcote and Pattishall was procured for a tented camp, based around Eastcote House, which provided offices and managers' quarters, with a hospital next door on Birdshill Road, and a staff canteen at Pattishall, in a hut that, until recently, served as the village hall. The camp was managed by the NSFU, while security was provided by civil police armed, appropriately, with cutlasses. It was reported at the time that by October 1914, many of these sixty seamen had been transferred to Alexandra Palace in north London, and had been replaced at Eastcote by German POWs, guarded by police officers with sidearms. The camp at Gretton, sometimes referred to as Corby, was a satellite of the civilian internment camps on the Isle of Man. Around a dozen camps catering for POWs were spread across the county, holding anything from between thirty to forty prisoners at Brackley or Yardley Gobion to a couple of hundred at Rothwell or Wakerley, and over 500 at Easton on the Hill. Many of these POWs were formed into work parties employed mainly in agriculture or mineral extraction. As was noted by the Oundle diarist, in 1917, seventy-five POWs were allocated to agricultural work locally. In March 1917, around 300 POWs from Gretton were assigned to work on the Corby iron stone workings, while others from Glendon and Rothwell were put to similar work in neighbouring pits. The POWs, perfectly understandably, appear to have preferred working in the peaceful English countryside to the dangers of the Western Front, but they still made demands on manpower. A detachment of the Royal Dublin Fusiliers was tasked with guarding them. Oundle's seventy-five POW farmworkers required a guard of thirty-five soldiers, probably from either the VTC or the Royal Defence Corps. Two German prisoners escaped from Corby in July 1917, making it to London where they were recaptured. As it became increasingly vital to convert more pastureland into corn-producing arable, a work gang of forty German POWs from Eastcote with ten guards was sent to Oundle in January 1918. They were meant to be put up in the workhouse, with their food being supplied from a central depot in Northampton, but until somewhere could be found for the unfortunate inmates, their arrival was delayed until March. By September, there were over 100 POWs in the Oundle area, with sixty in the workhouse and twenty at Winwick. One POW Camp, out of at least sixteen in the county, was in the grounds of Rushden House, holding, initially, sixty-two German prisoners carrying out tasks on the land. The guards were billeted in the town but their officers operated from an administration centre in Rushden House itself. At Yardley Gobion, the Potterspury Union Workhouse was used to hold up to fifty German POWs from May 1918.

Eastcote POW Camp's administration building.

Eastcote POW Camp's hospital in Birdshill Road.

The Interwar Years

The traumas of the war years were commemorated in a variety of ways: towns and villages erected war memorials, including that designed by Sir Edwin Lutyens, which now stands behind All Saints' Church in Northampton; memorial buildings such as the YWCA Hall in Castilian Street, Northampton, given by Mr & Mrs D. Taylor in memory of their son and the other young men who gave their lives in the Great War; and Lloyd George's Homes for Heroes initiative for honouring returning servicemen in a tangible way by building affordable modern housing for them. Throughout the interwar period new council estates were built in Far Cotton, Abington, Kingsthorpe, and Dallington. As the country optimistically entered a period of peace, it experienced a boom that unfortunately was not sustained. The armed forces underwent a radical and immediate reduction in numbers and would find it hard to survive the post-war slump with its strict limitations on public spending.

Some of those yeomanry regiments, which had enjoyed a continuous existence from their formation in the 1790s were able to retain their horses after the war. However, most of them, on the reincarnation of the volunteer forces as the new Territorial Army (TA) in 1920, faced life in a variety of new roles more suited to the demands of modern warfare. The Northamptonshire Yeomanry was lucky even to survive those years of depression and austerity, reduced to a single squadron now renamed 25th Armoured Car Company, the Tank Regiment, with HQ at Clare Street, Northampton. Equipped with unreliable Peerless 7-ton armoured cars, they attended annual camps at Bedford, Colchester, Dover, and Salisbury Plain. Budgets were so tight in 1933, that TA camps were cancelled altogether. By this time, they had been re-equipped with hand-me-down Rolls-Royce armoured cars, not significantly different from those used in the Palestine Campaign, twenty years earlier. Only in 1938, as the probability of a new European war intensified, was this skeleton unit expanded as an armoured yeomanry regiment, with a HQ and three fighting squadrons. It was next decided that the TA should be expanded by duplicating all existing units. So not only was a tiny nucleus of trained officers and NCOs required to establish a wholly new armoured unit, but must provide a cadre around which a second unit might be assembled. While even those regiments that had retained their full strength through the interwar years found this difficult, the Northamptonshire Yeomanry had no spare trained personnel at all, so had to manufacture this second new unit from 650 raw recruits under a newly promoted RSM. Nevertheless, by September 1939, both units, the 1st and 2nd Northamptonshire Yeomanry Regiments, were readied for the struggle ahead, the latter based in Brackley and Towcester.

The 1st Battalion, Northamptonshire Regiment, were the last British troops to leave the new Republic of Ireland in December 1922. They were deployed to the Middle East where they were involved in policing the British Mandate in Palestine, then to Egypt from where they were airlifted to Iraq in June 1932 in order to control a volatile situation. Their arrival in nine Vickers Victoria aircraft, appearing as if by magic, brought any emerging rebellion to an instant halt. The 2nd Battalion was involved in policing operations in India for much of the interwar period. In 1920, the volunteer units were re-established as the Territorial Army. The 4th Battalion was based in Northampton, Rushden, Wellingborough, and Kettering. A new 5th Battalion, using the former Huntingdonshire Cyclist Battalion as a basis, was formed centred on Huntingdon, Ramsey, and St Neots (all in historic Huntingdonshire). In 1927, the 5th Battalion HQ moved to Peterborough with 'B' Company based in Oundle with a drill station at Kingscliffe. In recognition of new tactics, in part dictated by improvements in weaponry, a restructuring of infantry battalions brought to the 4th Battalion in 1928 a newly created support company, armed with machine guns, mortars, and a LAA section. This new company moved in with HQ and 'A' Company at Clare Street in Northampton, with the remaining two companies at Wellingborough and Kettering. In 1935, the entire responsibility for the nation's AA defences was devolved to the TA. At the same time, there was developing in the Army what would turn out to be a bizarre misconception that the increasing use of technology in warfare would render infantry less important. Consequently, it was decided to convert some TA infantry to AA units. The Northamptonshire's 4th Battalion was one of those formally and diplomatically invited to change role—after all, they were volunteers. The invitation was accepted and they became, in 1937, the 50th (Northamptonshire Regiment) AA Battalion, RE (TA), equipped with AA searchlights, with two companies at Northampton, one at Peterborough and a fourth split between Wellingborough and Kettering. The duplication of TA units in 1938 provided the opportunity to establish the 5th Battalion's clone as a replacement 4th Battalion. Initially, its HQ was based in the depot's Isolation Hospital in Gibraltar Barracks, but it soon moved to a house opposite the barracks in Langham Place. Its four companies were based at Kettering, Raunds, Wellingborough, and Rushden.

The depot in Gibraltar Barracks consisted of a HQ and Administration Company; a Recruit Company; and, after the legislation requiring young men to undergo six months' military training was passed in 1938, a Militia Company that carried out basic training prior to allocating men to the regiment's home-based battalion of regulars. Gibraltar Barracks was becoming cramped and timber huts were erected to accommodate all these new functions so, in late 1938, it was decided to build a new regimental depot on a Greenfield site at Wootton to be completed by 1941. In the event, the outbreak of war postponed this project for a decade. The TA continued to use its established drill halls, under just as much pressure as the depot. The old Clare Street Militia Stores is listed in 1931 and 1936 as accommodating the offices of the Northamptonshire Territorial Association (TAA); 25th (Northamptonshire Yeomanry) Armoured Car Company; the HQ and two companies of the 4th Battalion; and the HQ of the 162nd (East Midland) Infantry Brigade. In October 1937, the War Office had allowed the TAA to buy 3 acres (1.2ha) of land behind the Militia Stores from the county council in order to increase the space for expanding units, particularly the newly mechanized Support Company of the 4th Battalion. The duplicate regiment of the Northamptonshire Yeomanry occupied the St Peter's Street drill hall in Brackley in 1938, and the Towcester drill hall, which had been built in 1925 in what is now Vernon Road. Rushden's new Victoria Road drill hall had been built around 1927 to effectively the same pre-1914 design used for Park Road, Wellingborough, but the new drill hall in Station Road, Kettering, opened in 1936, was a much more modern building, with characteristics common to many public buildings of the 1930s. It had a two-storey front block housing offices, armoury, stores, and messes, with a hall behind topped by a cupola. In Wellingborough, however, rather than building from new, the TAA acquired the Methodist manse to whose rear was added a large hall and garaging. As bases for two of the new searchlight companies, both Kettering and Wellingborough needed roomy training spaces with high ceilings for their night-sky simulations and doorways, which would allow access to bulky equipment on trailers. It appears likely that the new 4th Battalion, requiring accommodation in Raunds, took over the Golden Fleece PH, which had a clubroom of skating rink proportions.

As the vast army was demobilised in early 1919, Weedon ROD filled up again. The clothing was mainly transferred to Chilwell in Nottinghamshire to free up the three Nissen huts and the main storehouses for the storage of small arms, along with the Machine Guns Section, which arrived from Woolwich Arsenal in 1925. Combining the Cavalry and the RFA training establishments, the Army School of Equitation was set up in the barracks in 1922 with an indoor riding school and extra stables, the three pavilions functioning as their officers' mess. In 1930, the depot became the Central Ordnance Depot for Small Arms, Machine Guns and Bicycles. The eight storehouses were refurbished internally and given an exterior makeover, regaining some of their original elegance. Towards the end of the 1930s, improvements in access were made with concrete roadways replacing the tramway in recognition of the increasing role of motorised transport.

Rushden's Victoria Road drill hall opened in 1927 but remarkably similar in appearance to the 1906 drill hall in Great Park Street, Wellingborough.

Wellingborough, TAC, a converted Methodist manse.

Raunds: the 'Golden Fleece', in Rotten Row, with its large clubroom, provided a base for 'B' Company of the reformed 4th Battalion, Northamptonshire Regiment, from 1938, and for 'A' Company of the 8th Battalion, Northamptonshire Home Guard, from 1940.

Kettering, Station Road: this new drill hall was opened in 1936 for infantry and the new searchlight unit, with its cumbersome equipment and specialist training facilities. It later served as a leisure centre before being closed in 1993. (*Tony Smith and the Kettering Evening Telegraph*)

The RAF and Military Flight

Immediately when the fighting stopped, the RAF, still less than a year old but an enormous organisation, began to contract, amid concerted opposition from the other services allowing the politicians to pursue a policy of cuts. The Ten-Year Rule, which was predicated on the idea that it would take any belligerent power ten years to rearm, justified years of budget reduction. Only when it had become obvious by the early 1930s that German militarism was again becoming a threat were plans for an expansion of the RAF, with a reorientation of airfields toward the North Sea, implemented.

In light of governmental lack of concern for air defence, it was ironic, or maybe fortuitous, that post-war enthusiasm for flying increased. Pressure to establish a civil airport to serve Northampton threw up a number of possible sites, with Sywell being selected as the home of the Northamptonshire Aero Club. A combination of the annual pageant, the touring flying circus, the £10 government subsidy for pilot qualification, and the social life of the flying club all contributed to an increase in private flying and the build-up of a pool of experienced flyers. In 1932, the Aero Club at Sywell gave way to a new operation backed by Brooklands Flying Schools Ltd, who would lease a much

Sywell's *moderne* clubhouse of 1934 served an aerodrome that would train RAF pilots and function as an aircraft factory throughout the Second World War.

The Lindens in Northampton's Cliftonville became the local HQ for the RAFVR.

larger flying field and build permanent facilities. By 1934, a new clubhouse and hangar had been built in a *moderne* style, with further hangars added by 1938–40. At Daventry, there was a civilian landing ground listed by the Automobile Association in their guides published through the 1930s. Such private LGs offered little more than a flat surface and refuelling facilities.

The government had finally abandoned the Ten-Year Rule in 1932, but RAF growth remained only gradual, until 1934 saw a modest increase in the air estimates. Rearmament was under way and the RAF needed over 1,000 new pilots to be trained every year. It was decided to devolve basic flying training to civilian schools such as that run by Brooklands Aviation at Sywell, while developing the skills of the military pilot at the RAF Flying Training Schools (FTS). There were forty-eight pupils on each course lasting eight to ten weeks, with four courses each year. Successful pilots went on to complete their service training at RAF depots and flying schools. Sywell was No. 6 Elementary and Reserve Flying Training School (No. 6 E&RFTS), one of four dozen such schools across the country providing basic flying training for novice pilots, and refresher courses for reservists, in that crucial period between 1935 and the outbreak of war, when the RAF would need every pilot it could lay its hands on. A practice forced-landing ground for Tiger Moths of No. 6EFTS flying from Sywell had opened in 1931 at Earls Barton. In 1937, the RAF Volunteer Reserve (RAFVR) came into being. Local members flew service aircraft from Sywell and underwent ground tuition at their local HQ in 'The Lindens' at Cliftonville in Northampton. The RAF's airfield at Lilbourne had closed in 1919 and the GPO had built a W/T Station on the land. Not until 1938 would Northamptonshire see the commencement of work on planned, purpose-built RAF stations. Brackley LG became RAF Brackley and then RAF Croughton, which opened on the outbreak of war.

Air Defence, ARP, and Communications

A BBC high-power Long-Wave Transmitting Station was set up on Borough Hill outside Daventry in 1925, transmitting the BBC World Service from 1932 until 1992. A T-aerial was suspended between two 500-foot-high (154-metre-high) towers, standing 800 feet (246 metres) apart. Eventually, some forty-odd aerials would occupy the hilltop, and numbers of concrete plinths are still prominent all over the site. On 26 February 1935, Robert Watson Watt and A. P. Rowe, secretary of the government's Tizard Committee, exploring the development of an early warning air defence system, parked their van in a field at Upper Stoke, between Daventry and Weedon. Two dipole aerials were erected while a sensitive receiver connected to a cathode ray tube was set up in the back of the van. A signal on a 50-metre wavelength was transmitted from Borough Hill while a Handley Page Heyford biplane bomber flew 20 miles (32 km) backwards and forwards along the beam at 6,000 feet (1,846 metres). As the bomber approached the transmitter, a green spot, representing the bomber, appeared on the screen, enlarging as it approached the van, and diminishing as it flew away again, up to a range of 8 miles. This significant milestone in the development of Radio Direction Finding (RDF), later known as radar, would prove crucial to the country's air defence system, and would justify continuing experimentation at Bawdsey on the east coast. A memorial

BIRTH OF RADAR MEMORIAL

ON 26th FEBRUARY 1935, IN THE FIELD OPPOSITE

ROBERT WATSON WATT AND
ARNOLD WILKINS

SHOWED FOR THE FIRST TIME IN BRITAIN THAT
AIRCRAFT COULD BE DETECTED BY BOUNCING
RADIO WAVES OFF THEM. BY 1939 THERE WERE
20 STATIONS TRACKING AIRCRAFT AT DISTANCES
UP TO MORE THAN 100 MILES. LATER KNOWN
AS RADAR. IT WAS THIS INVENTION, MORE
THAN ANY OTHER, THAT SAVED THE RAF
FROM DEFEAT IN THE 1940 BATTLE OF BRITAIN.

The memorial erected in 2001 on the road connecting Litchborough to Watling Street (SP650557), where a plaque and an interpretation panel commemorate the first successful demonstration of Radio Direction Finding, later known as radar.

The Greatworth Signals Station opened in 1938 as a satellite of the RAF's main facility at Leighton Buzzard.

was erected in 2001 on the road connecting Litchborough to Watling Street, where the events are recorded by a plaque and an interpretation panel explains the process and its significance. Greatworth HF W/T signals station was set up in 1938 as a satellite of the RAF's main facility at Leighton Buzzard in Bedfordshire, later RAF Stanbridge. The equipment was accommodated in Nissen Huts and the transmitter itself was held in a larger version, the Tx Hall. RAF personnel were billeted in nearby Helmdon.

One of the key elements of LADA had been the network of observers on the ground, 'phoning in sightings of hostile aircraft to the control centre in Whitehall'. It was decided to develop this operation within Air Defence Great Britain (ADGB), beginning with the south-east of the country but eventually expanding to include the whole of Britain. The Observer Corps, becoming 'Royal' in 1941, was organised in groups under the auspices of the RAF. By 1935, there were, in Northamptonshire, fourteen posts under No. 12 Group (Bedford); with the network completed when Sutton Bassett opened under No. 5 Group (Coventry).

The least developed element of passive air defence during the First World War had been Air Raid Precautions (ARP). Throughout the 1930s, efforts were made to improve both the provision of shelters and the systems and procedures necessary to safeguard their users. An ARP department had been set up at the Home Office as early as 1935 to study the implications for the country of a bombing campaign using both HE and poison gas with the accent on shelters in domestic, public, and industrial settings. The official policy was that the majority of the population would shelter either at home, in domestic shelters, cellars, or basements, for which they were themselves responsible; at work, where employers had been issued with an ARP handbook in 1936 suggesting how they might protect their workforce; or in public shelters, provided for a meagre 10 per cent of the populace who might be caught out in the open during an air raid. In January 1938, legislation required local authorities to prepare ARP schemes for the construction of shelters and gas decontamination facilities, but the first concrete plans put forward by the government's ARP Department were for trench shelters to be constructed by factories. Local authorities were given no financial help, but in March 1939, an exercise was held across the county to test the blackout arrangements, particularly at the Corby and Islip steelworks; the response of the emergency services to aerial attack including the use of gas; and the TA's AA arrangements for identifying enemy aircraft using sound locators, basically big ear trumpets on trailers, and searchlights. On 13–14 July 1939, at almost the eleventh hour, Northampton's ARP system was again tested when French bombers flew overhead and were intercepted by Hawker Hurricane fighters from RAF Wittering. Eventually, a mixture of public and private initiatives produced viable designs for all three categories of shelter. The domestic shelter could be a sunken corrugated-iron Anderson shelter covered in earth, a brick-built surface shelter, or a strengthened basement room; for the general public, shelters could be brick-built on the surface or cut-and-cover trench systems; and for employees, shelters might be trench systems under factory floors, basements under shops, or concrete boxes built into steel-framed multi-storey mills. This latter solution seems to fit best with the typical premises of footwear manufacturers for instance. Although a certain amount of ARP activity occurred during the Munich Crisis of Autumn 1938, when trenches were dug on Northampton Racecourse, it is doubtful that much was done until war became a reality.

Munitions Production

Stewart and Lloyd set Corby up as a steel town producing Basic Bessemer-quality steel before 1934, and by 1939, the town's population had soared from 1,500 to over 10,000. The Kettering Iron and Coal Company was producing 100,000 tons of iron *per annum*. One of the challenges facing the expanding RAF was the supply of fuel to the new airfields. The Kelmarsh Air Force Distribution Depot (AFDD) was one of the first to be built, opening in 1937 to hold 2,000 tons (5,550 gallons or 25,000 litres) of aviation fuel in four D1 tanks, each with a capacity of 800 tons. These were kept topped up by rail tankers from the larger Air Force Reserve Depots (AFRDs), such as those at Misterton (Nottinghamshire) or Sandy (Bedfordshire), using the adjacent Northampton–Market Harborough railway line. Each AFDD was planned to serve about ten airfields using road tankers. While there was still a long way to go, at least a start had been made during the post-Munich period.

Surface features of the Kelmarsh Air Force Distribution Depot (AFDD), which opened in 1937 holding 2,000 tons (5,550 gallons or 25,000 litres) of aviation fuel in four tanks, each with a capacity of 800 tons.

6

The Second World War and the Cold War 1939–1990

Although land-locked Northamptonshire was distant from the invasion coast during the Second World War, it was little less involved than other counties: local units were heavily engaged in the conflict; it still figured in the national anti-invasion plans; it provided a suitable environment for training both army and air-force personnel; and it was a base for the production of munitions. Its inhabitants also faced the universal hardships of danger, privation, disruption, and loss. Almost everyone was in uniform, and every scrap of land was required for either military or agricultural exploitation. Agricultural production would be co-ordinated by the County War Executive Committee and its nine district committees, and the Women's Land Army was among the first of the voluntary organisations to be mobilised.

The Deployment of Local Units

The Northamptonshire Regiment

On the outbreak of war, the 1st Battalion, still referred to in regimental histories as the '48th', was stationed in India at Dinapore. It spent most of the war in Ceylon and India, crossing into Burma early in 1945, and was involved in the Battle for the Rangoon Road that spring. The 2nd Battalion (the '58th') did a lot of travelling in the 17th Infantry Brigade: first with the BEF in France, involved in the heavy fighting round Ypres in May 1940, and being evacuated from Dunkirk. Following two years on home defence duties, it became a component of Force 121 in May 1942, liberating Madagascar from the Vichy French. After that came a few months in Persia and Egypt prior to the Sicily landings, then back to the Middle East, followed by a return to Italy, and finally to Northwestern Europe for the last six months of the war. The 3rd Battalion staffed the Regimental Depot and the Infantry Training Centre (ITC), training recruits as drafts for the active battalions. The 4th Battalion remained in the UK for the duration as part of the 183rd Infantry Brigade, until the final year of the war when it was transferred into the 115th Infantry Brigade, forming Force 135 intended for the liberation of the Channel Islands, but fighting in North-west Europe instead. The 5th Battalion mobilised as part of the 143rd Infantry Brigade before transferring to the 11th Infantry Brigade in

January 1940 and fighting with the BEF in France. It then served in North Africa, Sicily, and mainland Italy, finishing the war in Austria.

From September 1939, Gibraltar Barracks became home to the Northamptonshire ITC, which moved in the spring of 1941 into a hutted camp known as Talavera Barracks on the old racecourse. It was then moved to Norwich where it became No. 2 ITC, and Talavera Barracks became No. 1 ATS Training Centre for the duration. Delapre Abbey had also begun to be used for training, probably Czech troops, as the 1st Czech Independent Armoured Brigade was based there in 1944. The regimental depot continued to support the increasing number of the regiment's battalions. In June 1940, the 50th Battalion was raised at Beccles (Suffolk) within No. 9 Infantry Holding Battalion, taking in untrained recruits and based at Euston Park near Thetford (Norfolk). This then became a new 6th Battalion tasked with anti-invasion duties in Suffolk, and remaining under GHQ Home Forces for the rest of the war. In 1941, a 70th (Young Soldier) Battalion was raised and based beside an equivalent battalion of the Leicestershire Regiment in Kettering. It was despatched to Cornwall to defend airfields against enemy landings. Although 1942 date stones were noted at the new Quebec Barracks in Wootton, it appears not to have been ready for full occupation until after the end of the war.

In the early rehearsals for war, two troops of what would become the 50th AA Searchlight Regiment (Northamptonshire Regiment) RA (TA), the former 4th Battalion, had been sent to defend Cardiff Docks armed with Lewis guns. In 1940, all four troops, by now badged as RA rather than RE, were deployed for the duration in the East Midlands in the Nottingham and Derby GDA, at Newark, Tuxford, Derby, Grantham,

Wooton, Quebec Barracks, was scheduled to open as a new depot for the Northamptonshire Regiment but was delayed by the Second World War. It then opened as Simpson Barracks, the Royal Pioneer Corps Depot.

and Nottingham. At the very end of the war, they were converted back to infantry and despatched to Norway on occupation duties following the German surrender.

The Northamptonshire Yeomanry

The 1st Northamptonshire Yeomanry started the war based in the drill halls in Northampton, Daventry, and Brackley, while the 2nd Northamptonshire Yeomanry had its HQ at Wootton Hall outside Northampton, with its three squadrons based at RAF Wyton near Huntingdon, Brixworth Hall, and Guilsborough Hall. Alongside training, mainly without vehicles, detachments guarded railway bridges and other VPs. In September 1940, they were despatched to Sussex. Unusually, from October 1940, both Northamptonshire regiments were brigaded together, along with the 2nd Royal Gloucestershire Hussars as the 20th Armoured Brigade, where they stayed until April 1942. While awaiting their promised complement of light tanks and armoured cars, the invasion scare of the summer of 1940, which had followed on the Dunkirk evacuation, saw a composite regiment with a few Vickers light (7-ton) tanks and the old Rolls-Royce armoured cars made ready to attack enemy armoured columns that might penetrate the defences on the coast. As the brigade gained from the materiel pouring out from the factories, it took its place in the 6th Armoured Division stationed in May 1941 in the Cambridge area to repel a German invasion of East Anglia and to protect the approaches to the Midlands. The 2nd Northamptonshire Yeomanry was based in Stow-cum-Quy between Cambridge and Newmarket, with personnel detailed to a number of different assignments. One officer and four crews with their Guy armoured cars became part of the most-secret 'Coats Mission', named after the major in charge. Stationed at Windsor Castle, it would fall to them to convey the Royal family to their bolthole in Worcestershire in an emergency. A second detail had been sent as signallers to link the two halves of the ill-conceived Norwegian expedition, while another went to the USA to help design the AFVs, which would come to Britain under the Lend-Lease scheme, some of them staying on in Canada as instructors. A steady stream of yeomanry officers was sent to the Middle East to stiffen the embryonic armoured formations fighting the Italian army in the Western Desert. All this was against a background of preparations for the Second Front. At this time, the regiments' assortment of armoured vehicles was replaced by proper tanks: first Matildas and Valentines, and then Cromwells. Within the 1st Northamptonshire Yeomanry, a Firefly, with its 17-pounder A/T gun, joined each trio of Shermans. The brigade was then sent to Wiltshire, training hard and absorbing the eighteen-year-old conscripts, not yet old enough to be sent overseas. In June 1944, both yeomanry units landed in Normandy, the 1st Northamptonshire Yeomanry being attached to the 50th Infantry Division to fight their way through the fields and hedges of Normandy. Following a few months' training with General Hobart's 79th Armoured Division (the 'funnies'), the 2nd Northamptonshire Yeomanry had joined 11th Armoured Division in March 1943, preparing for the savage fighting it would experience fighting its way out of the Normandy bridgehead a year later. In July's Operation Goodwood, they lost forty-seven of their sixty-two tanks, along with thirty-two officers and nearly 200 men. In August 1944, the survivors were drafted to the 1st Northamptonshire Yeomanry, continuing the advance, but now in support of the 51st Highland Division. Having fought their way over the Rhine in amphibious Buffaloes as part of 33rd Armoured Brigade, they ended the war in Zwolle, north of Arnhem.

Preparing to Resist Invasion, 1940–3

Following the evacuation of the BEF from Dunkirk in May 1940, a German invasion was expected daily, and the country's meagre defences were made ready to withstand it. Although the army was committed to a doctrine of mobility, the level of loss suffered in vehicles and equipment in France and Flanders dictated a strategy of static defence. Only once those deficiencies could be made good as the nation's factories moved on to a war footing might the strategy change. In the meantime, the plan was to delay the enemy on the coast until the capital ships of the Royal Navy, under an umbrella of RAF fighters, could sail down from its bases in Scotland to prevent the invaders' reinforcement and resupply. Coast batteries, anti-landing obstacles, and minefields were all employed to this end. The enemy's advance inland would be further delayed by continuous lines of anti-tank obstacles stretching the length and breadth of the country, from Somerset to Kent, and from Essex to Yorkshire and beyond. Behind these lines, mainly around Cambridge, Northampton, and Aldershot, would be stationed, from autumn 1940 until well into 1942, forces aspiring to an element of mobility. Known as the GHQ Reserve, these comprised embryonic divisions that were in process of reconstruction and training. The 1st Canadian Division had landed in Britain in January 1940, and been deployed between Aldershot and Portsmouth from 1 May. By the end of May, it had been sent to Northampton, with elements stationed at a number of locations in the county including Boughton House, Greens Norton, and Ecton Hall. It was one of three understrength infantry divisions forming the GHQ Reserve on a line drawn from Aldershot through north London to Northampton, but by July, it had been moved back to the Aldershot area. Elements of the 1st Armoured Division, which had lost all its armour in France, were based in the county prior to redeployment to the Cambridge area prior to a move to the Middle East in late 1941. The King's Dragoon Guards of 3rd Armoured Brigade spent time at Haselbech House, and the 22nd Armoured Brigade, consisting of the 3rd and 4th County of London Yeomanry (Sharpshooters), the 2nd Royal Gloucestershire Hussars, and the 2nd Battalion, King's Royal Rifle Corps (KRRC), were centred on Boughton House. At the end of 1940, the Northampton area became the base for the GHQ Reserve's 43rd Infantry Division, with HQ at Guilsborough House. In December 1940, a wholly new formation, the 9th Armoured Division, began to assemble, with its HQ at Cottesbrooke Hall. It would eventually comprise two armoured brigades, and a mechanised support group, plus divisional troops, with an infantry brigade joining in July 1942. A total of almost 10,000 troops was scattered across Northamptonshire and its immediate area. The 27th Armoured Brigade was based on Fawsley Hall from 1940–1943, with its three armoured regiments—the 1st East Riding Yeomanry, at Evenley Hall; the 4/7th Dragoon Guards at the Hinton Gorse Hotel and Woodford Halse; and the 13/18th Hussars in Litchborough's WI Room and Baptist schoolroom. The 1st Battalion, Queen Victoria's Rifles, KRRC, was attached as infantry. The 28th Armoured Brigade, with its HQ at Weston House, Weston Favell, included the 5th Royal Inniskilling Dragoon Guards, with its HQ Squadron in the Clare Street Drill Hall in Northampton, and the 15/19th Hussars and 1 Fife and Forfar Yeomanry at Weston House, Thorplands, and Guilsborough House. Their grand designations as armoured regiments, however, concealed their true state. The 15/19th Hussars had no tanks until March 1941, being equipped, in the meantime, with Austin cars armed with 0.55-inch Boys A/T rifles and Vickers 0.303-inch machine guns, the cars being supplemented by buses. When the regiment's tanks began to trickle in, they were from the first batch of A13 Mk III Covenanters. Around 2,000 of these were built for home defence, but they proved ineffective and unreliable, not only being under-gunned but also poorly designed mechanically. No sooner had the full complement arrived than they were recalled for essential modifications, disrupting training. The brigade's infantry element was provided by the 2nd Battalion, Queen Victoria's Rifles, KRRC. Each armoured division was provided with a support group consisting of a mechanised infantry battalion and field, A/T, and AA artillery. The 9th Support Group, with its HQ in Arthingworth Manor House, included the 11th Battalion, Worcestershire Regiment, based at Haselbech and Lamport Halls, and The Hemplow, Welford, with 6 Regiment RHA, 7 A/T Regiment, and 54 LAA Regiment. Divisional troops included 11 Field Squadron RE, which was billeted from March 1941, at Cottingham Hall (formerly Bury House) and the basement of a local factory, as well as in Burgess House (now Cannam House) and the Woolpack Inn, in next-door Middleton. In January 1943, the 1st Royal Gloucestershire Hussars joined the division.

Although there were strategic reasons for these formations to be based in the area as an anti-invasion mobile reserve, with a major exercise being held late in 1941, their primary role on a day-to-day basis was to train for operations overseas and, specifically, to prepare for the Second Front. There are still traces of the tank firing range and a tank turret trainer visible at Fawsley Hall where units of the 27th Armoured Brigade prepared for the Normandy landings. Every opportunity was taken for joint exercises with neighbouring units, which included the despatch riders of the Home Guard's 12th Battalion, the Czech Armoured Brigade, and 11th Battalion Home Guard from

Fawsley Hall, no stranger to military occupation having been a garrison in the Civil War, became the base for 27th Armoured Brigade in 1940.

Fawsley Hall: the remains of a tank gunnery trainer in the woods. A dummy tank turret was mounted on the steel framework, which was able to revolve by means of a toothed ring; the trainee tank gunner fired a 0.22-inch rifle mounted coaxially with the non-firing tank gun. (*Adrian Armishaw*)

Haselbech Hall housed elements of 3rd Armoured Brigade, including the Highland Light Infantry, King's Dragoon Guards, and 11th Battalion Worcestershire Regiment. Later, when these troops had moved on, it housed a POW camp.

Hardingstone. Training also extended to youngsters who took part in cadet camps both within the county, at sites such as Overstone with its very basic facilities, and with cadets from neighbouring Leicestershire at RAF Bitteswell near Lutterworth. The Northampton Sea Cadets purchased a 71-foot (22-metres) double-decker sailing barge to accommodate youngsters for weekend training sessions.

The Northamptonshire Home Guard and Local Defence

Despite the presence in the county of what were gradually becoming well-equipped and well-trained regular formations, it was recognised that their task lay elsewhere, so the responsibility for local defence would lie with the Northamptonshire Home Guard, whose shoulder flashes bore the 'NN' code. The county represented a sub-district of the East Central District of Eastern Command organised in four sectors with thirteen battalions, ordered 3rd–15th. The 1st and 2nd Battalions, based in the City and the Soke of Peterborough, were transferred to the Huntingdon Sector from August 1942. Over 20,000 men and women served in the force including the first volunteers (LDV) from May 1940; those otherwise exempt from military service who would be conscripted from January 1942; women volunteers who (officially) kept the books, manned telephones, and drove vehicles; and sixth-formers and school leavers awaiting their call-up.

In the days following the Dunkirk evacuation as the threat of imminent invasion hung over the country, embryo LDV units (Home Guard from July, 1940) focussed on securing vulnerable points against fifth columnists, parachutists, or any other will-o'-the-wisps who might appear. Consequently, many factories such as the Abbey Works or Express Lift Company in Northampton, and the Wellingborough Iron Company, formed their employees into dedicated platoons or companies to defend their own patches. The workforce of Stewart and Lloyd in Corby provided the nucleus of the 5th Battalion, and BBC staff at the Borough Hill transmitter site provided a company for the Daventry-based 10th Battalion. Similarly, the county's public utilities, the GPO and the LMS, all raised units, exploiting two very important advantages: familiarity with the terrain coupled with the leadership of their workplace managers. Early on, Northampton was the 12th Battalion's territory, but in July 1942, more of the independent units were brought together as the 15th Battalion with HQ Company, including a bomb-disposal section, coming from Express Lifts and 'A' Company made up of employees of the Electric Light and Power Company. The Bedford Road United Counties Omnibus Depot in Northampton was home to 2001 MT Company of East Central Home Guard Transport Column.

While a national anti-invasion strategy was gradually evolving based on coast defences backed up by continuous belts of A/T obstacles, inland counties were left to their own devices, and two significant strands quickly emerged. One concerned the construction of obstacles and checkpoints, which would control movement; the other was a network of permanently manned OPs, provided with Home Guard observers with access to police telephones and church bells, and messengers with bicycles who could together raise an alarm were parachutists or troop-carrying aircraft to be spied. These OPs occupied church towers as at Aston le Walls or Cosgrove; water towers as at Deanshanger or Yardley Gobion; windmills as at Blakesley or Braunston; or other suitably elevated structures, such as Davenports Brewery in Old Stratford or the power station in Northampton. At the behest of the county's Home

Guard commander and Central Midland Command, roadblocks were constructed in great numbers by the county council in July 1940, both around the major population and industrial centres and at selected spots on the county's more rural roads. Around Northampton, which had been designated an A/T Island, a ring of seventeen roadblocks sealed the town on an inner line, with a further ten forming an outer line. Each roadblock generally consisted of two elements: verges or pavements, permanently impeded by concrete blocks, brick walls, or stacks of sandbags, and materials for blocking the narrowed carriageway itself, kept ready for immediate use. Enormous numbers of concrete A/T Cylinders, over 700 in Northampton alone, were produced. These could be stacked by the roadside and rolled into place when the order was given. These cylinders were 3 feet (0.9 metres) high with a diameter of 2 feet (0.6 metres), and had vertical sockets into which could be inserted scaffolding poles temporarily aiding manoeuvrability, or iron pickets to which barbed wire could be permanently attached. The cylinders could also be linked together in chains by hawsers and laid horizontally. Slots in the roadway would take lengths of bent rail ('hairpins'), or RSJs could be dropped horizontally into slotted concrete cubes. Just south of the Eleanor Cross on London Road was a roadblock at the former junction with the Hardingstone turning. This was later upgraded as a Defended Locality (DL). In the boundary wall can be seen two loopholes, now blocked, which would have provided a protected position for riflemen defending the position. While this is the most obvious example, there would have been many others. The men manning these roadblocks, many of them from 'A' Company, 12th Battalion, would practise both closing the roadblocks themselves, and in view of the importance of timing, giving, and receiving the precise orders that would initiate the operation. In addition, four rail blocks—made up of combinations of concrete blocks and A/T Rails—had also been erected in order to stop enemy tanks penetrating the defences along the rail tracks. A platoon of guardsmen recruited from employees of the town's two fuel distribution depots was responsible for destroying any stocks left outside the perimeter if the roadblocks were closed.

In addition to roadblocks, measures were put in place to obstruct potential landing grounds for troop-carrying aircraft or gliders, particularly in the countryside. Any open area of land was obstructed with old cars or farm carts filled with rubble; posts sunk into the ground; or posts embedded in concrete-filled oil drums. This latter was the preferred option on Kingsthorpe golf course as it caused only minimal irritation to the golfers. Straight lengths of flat road were also seen as invitations to airborne landings, and on the A428, at the parish boundary between Brafield and Little Houghton (SP816589), a chain was suspended over the road above traffic height between two large ash trees.

While it had been important that something was being seen to be done, there were doubts about the effectiveness of these measures. Obstacles set up on the retreat to Dunkirk in April and May had proved as much a hazard to the defence as an impediment to the advancing enemy, and when Northern Command took over, this work was suspended, affecting roadblocks at Kelmarsh, Lamport, and Long Buckby, among others. Military thinking had long been committed to mobility and anything suggesting a static approach was anathema to the strategists. By mid-1941, it became possible to modify the hitherto unavoidable linear defence schemes by substituting an in-depth network of strongpoints backed up by mobile columns. At the regional level, this meant that in order to control important road and rail links, Wellingborough and Northampton, in September 1941, would be designated Nodal Points, a reworking of the earlier idea of A/T Islands, and would be given all-round defences. At the local level, defences would be concentrated on fewer but stronger DLs, again with all-round defences and generally straddling important bridges or key road junctions. Of Northampton's original seventeen inner roadblocks erected during the summer of 1940, only six would be retained and developed as DLs.

Wellingborough selected the density of its DLs on the basis of the resources available to man them. The garrison would consist of the Home Guard's 7th Battalion, a maximum of 1,150 men, supplemented by indeterminate numbers of US personnel who would be responsible for guarding only their own HQ and warehouse. Once a garrison of 180 men of 'B' Company for the keep and 'HQ' Company's 250 men as a reserve had been allocated, it was reckoned that up to seven DLs, each defended by a minimum of seventy troops, was sustainable. The Broad Green DL, the extension of High Street to the north-west of the town, was defended by two platoons from 'A' Company, armed with spigot mortars covering a complex of three roadblocks. Hardwick Road and Harrowden Road were each defended by a flame fougasse. The Finedon Road DL, held by elements of 'E' Company, consisted of a roughly circular wired area around 300 yards across, centred on the T-junction with Eastfield Road, and sealed by three roadblocks. All the approaches were mined and covered by spigot mortars, light machine guns, and Northover Projectors (see below). Outlying bridgeheads were defended at Ditchford Mill and Little Irchester, as was the river crossing at Irthlingborough. Large numbers of A/T Blocks can still be seen in Wellingborough: over 120 incorporated in a revetment in Croyland Road, and nearly 200 within the allotments in Doddington Road opposite the Royal Oak PH.

Loopholes, now blocked, in a boundary wall at a Defended Locality near the Mereway roundabout in Northampton (SP75455814). (*Adrian Armishaw*)

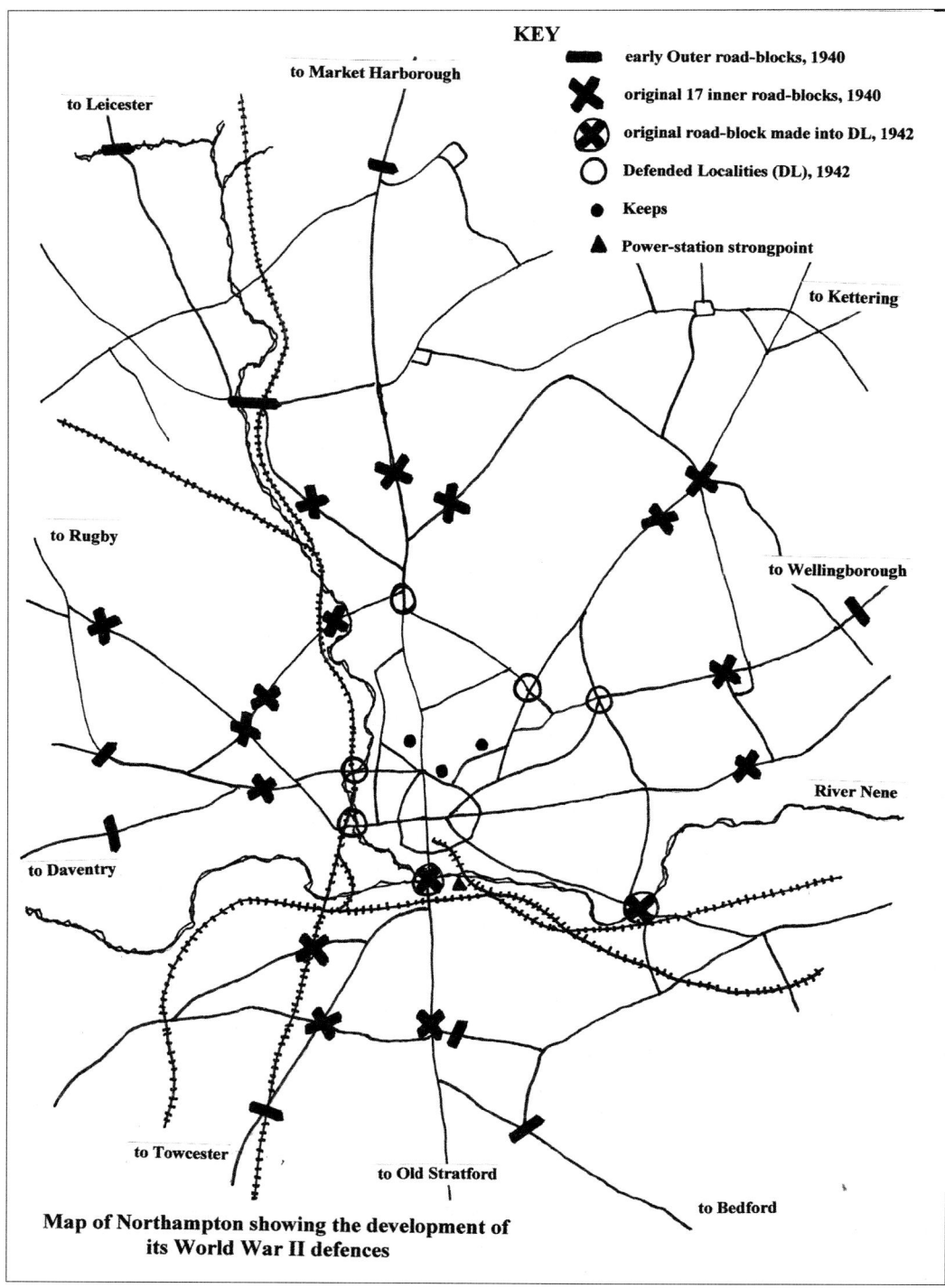

KEY

▬▬▬ early Outer road-blocks, 1940

✖ original 17 inner road-blocks, 1940

⊗ original road-block made into DL, 1942

◯ Defended Localities (DL), 1942

● Keeps

▲ Power-station strongpoint

to Market Harborough

to Leicester

to Kettering

to Rugby

to Wellingborough

River Nene

to Daventry

to Towcester

to Old Stratford

to Bedford

**Map of Northampton showing the development of
its World War II defences**

Sketch map showing the defences of Northampton in the Second World War.

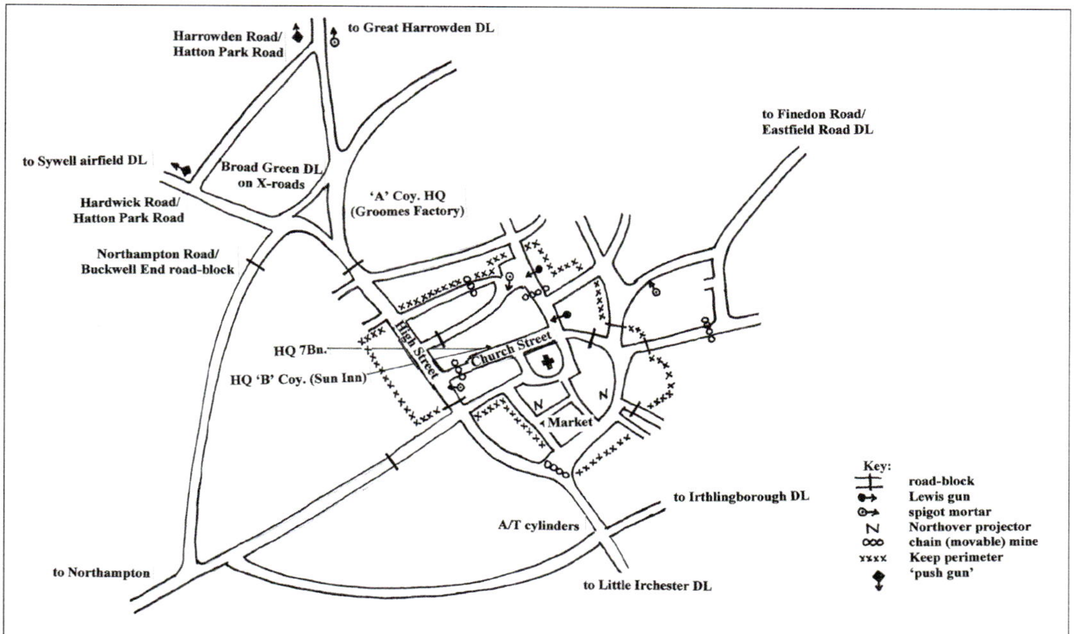

Sketch plan of the Wellingborough 'Keep' & inner defences (1941)

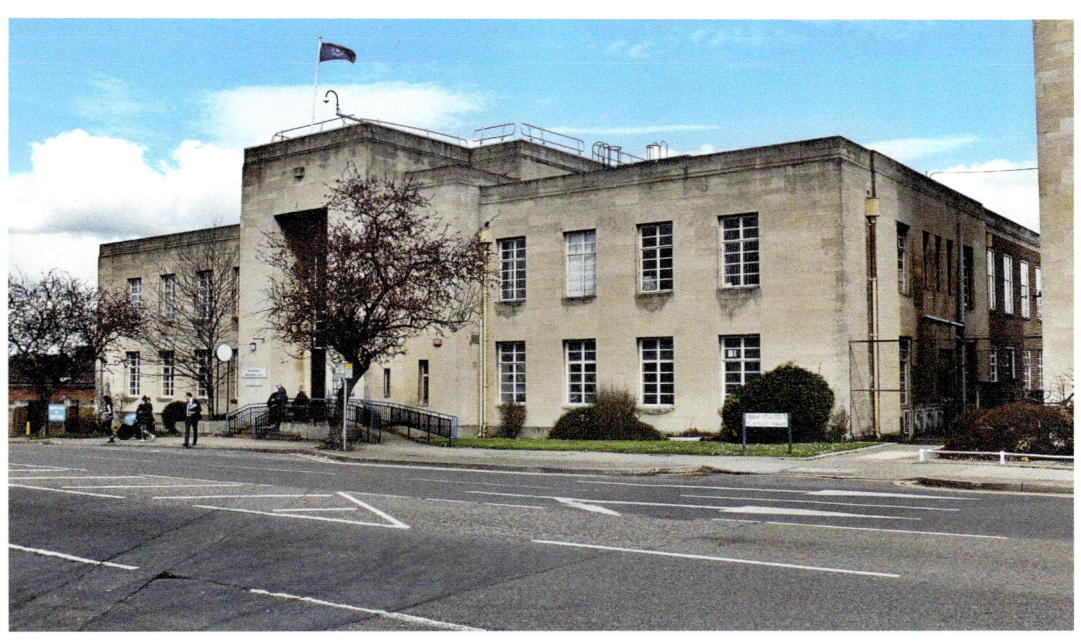

Sketch map showing the defences of Wellingborough in the Second World War.

Northampton, The Mounts: the recently opened police station served as one of the three keeps in the Home Guard Defence Plan of 1941.

Aston-le-Walls: the tower of St Leonard's Church was taken over by the local Home Guard as an observation post.

Within the area defended by the DLs was the keep: the position prepared for the garrison's last ditch defence. Northampton was considered to be so large that three keeps were established: at the police station on The Mounts; at Gibraltar Barracks; and at the Clare Road drill hall. These three positions were prepared for all-round defence by blocking the approaches with wire, A/T obstacles, and mined areas, all covered by emplaced weaponry with interlocking fields of fire. Down on the riverbank by the power station, two very rudimentary concrete pillboxes fashioned from sewer pipes gave a modicum of protection to their garrisons who commanded the approach with Lewis guns and rifles. Wellingborough's Keep was centred on Church Street, taking in Market Street and the lower part of High Street. Access points were blocked with mines and A/T obstacles, covered by spigot mortars, light machine guns (still the old Lewis guns in 1942), and Northover Projectors.

The Home Guard Armoury

While the earliest days of the Home Guard are characterised by blunderbusses, shotguns, and pikes, an eclectic assortment of effective weaponry was quickly amassed. This included US and Canadian 0.303-inch and 0.300-inch rifles, causing all sorts of problems over the allocation of the small amounts of the right ammunition available for each calibre. An allocation of seventy 0.300-inch Lewis guns arrived in September 1940, the first automatic weapons to reach the Home Guard, causing great excitement for those who had used them in the previous war. Later there were Bren and Sten guns, and Vickers medium machine guns, including some at Thrapston for which trailers were ingeniously constructed. In order to increase the Home Guard's firepower, a whole range of sub-artillery was developed. The Northover Projector fired Self-Igniting Phosphorous (SIP) grenades, and was basically a length of drainpipe on a tripod. These projectiles were later dubbed Molotov cocktails, but the official name was the Albright & Wilson (AW) bomb, which was also issued to bomb-throwing parties in ambush positions. The Blacker Bombard, or 29-mm spigot mortar, which fired a 14-lb (6.4-kg) anti-personnel, or a 20-lb (9-kg) anti-tank bomb, up to 400 yards, was designed to be fired from fixed mountings consisting of a domed concrete pedestal set in a circular or hexagonal pit with ready-use bomb lockers built into its sides. The pedestal contained a steel reinforcing frame, or 'spider', whose apex was a stainless steel peg that protruded from the domed top and held the mortar, which was stored off-site. Although the Northampton defences used spigot mortars, no permanent pedestals have been reported. The Wellingborough Home Guard sited three spigot mortars to defend their keep in the centre of town, and further ones in their outlying defences including three in the Finedon Road DL. Reference is made to spigot mortar squads, and planning documents appear to point to a flexibility of positioning these weapons. This would suggest that Northampton's 12th Battalion and Wellingborough's 7th Battalion both opted for the alternative mobile mounting, which consisted of a low tripod of scaffolding poles with spade-grips for stability. Only at Oundle can a fixed pedestal mount be seen, covering the bridge on the Stoke Doyle road. Another extemporised weapon was the Smith Gun, a piece of field artillery firing a 3-inch (75-mm) shell. The gun was mounted on a wheeled carriage, and was designed to be towed into action behind a small saloon car. It was then turned on its side with one of its dustbin lid-shaped wheels providing overhead cover while the other acted as a turntable. These guns were sometimes kept in the explosives and inflammables Stores that were designed for Home Guard use. One of the pair behind the drill hall in Oundle has large steel double doors, which may suggest such use. There is a further pair of stores at Bulwick, and single stores exist across the county, usually partitioned across the middle and double-ended, like that maintained at their Barnwell range (now the Shooting Club) by Oundle Home Guard. The storage of explosives posed a constant problem, highlighted when the store at Dulley's Brewery, Wellingborough, HQ of the Home Guard's 7th Battalion, and containing large stocks of SAA and SIP grenades, was bombed. Smith Gun ammunition had a reputation for instability, and the RAF Regiment, also issued with this unpopular weapon after 1942, stored its ammunition as far away as possible from other explosives.

While those improvised weapons were supplied from central sources there was still scope for local initiative. Large quantities of explosives were stored at the Thingdon Mines at Finedon and employees, who were members of the local Home Guard, improvised a range of devices that could be used against enemy tanks. These included mines, both static and mounted on trolleys; grenades; and fougasses, which could be triggered to hurl flaming oil, shrapnel, or rocks over passing troops or vehicles, to a distance of up to 180 yards. These devices attracted the attention of the North Midland District HQ at Nottingham and demonstrations were laid on for senior Regular Army and Home Guard commanders. These Thingdon experiments may thus have influenced the design of A/T weapons including the Hanworth Torpedo, subsequently developed by RE officers in Nottingham. However, gelignite was found to be unstable and after

Wellingborough: a collection of over 100 A/T cylinders used as a revetment in London Road.

Oundle: the pair of Home Guard Explosives and Inflammable Stores behind the drill hall, one of which may have housed a Smith gun.

Oundle: the spigot mortar pedestal overlooking the bridge on the Stoke Doyle road (TL03558811).

casualties were sustained in tests, production was suspended. Also deemed to be more dangerous to its operators than to the enemy was the Harvey flamethrower. A dozen of these pieces of equipment were issued to the 12th Battalion but were quietly forgotten about and stored in the LMS sheds at the railway station for the duration. Flame fougasses, nevertheless, figure in the planned defences of DLs in Wellingborough.

The Home Guard, as we have seen, requisitioned vantage points as OPs, and both public and private premises for HQs, unit bases, and training spaces. Public houses or village institutes provided bases for rural platoons. Long established 600-yard ranges such as Nobottle or Sywell were used for shooting practice, along with local 25-yard ranges both indoor and outdoor. There was a range for the conventional 2-inch mortar at Kelmarsh, but there were also ranges for the more volatile pieces of sub-artillery such as that for spigot mortars and Smith Guns at St Peter's Bridge and Clifford's Hill in Northampton, and at Finedon. Unavoidable, but extremely dangerous, grenade-throwing practice tended to be carried out in locations such as Castle Dykes at Farthingstone, or quarries where blast could, to some extent, be minimised. Battle training was carried out on a number of isolated sites including in the ruins of the former First World War munitions factory at Warkworth.

Vulnerable Points (VPs)

The fear of invasion in May 1940 prompted a frenzied building activity to construct fixed defences, the majority of the effort going into the fortification of the Coastal Crust backed by the GHQ Line. However, to complement the A/T islands, it was necessary to identify further strongpoints that could become centres of resistance if it came to it. At the time, AA searchlights (S/L) were deployed in a grid of permanent sites about 3 miles apart in all directions. The local OC 40th AA Brigade issued an instruction that a concrete pillbox should be constructed on each S/L site and that a barbed-wire apron, strengthened by weapons pits should be laid. The site personnel should then defend that site following the orders of the local field force commander. At least six pillboxes, including those at Gretton and Pipewell, are still extant from such sites and others, such as Woodnewton, are known to have been built. This origin explains what otherwise appear as randomly distributed pillboxes with little purpose.

Other elements of these early defences were more *ad hoc*. At Great Addington, just south of the church, a garden wall has been heightened to accommodate a pair of loopholes. Another pair of what appear to be similar loopholes overlook Waitrose's carpark in Oundle, facing the bridge over the Nene. Brigstock Camp was built in the 1930s as a work camp for the unemployed. It was taken over by the military and may have been a S/L HQ. In a hedge line on the camp's western perimeter is a standard DFW/3 Type 22 pillbox, reportedly one of a trio (SP9346 8642). The perimeter of Corby steel works was patrolled day and night, with permanent guard posts set up. These may have been brick-built like Wardens' Posts or, more likely, they could have been constructed out of sandbags, roofed in tin and earthed over. The BBC building on Borough Hill has an OP/guard post high up on one wall overlooking the station's approaches.

East Carlton: a weak, badly constructed DFW3 Type 22 pillbox on a searchlight site (SP824896); it has not yet fallen down, eighty years on.

In early 1941, the construction of fixed defences was stopped, with just one major exception: airfields. After the German airborne attack on Crete, whose initial objective had been the capture of an airfield, there was a fear that such an assault might be replicated in Britain but on a far larger scale. In May 1940, the RAF invited Major-General Taylor, Director of Fortifications and Works at the War Office, to formulate a policy for the defence of airfields. Taylor prioritised as Class I airfields, those most involved in efforts to repel an invading force, and those closest to vulnerable ports or nearest to potential invasion beaches. Unsurprisingly, Northamptonshire's airfields failed to meet these criteria, so Collyweston, not in the frontline of a counterattack but nevertheless of operational significance, came into Taylor's Class IIa category, along with Kingscliffe, noted as still under construction. The remainder, including Sywell, were categorised as Class III. At the time of the Taylor Report's publication, many of the county's other airfields were still barely past the planning stage. In the early days, airfield defences were composed of pillboxes: an inward ring facing the flying field and another facing outwards, along with weapons pits and wire. These defences were manned by regular troops and RAF ground crew. With a specific role in airfield defence, the RAF regiment was formed in 1942, coinciding with the end of a review of tactics. Paralleling the replacement of linear defence systems across the country by Nodal Points and DLs, airfields adopted a system of DLs, a change exemplified, in different ways, by Sywell and Kingscliffe.

Sywell as a Class III airfield might be expected to be defended by up to a maximum of ten to sixteen pillboxes. The 1941 plan records seven pillboxes, four AA posts, and four road barriers distributed around the perimeter of the aerodrome. Additionally, a BHQ was built into an existing barn a little distance outside the perimeter, with loopholes in the gable ends and a strengthened core. It would appear that the surviving pillbox located opposite the access road to Sywell Grange is a later addition to the original defences as it is shellproof with 36-inch-thick (0.9-metre-thick) walls, and a reduced number of three loopholes, design requirements only introduced by the AM in 1941. Sywell Airfield officially constituted a Home Guard DL in its own right, manned by 'E' Company, 9th Battalion, and equipped with a Smith gun, stored in its own shed on the western perimeter.

Kingscliffe, by contrast to Sywell, only opened at the end of 1941 and has defences based on the new orthodoxy. Two new structures were widely introduced by the Air Ministry in 1941. One was a purpose-built BHQ (11008/41) consisting of a concrete cupola over a 360-degree observation slit, with PBX and crew rooms underground, accessed via steps or a hatch above rungs. Located on a vantage point overlooking the flying field its purpose was to allow a defence commander to maintain visual control of his forces. The other was the F. C. Construction pillbox (9882/41), often referred to as the Oakington, Fairlop or simply, as on the AM plan of Kingscliffe, 'mushroom' pillbox. This had a domed roof cantilevered over a sunken, circular chamber, with a pair of Vickers 0.303-inch machine guns clamped on to a tubular bar running round the wall below the firing slit, allowing them to fire in any direction. Kingscliffe appears never to have received the fifteen to twenty-four pillboxes to which its IIa status entitled it, but there are fourteen E-shaped fighter dispersal pens (FCW4513) ranged around the perimeter. Each of these consisted of earth-covered Stanton shelters for pilots and ground crew, with outward-facing loopholed walls, providing firing positions for the airfield's defence force. There were, additionally, two DLs, one with two mushroom pillboxes and the other with two more mushrooms and the BHQ.

A further new defence work was the brick-lined 'seagull-trench', in the shape of a flattened 'V' or 'W', designed to hold machine guns and rifles, constructed at Hinton-in-the-Hedges and Croughton. The mushroom pillbox proved particularly popular in Northamptonshire, with examples, in addition to Kingscliffe's four, at Chipping Warden (one), Grafton Underwood (two), Croughton (one), Hinton-in-the-Hedges (three), and Collyweston (one), where they often, as at Kingscliffe, formed components of DLs. At Hinton-in-the-Hedges, a group of three seagull trenches, two mushroom pillboxes, and the BHQ defends the eastern side of the airfield, and Croughton's north-east corner was defended by a group composed of two seagull trenches and a mushroom pillbox. However, at Grafton Underwood, the BHQ is distant from the mushroom pillboxes, which are themselves some distance apart from each other. Chelveston also had a BHQ, but, apparently, no pillboxes.

These three structures—BHQ, mushroom pillbox, and seagull trench—did not entirely replace earlier designs. Hinton-in-the-Hedges has a hexagonal pillbox with the DF Homer on its roof, while Polebrook opened in 1941 but appears to have been given linear defences. There is a BHQ at one corner, and three surviving hexagonal pillboxes. One lies at the north-west corner but two more straddle the southern ends of two of the three concrete runways fully operational by June 1941. All three pillboxes are hexagonal but two are most unusual in that they have two loopholes, one above the other, in two of their six faces, with single loopholes at orthodox height in others.

Hinton-in-the-Hedges: the Battle HQ on the defended locality at SP550372.

Croughton: an F. C. Construction (or 'mushroom') cantilevered pillbox.

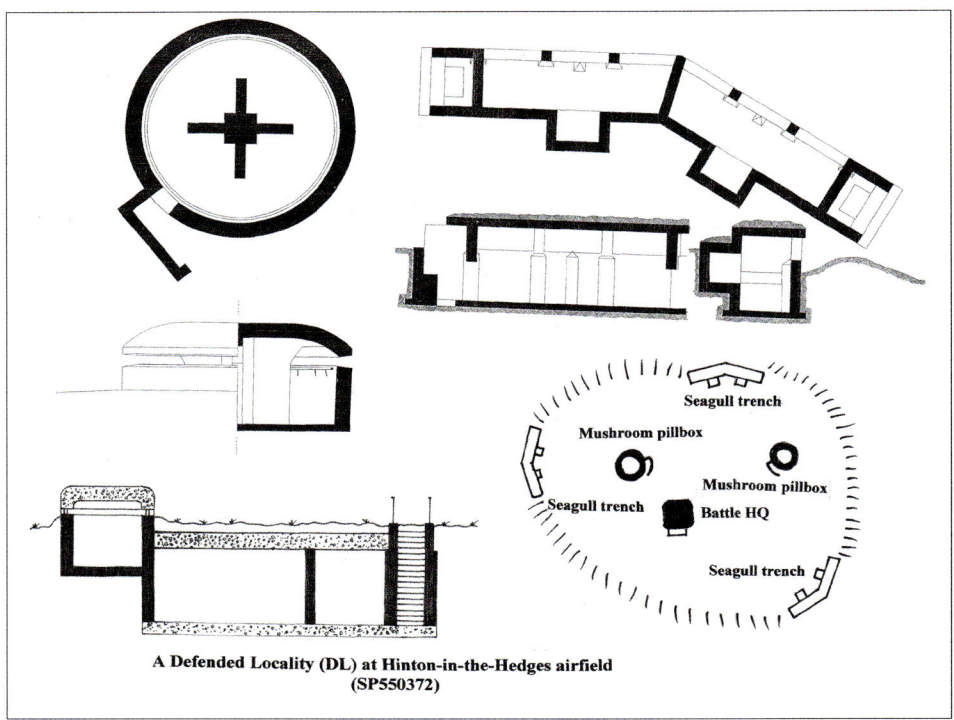

A Defended Locality (DL) at Hinton-in-the-Hedges airfield
(SP550372)

Hinton-in-the-Hedges: sketch plan of a defended locality. (*Adrian Armishaw and author*)

Kingscliffe: one of the defended E-pens showing the loopholed wall and an entrance to the shelter.

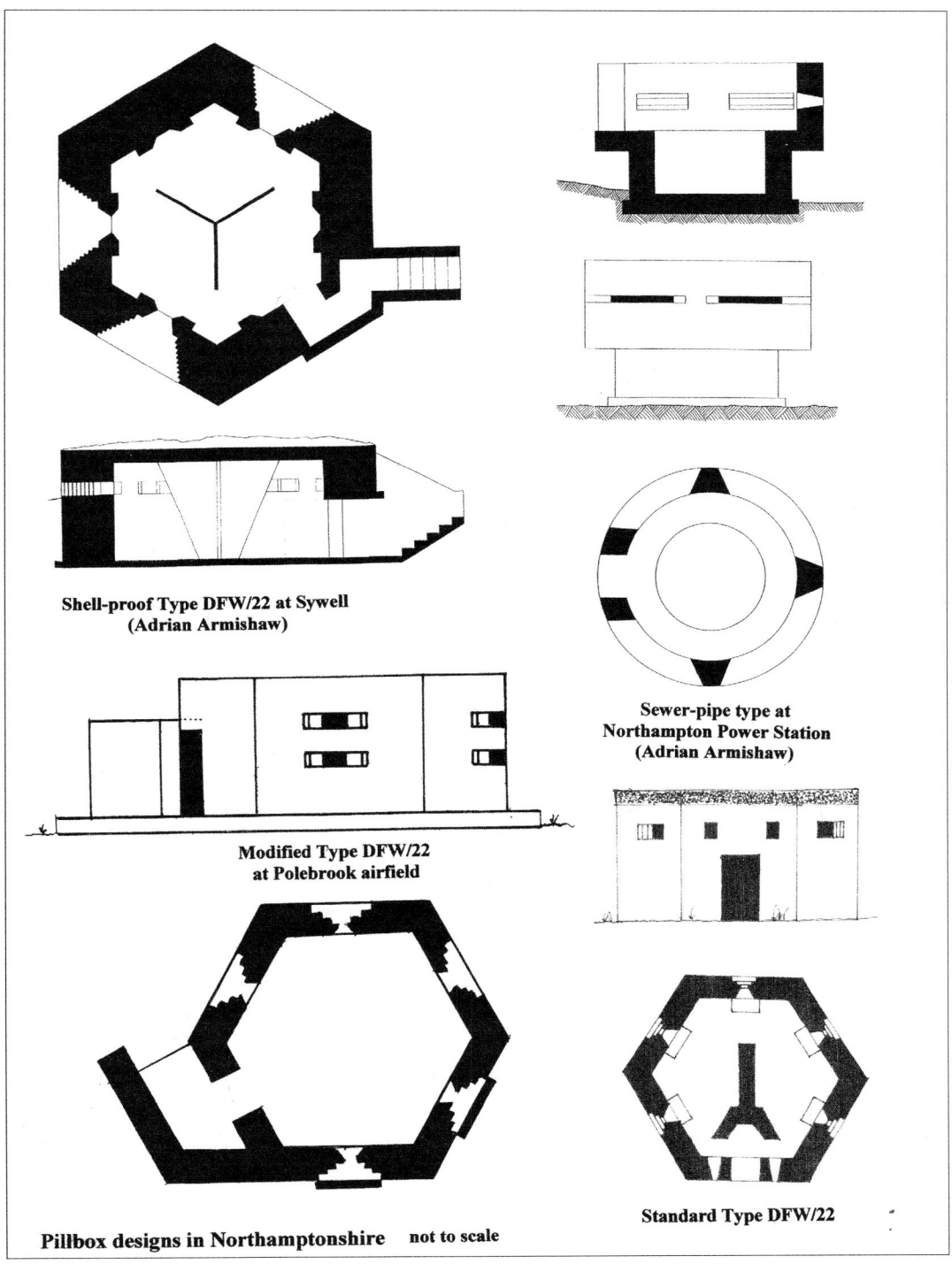

Shell-proof Type DFW/22 at Sywell
(Adrian Armishaw)

Modified Type DFW/22
at Polebrook airfield

Sewer-pipe type at
Northampton Power Station
(Adrian Armishaw)

Pillbox designs in Northamptonshire   not to scale

Standard Type DFW/22

Plans of Northamptonshire pillboxes. (*Adrian Armishaw and author*)

Polebrook: a pillbox on the airfield with two loopholes in one face but a single in another. The lower loop may have been for the Boys 0.55-inch A/T rifle, ineffective against armour but lethal against enemy troop-carrying aircraft attempting a landing.

Their current isolated situation does not, of course, preclude the possibility that they each formed the centre of a DL composed of long disappeared weapons pits and wire. It would appear that the half a dozen airfields, including Silverstone, Desborough, and Spanhoe, which did not become operational until 1943 or even later, received no fixed defences at all, but there was a practice, especially on USAAF airfields, of mounting 0.5-inch Browning aircraft machine guns on jeeps as a mobile, dual-purpose defence against both ground and air attack.

Military Airfields and Flight in the Second World War

As war broke out, few airfields in Northamptonshire were anywhere near operational, a few more were nearing completion, but the number of those well equipped to meet the demands of modern warfare would increase only gradually. Sywell and its Relief LGs at Brafield-on-the-Green/Denton and Earls Barton, were all grass fields geared to the operation of biplane trainers. Wittering's satellite of Collyweston was prepared for flying operational fighter aircraft, but its other satellite, Kingscliffe, would not be ready until 1941 and would then only get its concrete runways and upgraded hangars in 1943. Croughton and Hinton-in-the-Hedges both opened in 1940 with grass fields as satellites of, respectively, 16 OTU at Upper Heyford and 13 OTU at Bicester (both in Oxfordshire). Hinton would later gain hard runways, but Croughton would stay as grass until the end of the war. Opened in 1941, Chipping Warden, Polebrook, and Chelveston were built to an eve-of-war standard, with J-type hangars, but the concrete runways of all three of them still required to be extended, even though Polebrook was deemed suitable to host the RAF's first operational Flying Fortresses, obtained from the USA in 1941. The arrival of the 8th USAAF in early 1942 accentuated the need to speed up the construction of ever more airfields: Grafton Underwood in 1942, with Deenethorpe and Harrington following a year later. Desborough and Silverstone also opened as RAF OTUs in 1943 and the final addition came at Spanhoe in 1944.

Northamptonshire's airfields performed a wide range of roles. The well-established tradition of training, begun in the First World War and continued at Sywell throughout the 1930s, was extended by the use of first Croughton and Hinton-in-the-Hedges, and then Desborough and Silverstone as bases for OTUs. Croughton went on to become a specialist centre for glider pilot training, and Hinton-in-the-Hedges was involved in the development and testing of electronic landing and navigation aids such as GEE, Oboe, H2S, and LORAN, which were being rolled out for operational use. Under the aegis of the Signals Development Unit, the operation of airborne radio stations for use in battlefield command and control was perfected. The Wellingtons of 12 OTU at Chipping Warden flew bombing missions over France and Germany, suffering heavy losses in the process. Silverstone opened in March 1943 as 17 OTU, carrying out leaflet dropping, bombing raids, and diversionary incursions over France. September 1943 saw the opening of Desborough as 84 OTU training five-man crews, eleven at a time, in Wellington bombers. The OTUs contributed at least twenty aircraft from Northamptonshire's airfields to the first 1,000-bomber raid on Cologne. Chelveston was also intended as an operational bomber station, but until its runways could be completed, it became home to first the Central Gunnery School and then the Airborne Forces Experimental Establishment, carrying out suitability trials of glider-towing aircraft. An unofficial delegation of USAAF engineer officers had visited during the airfield's construction, but only in mid-1942 did the airfield become an operational USAAF bomber station, carrying out daylight raids on France. Polebrook, opening in 1941, was selected on the basis of its concrete runways, to operate the RAF's twenty B17 Mk I Flying Fortresses. Bombing practice by 90 Squadron was carried out on Ashton Bombing Range near Oundle, and despite their initially disappointing results, useful lessons were learned from their officially neutral USAAF mentors. It was subsequently handed over to the USAAF to continue the good work. The very first USAAF arrivals had been in May 1942, when a QM Company took up residence in Wicksteed Park, and a bomber squadron at Grafton Underwood commenced the first wholly USAAF bombing operation from British soil with Deenethorpe following the next year. Harrington, a satellite of 84 OTU at Desborough until March 1944, was handed over to the two USAAF squadrons that would fly their matt-black Liberators in support of OSS Carpetbagger operations. The USAAF 422 Bomb Squadron at Chelveston trained in night attacks, and some of their operations involved parachuting OSS operatives into occupied France. Collyweston operated fighters throughout the war and was officially absorbed into the coterminous Wittering in 1942. Kingscliffe was the base for RAF fighter squadrons equipped mainly with Spitfires, but from January 1943, a USAAF fighter group moved in for a few months. When they left for North Africa that May, the opportunity was taken to improve the airfield's infrastructure by laying concrete runways. In August, the USAAF 20th Fighter Group arrived with twin-engined P-38 Lightnings, capable of carrying out operations up to 600 miles (960 km) away, escorting the bomber force deep into Germany and conducting their own bombing and strafing attacks on enemy airfields. Later, in 1944, both squadrons of the 20th converted to P-51 Mustangs. Between 1942 and 1945, the four main 8th USAAF Bomb Groups flew a total of 1,216 missions involving 34,609 aircraft sorties, losing 531 aircraft. The 20th USAAF Fighter Group flew 312 missions involving 14,764 sorties, losing 132 aircraft. The strangest role, and possibly no less dangerous than operational flights, was Collyweston's, which included maintaining and operating the growing collection of captured enemy aircraft that could be flown around the country for training and identification practice.

The build-up to the Normandy landings saw the Dakotas of 315th Troop Carrier Group (TCG) moving into the newly completed Spanhoe, from whence, on D-Day, the 505th Parachute Infantry Regiment of the 82nd Airborne Division was delivered to targets in Normandy. As part of Operation Market, sorties from Spanhoe dropped more of these airborne troops near Nijmegen, and the 315th TCG was involved in operations to cross the Rhine in March 1945. Sadly, in October 1944, No. 1 Glider Training School had been forced to reform at Croughton to make good the losses sustained at Arnhem. The Normandy landings had seen the formation of one of the war's stranger units. The Allied air forces supporting the landings had realised that any aircraft overflying the armada was seen as hostile and in real danger from trigger-happy AA gunners. A detachment of the ROC (Seaborne), including volunteers from Northamptonshire, was recruited to serve as on-board aircraft spotters to attempt to ensure that only those aircraft positively identified as hostile were fired on.

Airfield Design and Architecture

The neo-Baroque architecture of the RAF's expansion period of the 1930s is entirely missing from Northamptonshire's airfields. Towards the end of the decade, urgency was injected into airfield construction and new designs were both less extravagant in their use of materials and more hurriedly built. A stopgap hangar, bridging the gap between the C-type and new prefabricated hangars, was the bowstring-roof J-type (5836/39) that was erected at Chelveston, Chipping Warden, and Polebrook. The first of a range of prefabricated hangars was the Callender-Hamilton (6637/37) put up at Kingscliffe, but the most used was the T2 (8254/40), which appeared in great numbers and could be transported from one site to another, and in an emergency, it was capable of erection by twelve men in ten days. Designed and supplied by Lord Beaverbrook's Ministry of Aircraft Production (MAP) for on-the-spot repairs to operational aircraft by civilian staff, many airfields also had a B1 hangar. Examples were built at Desborough, Hinton-in-the-Hedges, and Silverstone. A further MAP design was the much larger R-type hangar, which was used for aircraft manufacture and can be seen at the Armstrong Whitworth factory at Sywell. The most numerous hangars were the various marques of Blister hangars that were built at Kingscliffe (twelve), Sywell (five), and Denton (ten).

The new austerity extended to all the other buildings on an airfield, so temporary brick (tb) and Nissen huts became the norm. A design for the watch office (518/40) was paired with the J-type hangars at Chelveston, Polebrook, and Chipping Warden, upgraded at Polebrook in 1942. A new design for the watch office complex (Type A 15898/40) designed for bomber satellite stations, including a two-storey block with control and signals rooms, and an attached Nissen hut as a crew-briefing room, was built at Grafton Underwood and Hinton-in-the Hedges. Further watch offices were designed for specific purposes, such as for night fighters at Kingscliffe (FCW 4514), for OTU Satellites (13726/41) at Desborough, or a general-purpose prototype (12779/41) at Croughton, ultimately to be developed as the Watch Office for All Commands (343/43) subsequently built at Harrington, Deenethorpe, Silverstone, and Spanhoe. From 1939, virtually all structures were utility from the synthetic training buildings at Silverstone (11023/40 and 1739/41), to Deenethorpe's or Harrington's operations blocks (228/43) or the chapel and gymnasium (14604/40) at Kingscliffe or Desborough, and the Crew Procedure Centre (9116/41) at Chipping Warden, all constructed in tb, with walls of only a single brick's depth with brick buttresses. The ubiquitous Nissen hut housed everything from living quarters at Desborough to small arms ammunition (SAA) and pyrotechnics at Chelveston. Romney huts were larger versions of the Nissen used in pairs for main stores and workshops. A dozen further prefabricated hut types were used, including Desborough's Handcraft hut. Most of the original building work, as well as later upgrading, was carried out by British civil engineering firms such as French, Laing, Wimpey, Mowlem, Tarmac, and Taylor-Woodrow, with only Harrington being built by a construction battalion ('Seebees') of the US Army Engineer Corps. Apart from

Polebrook: a J-Type hangar.

Chipping Warden: a T2 hangar, transportable and speedily constructed.

Sywell: one of two R-Type hangars erected for aircraft production.

the shift to utility structures, the biggest change to airfields came in their layout. Until 1939, airfields had been planned as tight complexes of hangars, technical site, training buildings, and accommodation, all grouped together in one corner of the flying field, but in order to lessen the effects of aerial bombardment, all these elements would now be dispersed: fighter aircraft would be hidden behind camouflaged, earthed-up traverses and bombers would be parked out on frying pan or spectacle-shaped hard-standings scattered all around the perimeter. Operations blocks and munitions stores would be isolated from other buildings, and communal sites were banished some distance from the airfield itself, making bicycles or, later on, Jeeps essential for the maintenance of daily life. Shelters were provided onsite for those caught in an air raid.

One aspect not to be underestimated was the impact made on the rural landscape by, particularly bomber, airfields. These effectively constituted small towns with up to 2,500 or more personnel at each one, so their superimposition on the landscape was totally obtrusive: destructive of agriculture and disruptive of the local social dynamic. By the end of the war, the Air Ministry's requirements came to a total of 740 airfields across Britain, so given the unsuitability of some of the existing ones, a hunt for new sites was always under way. Culworth was identified in 1942 as an Advanced Flying Unit and OTU Parent for Flying Training Command. The land requisitioning notices were sent out, but despite only minor adjustments to the original plan being necessary, it was judged to be too near Chipping Warden and Silverstone, so was dropped from the

Silverstone: a synthetic training structure—a triple AM Bombing Teacher.

Kingscliffe: the night-fighter-type watch office.

Desborough: the gymnasium/chapel on a communal site.

official list. A site at Finedon was identified as a possible USAAF base, but it overlapped a tank-training area that the War Department declined to relinquish and, anyway, the slow progress being made on current builds during 1942–3 forced a postponement of new starts, particularly on sites with complications. A third site at Yardley Gobion was identified as a possible medium-bomber station, but it was never followed up.

Bombing Training

Those of the county's airfields that were bases for OTUs needed easily accessible bombing ranges. We have seen how RAF 90 Squadron, flying the early Fortresses from Polebrook, used Ashton Bombing Range near Oundle, and there were at least three others in the county: at Preston Capes, used by 16 OTU; at Shutlanger, also referred to as Alderton (SP729477), used by 17 OTU; and at Bearshanks Wood (SP994860), Pilton near Brigstock. Here, bombing crews dropped real 4-lb (1.8-kg) flash bombs on simulated targets and were closely monitored by observers who measured and reported on their accuracy. These observers were positioned in two-storey, brick and concrete quadrant towers, built to overlook the target area. One such tower still stands at Preston Capes (SP591555). Airfields often had their own local range in an adjacent field, where bombardiers could practise low-level bombing by dropping unarmed bombs or even sandbags on a target. People have described how as children they would observe this fascinating activity at Polebrook, rushing in to retrieve bomb fragments after it had gone quiet. The Eyebrook Reservoir is reputed to have been used by the Dambusters as one of a number of practice locations.

One of the US Navy's contributions to the Allied war effort was the invention of the Norden bombsight, but fearing that this precision instrument might come into the possession of the enemy, its use was initially denied even to the USAAC. So it came as no surprise that the RAF was emphatically denied a supply. Security was so tight that, even after the USA had entered the war in Europe, dedicated stores manned by specialist technicians were built on USAAF bomber airfields for this equipment. One such store, from which the Norden sights were issued prior to each sortie and checked back in on safe return, still stands in woods at the north end of Grafton Underwood (SP931837). Ironically, only 50 yards from this secret and sensitive bombsight store is a structure with an apparently protected elevated viewing platform, possibly built to observe local bombing practice.

Problems attached to using necessarily isolated bombing ranges meant alternatives were sought. One solution, developed by the RAE at Farnborough (Hampshire) by 1939, was the infrared target projector. This was located as a notional target that the bomber approached and 'bombed'. A camera in the aircraft loaded with infrared film recorded the bomber's approach, the fall of the 'bomb', and its precise landfall in relation to the target. This system replicated the conditions under which a real operation would be conducted, testing the navigator's skill in finding the target, and the bomb aimer's skill in hitting it. One such projector was located at Northampton Power Station (SP764597), one of only three urban examples in the initial scheme; however, the need for regular monitoring of the equipment by dedicated personnel onsite meant that further urban locations such as Peterborough, Leicester, and Cambridge would be added to the network at the end of 1943.

Left: Preston Capes: a quadrant tower for recording accuracy and giving feedback to bomb aimers on this bombing range.

Below: Grafton Underwood: a secure store for the top-secret US Norden bombsight.

Fuel Supply

It was vital to the war effort that a constant and consistent supply of fuel was maintained, particularly to keep up the intensity of the bombing offensive against targets from Scandinavia to the Alps. Britain's bomber airfields were using anything up to 12,000 tons or 3 million gallons (13.5 million litres) of fuel on a single raid, which meant that bomber airfields such as Grafton Underwood, Polebrook, or Chelveston required frequent, at times daily, replenishment from the AFDD of up to 75,000 gallons (340,000 litres) at a time. By 1945, across the country, there were forty-two of these AFDDs, like that at Kelmarsh supplying Britain's 700-plus airfields in an operation co-ordinated from Shell-Mex House in London, and using a combination of pipelines extending the length of England, the railways, and the road network. The original four D1 tanks at Kelmarsh AFDD, each held 500 tons, but by 1942, these had been supplemented by a further three C2 tanks, each holding around 4,000 tons, thus bringing the total stored to 15,200 tons (3.8 million gallons, or 17 million litres) of aviation fuel. Rail access into the site was via three sidings, necessary for handling the vast numbers of fuel wagons that arrived daily from the AFRDs.

This operation had been extended to the continent in the follow-up to the D-Day invasion by the Pluto project, in whose development the Corby steelworks had been instrumental. One of two types of pipeline, HAMEL (its two inventors were called Hammick and Ellis) had been manufactured by Stewart and Lloyd, who produced 1,000 miles (1,600 km) of 3-inch-diameter (7.5-cm-diameter) pipe, which was wound around steel drums, 30 feet (9 metres) in diameter and 50 feet (15 metres) long. These drums, known as Conundrums, were then mounted on specially adapted barges, from which they could be uncoiled from coast to coast. Stewart and Lloyd also became agents for the Ministry of Fuel and Power's Petroleum Division and ran the Tilbury Docks end of the operation. Pipe would arrive at Tilbury by train from Corby to be offloaded on to a roller-way in a purpose-built factory, where it was welded into 4,000-foot (1,230-metre) lengths. It was then wound on to a Conundrum and towed out to sea by tugs to be laid on the seabed. Pipelines from the Isle of Wight to Cherbourg and from Dungeness to Calais operated until the end of the war, with varying degrees of success due to both technical and environmental problems. When running at peak efficiency, the seventeen lines from Dungeness to Calais would pump over a million gallons a day for weeks on end. Aynho Park is also recorded as a major fuel dump in 1940, showing up on later aerial photographs, and its use may have continued throughout the war.

Corby: a recent view of part of the Stewart & Lloyd steel works.

The Secret War: Intelligence, SOE/OSS, and Communications

Daventry was home to the transmitter used for the BBC World Service and 'Daventry calling' would be listened to attentively all over, especially, occupied Europe. It was this facility that had enabled the early experiments with radar to be conducted from here. Early in the war, the RAF recognised the value of the site for developing a number of electronic aids. Three aerials were erected by the Air Ministry and RAF staff moved on to the site. On the south-western outskirts of Daventry, Staverton Radio Relay Station opened in 1940. Its buildings accommodated the staff of RAF Daventry on Borough Hill who belonged to the highly secret RAF 80 Wing, operating the beam-bending operation set up to corrupt the Luftwaffe's directional systems such as *Knickerbein*. Three brick and concrete wartime buildings survive at the north end of the Borough Hill site. One appears to be a fairly standard RAF Standby-set house for a generator; another is very similar to the standard explosives and inflammables store and may have been used to store fuel for the generators; the third consists of an open-roofed compound surrounded by blast walls of the type used to house mobile transmitter units. This may have held trailers containing either the equipment for running the radio-beam system known as GEE, which directed allied bombers, or that used to jam or deflect the German beams. GEE (or Gee) was developed, early in 1942, as a way of directing aircraft on to their targets by using radio signals with a time delay. Two transmitters, 190 miles (300 km) or so apart, provided a baseline that enabled the navigator, receiving blips on his oscilloscope, to plot a number of curves. The two points at which the curves intersected indicated possible positions, and parallel navigation techniques such as dead reckoning allowed him to select the correct one and thus fix the position of his aircraft. Accuracies of 200 metres at distances of up to 350 miles (560 km) could be achieved. The system was organised in geographical Chains, with the transmitter at Daventry, acting as Master of the Eastern Chain. Daventry's signals on 48.75 MHz took 1 millisecond to reach Slaves at Clee Hill in Shropshire, Stenigot AMES (Radar) site in Lincolnshire, or Gibbet Hill at Hindhead in Surrey, to be retransmitted and picked up by the aircraft. This Eastern Chain, code-named Virginia, was monitored from RAF Barkway near Royston in Hertfordshire. GEE commenced operations from Daventry in June 1942, providing guidance for bombers over targets up to 400 miles (640 km) away in Germany. In December 1944, two of the AM's three aerials were fouled by two bombers returning from a raid in thick fog. One of the B-17s managed to extricate itself, trailing wires behind it, but the second aircraft crashed, taking down the GEE chain for fifteen minutes until the standby system could be triggered. There was a further RAF transmitter at Greatworth (SP554433) that served Bletchley Park from 1943. The communications station, a satellite of the main RAF signals establishment at Leighton Buzzard, covered 90 acres (36 ha). There were five Nissen huts as billets, plus ablutions and a Mess/NAAFI hut, and additional billets in the village of Helmdon.

Northamptonshire provided important elements of not only the training system that produced secret agents to work in Europe, but also the operational system that delivered them and kept them supplied. Brockhall Manor (STS 1) was one of six SOE depot schools in use from 1940–44, and was then used by two OSS units: the Norwegian Special Operations Group (NORSOG) and Force 12, recruited in 1942 from expatriate enemy aliens. Prior to OSS taking over, agents of eleven different nationalities were already reported as having passed through the school. Several sources list Grendon Hall as a training centre for SOE & Free French agents, who would be dropped in occupied France. There may be some confusion here with Grendon Hall (STS 53a) at Grendon-Underwood near Aylesbury, which was a radio-receiving centre for SOE's French agents. Both locations may have served, with French SOE agents receiving their general training in Northamptonshire, and their specialised radio training in Buckinghamshire. The First Aid Nursing Yeomanry (FANY) was an all-female military unit that had been formed in the First World War, and from 1940 provided cover for SOE's volunteers in the, subsequently forlorn, hope that their military status might provide some protection. Overthorpe Hall became their induction centre. Sunnyside House in Northampton was a holding house for SOE and OSS agents awaiting flights to France. One possible location has been put forward at Kingsthorpe, now a PH, but a more likely candidate would appear to be Sunnyside House in Cliftonville, a large Victorian mansion of 1865, now a children's nursery. Harrington became the base for the 'Carpetbaggers', the USAAF squadrons working for the OSS, making clandestine flights to the continent. In their matt-black B-24 Liberators, equipped with enhanced electronic navigation aids such as GEE, LORAN, and Rebecca, they made pinpoint supply drops to the French resistance and delivered agents and radio operators by parachute. After D-Day, they dropped the uniformed three-man Jedburgh teams, which had the task of focusing the Resistance in their efforts to delay the arrival of German reinforcements. A further, Chelveston-based USAAF bomber squadron trained for

Daventry radio station's original buildings.

Greatworth radio station.

Brockhall Manor (STS1) was a training base for SOE operatives.

Northampton, Cliftonville, Sunnyside, was used by SOE operatives prior to embarking on secret missions.

Overthorpe Hall was a training centre for FANY personnel, many of whom were employed by SOE.

night attacks, and would often parachute OSS operatives into occupied France during operations. The Carpetbaggers practised their parachute drops at Fawsley Park. Some of the SOE agents and Jedburgh teams waiting to fly out from Harrington or Tempsford (Bedfordshire) gathered at Finedon Hall.

Air Defence

In terms of air defence, the priority when war broke out was to ensure that maximum numbers of AA weapons were available to defend against the aerial bombardment daily expected, but there was not nearly enough of even the inadequate weaponry on issue to go round. In October 1939, HQ 41 AA Brigade based mainly in East Anglia sent out instructions that all Lewis gun bipod mountings, held by LAA or searchlight batteries, should be sent to Barnwell Ordnance Depot for reissue to infantry units. In December, units were notified in rotation of the order to return to COD Weedon, all Bren gun tripod mounts, on LAA or searchlight battery sites, for modification and reissue. General mobilisation saw the RASC company attached to 40 AA Brigade ordered to Barnwell, presumably to collect equipment being shuttled back and forth to AA units. Across the country, AA weapons of any type were scarce, particularly so in the East Midlands. In September 1939, 40 AA Brigade's Order of Battle records that 401 Company of 50 AA Battalion (RE) was based at Thrapston Militia Camp. Shortly after, 78 HAA Regiment, 41 AA Brigade, set up its RHQ there, along with 245 Battery. This regiment covered large tracts of East Anglia defending, for the most part, airfields and the industry of Norwich. In the summer of 1940, the only site in Northamptonshire with any real AA protection was the BBC transmitter at Daventry, where, from 26–27 May, two sections of 244 Battery, 78 HAA Regiment, with four 3-inch, 20-cwt guns of First World War vintage, was stationed, accompanied by 425 Battery of 58 S/L Regiment. These AA units were involved in an apparently never-ending redrawing of operational areas with consequent reordering of AA units. In October 1940, for instance, 40 AA Brigade's war diary records the arrival of 501 Battery, attached to 72 Searchlight Regiment in the new 257 Company Area with its HQ in Easton Neston Lodge near Towcester (TNA WO166/227-8). Daventry may have had an element of HAA cover, but all other targets in the county were given only light cover: Lewis guns at Weedon COD and thirty-four more at Corby protecting the steel works. Not until May 1942 did Corby get anything approaching adequate cover with two batteries of four 3.7-inch, static HAA guns at Weldon and Rockingham, with GL radar and manned by a battery of 136 HAA Regiment, its instruments operated by women of the ATS. The Weldon site, now under a farmer's field, was configured in the normal way with an arc of four circular gun pits facing east along the Oundle road, arranged round the rectangular command post. The camp lay to the south-west, with living huts, gun store, messes, workshops, and garages. The ablutions block stood where the present holiday park's centrepiece bungalow now stands. Close AA defence of Stewart and Lloyd was provided by 'Y' Troop, No. 534 (Home Guard) LAA Regiment, part of 6th Battalion. In October 1942, 244 Battery, 20 LAA Regiment, was deployed to Wellingborough. Thrapston Militia Camp, its site now under the vast warehouses alongside the A14, continued as an AA training camp throughout the war. In February 1944, LAA units such as 475 Battery, 134 LAA Regiment, 50 AA Brigade, arrived at Thrapston from Wakefield, followed by 455 Battery, 129 LAA Regiment, both sent to Thrapston for training on mobile AA guns prior to D-Day.

In the first year of the war, searchlights were deployed singly, spaced at roughly 3-mile (4.8-km) intervals as a carpet. Experiments were then carried out in clusters of six or so, and then into three belts: the first, 12 miles (20 km) deep, with single lights at 10,000-yard (5.7-mile, or 9.1-km) intervals to indicate the approach of hostile aircraft; the second, 16 miles (25.5 km) deep with 3.4-mile (5.5-km) spacings to aid night fighters; and the third in gun-defended areas (GDA) around conurbations. Some 100–110 S/L sites have been identified in Northamptonshire, not all in simultaneous operation, giving some indication of those changing deployments. Only a few of the earliest sites were provided with pillboxes, and the majority of S/L sites would finally consist of little more than a ring ditch around a low mound. Living structures would be either of timber or wrinkly tin, with slit trenches for air-raid protection. As the RCHM points out, many supposed prehistoric 'ring ditches' such as some at Brixworth, in fact represent AA sites. At Titchmarsh, there were, at some time, AA guns and S/Ls in the fields near the Mill in Oundle Road and in Town End Close at the bottom of Church

Street, where such earthworks have been noted. The Wellingborough Gas Works was one of many such facilities supplying gas for the Barrage Balloons largely operated by the WAAF.

Royal Observer Corps Posts

With the opening of Sutton Bassett in 1939, there were fifteen Observer Corps posts spread across the county. They ranged from Blakesley windmill to a post at Raunds consisting, as many others did, mainly of sandbags. The standard post, issued by the Air Ministry, was a very basic garden shed, often referred to by observers as the 'rabbit hutch'. The Cogenhoe post on Station Road supplemented this shed with a timber, two-storey tower, accessed by external stairs. Around its top were fixed old bus windows, which gave some protection against the wind without impairing vision, and a narrow strip at one end was roofed and furnished with two old bus seats. The shed contained bunks, a stove, a folding table for maps, and storage for the essential beverages that might aid wakefulness in the long winter nights. The whole structure was surrounded by a rampart and ditch that could have been no more than a gesture of defiance, although at the time that the LDV was being formed, two rifles were issued to each observer post. Observers were warned to wear their badges at all times as these would allow them, while remaining civilians, to assume combatant status. Despite all the other concerns, learned judges found the time to debate the issue, deciding that a few pot-shots at the enemy did not breach the rules of war. Plans to incorporate observer posts into a network of anti-invasion strongpoints in 1941 fell down as tight rotas and lack of manpower found too few observers on duty at any one time.

Posts will have added extra shelves for the radios, which appear to have arrived by the summer of 1942. Reporting on first-hand information from an observer who was present, Steven Hollowell has related how on 3 August, the observers in the Cogenhoe post were put in direct contact with a Spitfire pilot of 485 Squadron from Kingscliffe who subsequently shot down one of several Dornier 217s that had been bombing Wellingborough. A constant problem assailing the RAF and USAAF bombers was getting back to base with damaged aircraft or in low visibility. A number of aids were developed, including 'Darky', which used radio to talk pilots down; 'Sandra', which projected searchlight beams for aircraft to follow; and 'Granite', which was a shower of red flares warning pilots of their proximity to high ground. This last was installed in the Chipping Warden post. There are a few examples in other counties of robust brick-built posts, so it is quite possible that the Sutton Bassett post dates from the war years. It is rectangular with a door and a window, and a flat roof with a low parapet. As we shall see, more aircraft-spotting posts were built in brick before the standard concrete post-war model was adopted.

Bombing Decoys

Beam-bending was one way of diverting enemy bombers from their intended goals, and another way of fooling them was to fabricate fake targets. These bombing decoys were built just close enough to operational airfields to be plausible, and simulated the activities of airfields by moving dummy aircraft around on 'K' sites, or by replicating the lights of both runways and of individual aircraft on 'Q' sites. The set and prop technicians of the film industry, notably from Shepperton Studios, were employed to produce realistic dummy aircraft. Decoys for Polebrook at Little Gidding, and for Kingscliffe at Warmington and Alwalton, two of those three in Cambridgeshire, were built as was one at Swineshead in Bedfordshire for Chelveston. The only significant structure on these sites was a control blockhouse of brick and concrete, and a Stanton-type shelter housing a generator and fuel tank, like that surviving at Warmington. It would appear that these decoys, specifically for airfields, were stood down by the middle of 1942.

Weedon COD was provided with a decoy at Preston Capes under the Army Series 'A', but as the war progressed, further needs for the protection of civil and industrial targets were recognised. Special Fires ('SF' or 'Starfish') decoys consisted of concentrations of flammable materials linked by oil-filled trenches and seeded with sudden flare ups, simulating burning buildings in towns. On the approach of enemy bombers, these were ignited to represent incendiaries dropped by target-marking aircraft. Such decoys, defined as 'Permanent' and remaining active until the spring of 1943, were provided for Northampton at Kislingbury and Hardingstone, and at Barby and Claycoton, for Rugby. Intended for the protection of specific targets with identifiably individual characteristics, the Civil ('C' Series) lights ('QL') or fires ('QF') decoys used ingenious techniques. The lights of the marshalling yards ('MY') and factories ('FL') at Kettering, Wellingborough and Corby, and the added glows of locomotive fire boxes ('LG') at Corby and Kettering, were all simulated by systems of lights and fires. In this way,

Warmington (TL082919) the blockhouse for the bombing decoy serving Kingscliffe airfield.

bombers aiming for Stewart & Lloyd at Corby, or the Islip ironworks could be lured into dropping their bombs on open countryside. As with any preventative measure, it is impossible to gauge effectiveness, but decoy sites across the land received a significant number of bombs that would otherwise have been directed at vulnerable targets. As a complement to the decoys, many sites, such as Stewart & Lloyd steelworks at Corby, were camouflaged with paint schemes devised by specialists at the camouflage HQ at Leamington Spa in Warwickshire.

Air Raids and ARP

Despite fears that aerial bombing would be instantaneous on the declaration of war, it would be almost twelve months before air raids came to Northamptonshire. In May 1940, Northampton was one of three towns to feature in an ARP exercise carried out across the East Midlands, but within three months, the attacks would be real. Bombs were dropped on Kilsby and Duston, resulting in one fatality, and the next month, parachute mines were dropped on Towcester. On 3 October, bombs fell on Rushden, killing seven children in a school and three adults in a factory, and heavy bombing and strafing continued for the rest of the month. In the middle of November, two of the bomber groups attacking Coventry were reported by Observer Corps posts as they flew over Northamptonshire. This was the peak month for bombing, with over 1,000 HE or incendiary bombs dropped, resulting in five more deaths in Rushden and another in Easton-on-the-Hill, and Titchmarsh was the target of incendiaries. In May 1941, two people were injured in Corby, and there were attacks on Chipping Warden, Croughton, and Polebrook airfields. A total of 7,800 bombs fell on the county in the course of the war, almost 85 per cent of which were incendiaries. Nearly 2,000 buildings were damaged, one-fifth of them through Allied accidents and errors. Bombing caused thirty-six deaths and 212 serious injuries, with the Wellingborough and Rushden areas suffering the majority. In July 1944, a stray V1 rocket crashed at Creaton, injuring five people, an event reported by the ROC. Just two more followed including one, air launched and aimed at Manchester, which landed at Woodford, and the third, which fell outside Irthlingborough. Throughout the onslaught of the V-weapons, missions to destroy their launching sites were being continuously conducted by aircraft from the county's airfields.

As early as September 1938, the Munich Crisis precipitated precautionary measures against aerial bombardment on Northampton racecourse. Initially trenches, but then five large underground shelters were dug. By early 1940, flimsy brick shelters were constructed in the street; individual households were digging Anderson shelters into their gardens; cellars were strengthened; and families combined to burrow deeper shelters. Public buildings were masked by walls of sandbags, and decontamination centres were built in the expectation of gas attacks. Firms were responsible for their own employees so provided their own shelters on site. In 1940, Stewart and Lloyd built an underground ARP Centre with two entrances at their Corby steelworks. It comprised a first aid post, telephone exchange, stand-by generator, and ventilation plant, and it also housed an ambulance in one of the tunnels. A decontamination centre that stands in Oundle may date from then or a later post-war period.

While the Observer Corps looked out for aircraft in order to direct the fighter defences, it was the job of a parallel system of ARP watchers to warn the public of air raids in order that they might take shelter. Observation posts were established not only in existing structures such as Titchmarsh church tower or in windmills, but also in purpose-built or adapted rooftop firewatchers' posts such as those at Kingsthorpe, Billing, or the old County Hall in Guildhall Street, Northampton. Similarly, wardens' posts occupied empty properties as in Oundle, or purpose-built cabins very similar to the stores of the Home Guard. A steel one-man shelter for ARP wardens or police officers, one of which stands by the old railway station in Rushden, looked like a giant salt cellar and was marketed as the 'Consol'. Following the amalgamation of myriad hitherto independent local fire brigades into a National Fire Service, Northamptonshire was included in Fire Force Region No. 9, administered from Leicester, with the local HQ at The Mounts Fire Station in Northampton. In 1941, a national system of Civil Defence regions was established by the government with Northamptonshire as part of Region 3 centred on Nottingham.

Oundle: this decontamination centre was built in anticipation of gas attacks in the Second World War then became part of Civil Defence precautions in the Cold War.

Rushden: this one-man air-raid shelter for police or ARP wardens was marketed as the Consol.

Army Camps in the Second World War

Across the land, established barracks and camps proved grossly inadequate for the needs of rapidly expanding armed forces. Even though Northampton racecourse was pressed into service as an overflow barracks, and work had begun on a wholly new barracks at Wootton, these fell far short of meeting the needs. Northamptonshire, with its profusion of country houses and parklands, would provide camps for many British and Allied army units throughout the war. A militia camp for the training of young men prior to the outbreak of war was set up at Thrapston; Haselbech Hall took in the King's Dragoon Guards after Dunkirk; Boughton House was home to newly arrived Canadians in 1940; Arthingworth hosted an armoured division support group when invasion was expected; Fawsley Hall accommodated the nucleus of an armoured brigade and provided its training facilities until 1943; Delapre Abbey was an infantry training camp and Rushton Hall trained officers for the RAOC; troops heading for the Normandy beaches in 1944 assembled in Guilsborough Park; Polish Airborne troops were based at Blatherwyke Hall before the Arnhem operation; and Wicksteed Park absorbed a large US Army Quartermaster's Stores and transport unit. The normal pattern of use was for the main house to be used for unit or formation HQ and offices; officers' mess and quarters; and ATS quarters. Workshops, garages, and an armoury would occupy the stable block, and troops would be accommodated in Nissen huts, or even tents, in the grounds. If the owner's family remained in residence, they would be assigned private quarters in a remote wing of the house. It has been suggested that only large houses furnished with electric power and light would be requisitioned for use by the armed services or decentralised government departments. However, Deene, with only coal fires and gas lamps, was occupied by the military after 1940, becoming a home at various times to Greek, Polish, and Indian units, while Czech troops were at Billing Hall and Free French ones at Grendon and Finedon. Castle Ashby became an important training centre for the expanding ATS. Many houses suffered very badly from occupation by the military. Is it coincidence that Norton Hall was blown up in 1945, and Blatherwyke Hall, badly damaged by its military occupants, was demolished in 1948?

Munitions Production

As industrial enterprises across Britain adapted to a war economy, the whole range of these operations can be seen in Northamptonshire. This included the heavy industry of Corby's steel working; the purpose-built aircraft factories of Sywell, Burton Latimer, and Moulton; the switch to military customers made by the footwear and clothing factories; a new focus on aircraft or weaponry parts adopted by small engineering or automotive workshops; and the cottage industry of dozens of small concerns meeting contracts issued by Weedon COD. The RAOC organised a Home Industries Scheme for packing small stores for issue at home or overseas. Completed orders were collected in the network of small stores, which received items packed in cardboard boxes for onward distribution. Such stores, utilising existing buildings such as the village halls at Blisworth and Clipston, were established in thirteen locations, mainly in the west of the county and near to Weedon, including Crick, Daventry, Watford, and West Haddon.

Fawsley Hall was a base for tank units prior to D-Day and a practice drop zone for the secret Carpetbaggers operations.

Rushton Hall was an auxiliary hospital in the First World War, and an officer cadet training unit for the Royal Army Ordnance Corps in the Second World War.

From 1940, Brooklands Aviation at Sywell, already with a history of involvement in RAF pilot training on the airfield, opened a CRU. Its main purpose was to repair or convert Wellington bombers, built by Vickers at Brooklands in Surrey and, owing to the aircraft's revolutionary geodetic construction, needing specialist repair facilities. An Air Ministry map of 1941 shows the Brooklands operation occupying the two side-opening hangars behind the FTS buildings and a large hangar on Holcot Lane. The second hangar on Holcot Lane was in use by MAP, which also shared some of the Brooklands factory premises as well as using the Bellman hangar. Throughout the war, some 1,841 Wellington bombers were repaired using a purpose-built facility at Buttocks Booth, Moulton, as well as workshops and garages in Desborough, Earls Barton, and Kettering. A large hangar was erected on Polwell Lane, Burton Latimer, for the overhaul of the bulkier wing sections.

At the beginning of the war, the Armstrong Whitworth Aircraft company (AWA), based at Baginton, now Coventry Airport, dispersed some of its Whitley production to Northampton, taking over some local premises to manufacture components, using an established factory in Bedford Road as the nucleus of a network of small workshops producing parts for assembly elsewhere. These included shoe factories such as Barratt's, Manfield's, and the Cantilever Shoe Co., as well as the Corporation Bus depot and Airflow Streamlines. When manufacture of the unsatisfactory Manchester bomber was aborted and the Whitley had run its course, production was switched to the Manchester's successor, the Avro Lancaster four-engined heavy bomber. AWA was involved in developing the Mk II Lancaster with the Bristol Hercules radial engine. It was now necessary to provide a more suitable factory area, so two R-type hangars were built on the south-western edge of Sywell airfield. Here, it would appear that the first ten prototypes were assembled with parts from A. V. Roe in Manchester, but over 100 subsequent aircraft, part of an order placed for 300, were assembled at Sywell from parts manufactured in Northampton's workshops, factories, and garages. These Mk II Lancasters were flight tested at Sywell and then flown off, weather permitting, from the grass field for delivery to Baginton. In 1943, the main assembly line was transferred to Bitteswell on the A5 road near Lutterworth in Leicestershire, now Magna Park. Concrete runways had just been laid there, and AWA was allocated a large factory site on the edge of the airfield in which nearly 1,000 Lancasters would be built. Parts were still made in Northampton with fuselages being assembled in the bus depot at St James and Airflow Streamlines making engine cowlings both for Lancasters and a variety of other aircraft. Companies in Rushden, Kettering, Earls Barton, Desborough, Daventry, and Wellingborough were also involved in the Lancaster programme along with Express Lifts in Northampton. Beside the former Northampton power station is an unusual structure, the shape and size of a Nissen hut but constructed out of reinforced concrete, 6 inches (15 cm) thick. It has been suggested that its purpose was to test jet engines but this theory awaits corroboration.

The Lee Enfield SMLE 0.303-inch Mk IV rifle, of which millions were produced, was the standard weapon of the British, Commonwealth, and other Allied forces. Vast quantities were turned out by the Royal Ordnance Factories, the several BSA plants, and by Weedon itself, but a significant amount of output came from small engineering companies mass-producing particular parts. In Northamptonshire, rifle components were manufactured, and rifles repaired to the 'Weedon Repair Standard'. Parts made in Northamptonshire included magazine catches by Standard Rotary Machine Co. Ltd of Rushden; back-sight beds by Timson, Bullock, Barber Ltd of Catesby Road, Kettering, and bolt heads by Hanwell Engineering Co. of Northampton. Also involved in the production of Lee–Enfield rifle parts was Job Lee, Premier Engineering of Kettering. As well as producing a range of aircraft parts and several types of hoist in their various factories, Express Lifts also made 7.2-inch howitzer shells. The Air Ministry had a testing station at Wellingborough Gasworks to process gas cylinders for use with AA Barrage Balloons.

Stewart & Lloyd greatly expanded their operations and moved their administration offsite to Brigstock Manor, where temporary buildings were erected as offices, and to East Carlton Hall, which became the company's wartime HQ. Although they produced scaffolding for beach anti-invasion defences early in the war, their most high-profile wartime achievement was the production of 1,000 miles of initially 2-inch (50-mm) and then 3-inch (75-mm) steel pipe for the Pluto operation (see above). Another distinctive contribution to D-Day came from Bassett-Lowke, famous for their model railways, which made precisely detailed scale models of the prefabricated Mulberry Harbours both for testing and for training purposes. Other of their models included Inglis and Bailey bridges and dive-bombers for training, respectively, REs and AA gunners. Many firms, which ran munitions factories in cities that were frequently and heavily bombed, established shadow factories to produce vital materiel in less vulnerable locations. In 1941, British Timken set up such a shadow factory in Duston to produce roller bearings, just in time as, a few months later, the parent factory in Birmingham was severely damaged by bombing. A Royal Ordnance Factory was built in Northampton

Desborough bus garage was one of a number of dispersed workshops involved with aircraft production.

to manufacture explosives but the plans for its companion, a projected Filling Factory No. 20, remained on the drawing-board.

Just as in the previous war, Northamptonshire's footwear factories fulfilled endless orders for standard boots and shoes, but one unusual order came to Haynes & Cann from MI9 (Escape & Evasion). This was for flying boots that could be converted into civilian shoes. In their Kettering, Burton Latimer, and Corby factories, Kaycee produced half a million garments for British and Allied military forces, while in Cottingham and Kettering, many of the 200,000 garments manufactured by Wallis & Linnell were for the women's uniformed services, mainly the ATS and the WAAF.

Storage and Distribution Depots

While the factories were turning out the goods and national organisations, military, and civil were gathering equipment and commodities, their distribution required a network of specialist depots for storage and issue to their end users. Distributing maps from the store occupying the buildings of Towcester Racecourse might have been a straightforward, if fiddly operation, but most others were not so simple. First of all, the necessary infrastructure, especially on the railways, had to be provided. New sidings were laid at the RAF Depot at Croughton; at the RAF Repair, Air Ministry Works Department, and Royal Ordnance depots on Oundle Road, Barnwell; and at RAF Roade's Ground Equipment storage facility in Salcey Forest. The line from Kettering through Cransley to Loddington was confined to freight only, and new stations at RODs Weedon Bec and Yardley Chase were built exclusively for military use. For obvious reasons, bombs and ammunition had to be stored securely and as far as possible away from populated areas. In Yardley Chase, explosives were stored, from 1942, in several dozen moated and traversed rectangular sheds. On a smaller scale, the three ammunition stores at Isham are robustly traversed. Ammunition was stored in Nissen huts at Parkhill Farm, Castle Ashby, and, once the bombing threat had become much reduced, munitions were stored in roadside shelters throughout the East Midlands, an example being Great Billing. As the bombing offensive had gathered pace the RAF 223MU opened a bomb store at Braybrooke. This was then handed over to the 8th USAAF as Station 21, with a capacity of 17.5 kilotons of bombs, storing the bombs and ammunition for fifteen bomber airfields, as well as the fighter fields at Atcham (Shropshire) and Goxhill (Lincolnshire). SAA and pyrotechnics were stored at Loatland Wood. The station was manned by 2107 Ordnance Battalion (Aviation), 1906 Ordnance Ammunition Company (Aviation), and 2222 Ordnance Truck Company (Aviation).

As well as stockpiles of ammunition, the preparations for D-Day required whole fleets of vehicles to be assembled. Castle Ashby was established as No. 21 Vehicle Replacement Depot, a satellite of the main operation at Chilwell in Nottinghamshire, and pre-D-Day, there were 6,000 vehicles parked in the grounds. To oversee construction and maintenance works on both RAF and USAAF stations, the Air Ministry set up one of its countrywide network of twenty-five works depots, co-located with the Royal Ordnance Depot at Barnwell in 1939. The Air Ministry's main stores depot was 25MU at Hartlebury (Worcestershire), but in 1941, 72MU at Roade was established as a Ground Equipment Depot taking on one of Hartlebury's previous functions

Yardley Chase: the administrative buildings of this extensive ordnance store.

Isham: one of three remaining ammunition storage buildings standing within high earth and corrugated-iron traverses.

Barnwell Royal Ordnance Depot stored AA equipment for distribution to TA units, and carried out routine maintenance.

New Duston: Ministry of Supply (later MAFF) depot stockpiling sugar for onward distribution.

and occupying thirty-two large sheds dispersed in Salcey Forest. In 1942, 204MU, a satellite of Hartlebury, was set up in Harborough Road, Rushden, as an equipment park for the local distribution of airborne stores. In Stamford Road, Kettering, was 236MU, a RAF vehicle-servicing unit. The US Army established Q-101, an extensive quartermaster depot at Wicksteed Park. Harrington Museum's indispensable list of military sites within a 30-mile (48-km) radius logs several dozen US Army QM, Truck, and Bakery units based there at different times serving the local USAAF stations. The Ministry of Supply (MoS) also operated a network of stores of food for distribution to civilians, with their characteristic buildings with hipped-roof and clerestory at Boughton Crossing, New Duston, and Barby.

Hospitals

As in the First World War, many civilian hospitals and private houses entered temporary service as military hospitals or convalescent homes, many of the latter under the auspices of the British Red Cross and the St John's Ambulance who combined their resources. With the arrival of large numbers of USAAF personnel into the county, a dedicated medical service was set up. Lilford Hall was taken over as the US 16th Station Hospital, accommodated in huts with nurses' quarters in the hall, with 303rd USAAF Station Hospital in the park. A railway siding at Barnwell served as the base for Nos 21, 43, and 45 Hospital Trains, lined up for service in anticipation of heavy casualties resulting from the Normandy Landings (see Appendix XI)

Prisoner of War (POW) Camps

Camps were run throughout the war for both German and Italian POWs. As the tide turned, more POWs were captured and more camps needed to be improvised. Former WLA Hostels at Greens Norton and Yelvertoft were taken over, as were vacated communal sites on airfields as at Kingscliffe and Harrington (see Appendix XV)

Feeding the Nation: Agriculture

During the course of the war, the county's total arable acreage was increased from 112,000 acres (44,800 ha) in 1939 up to almost 300,000 acres (120,000 ha) by 1945, a momentous achievement when the large-scale requisitioning of land for airfields and training areas is taken into account. Agriculture was overseen by a War Agricultural Executive Committee, which had the power to tell farmers what to grow and where. The county was split into nine districts based on local authorities. There were five depots for storing agricultural machinery for hire out to farmers at Northampton, Thrapston, Kettering, Daventry, and Towcester, with a sixth added later at Brackley. Training courses for farmers, such as that held in Oundle's Victoria Hall in 1942, were intended to provide ways of increasing yield and ensuring appropriate use of the land. Women were directed into the Women's Land Army (WLA) and could attend courses held at

Right: Byfield POW Camp's characteristic water tower.

Below: Yelvertoft: the WLA hostel later used as a POW camp, and now the village hall.

the Northamptonshire Institute of Agriculture at Moulton. The county's complement of 1,000 or so land girls either stayed on the farms where they were working or in hostels, with some of the twenty or so across the county being run by the YWCA. Hostels tended to be built in temporary brick or from prefabricated sections. Some, such as Greens Norton or Yelvertoft, became POW camps at the war's end and then village halls. The WLA mobilised all available resources, for instance, training boys from Oundle School to drive tractors, and groups of boys were billeted at Hemington, Lyveden, Lilford Hall, and Apethorpe to work on the land. Some stayed on at school through the summer holidays to help with the local harvest. Summer camps were also held for the Scouts. Many POWs were encouraged to work on the land and over twenty labour officers were trained at Brixworth to supervise working parties of German and Italian POWs working in agriculture or forestry, particularly on ditching and drainage schemes.

The Cold War, 1945–1990

The Regular Army and the TA

In 1947, the joint ITCs such as that at Norwich were reorganised and a new No. 48 Primary Training Centre was opened at Gibraltar Barracks for the flood of recruits and National Servicemen. Talavera Barracks on the racecourse was demolished in 1948, and Quebec Barracks gradually took over, but not until 1980 were two-thirds of the Barrack Road site sold to the GPO. The reformation of the TA in 1947 saw an extensive reorganisation of the yeomanry regiments. The Northamptonshire Yeomanry reverted to being an armoured car regiment equipped with Ferrets and Dingoes. Successive cuts to the TA brought amalgamation with the Inns of Court Regiment as 'D' Squadron in 1958, with a complete change of role four years later. Now as 250 (Northamptonshire Yeomanry) Independent Field Squadron, RE (TA), their focus was bridge building. By 1967, when this latest unit was phased out, a few personnel were absorbed by the Northamptonshire Regiment and thence into the Royal Anglians, but the days of the yeomanry in Northamptonshire were past. The 5th Battalion had been reduced to a cadre in 1948 with drill stations in its old recruiting area but retaining a county presence in Oundle and Rushden. The 50th Searchlight Regiment reformed in 1947 as 585 Searchlight Regiment RA (TA), with bases in Northampton, Kettering, and Wellingborough. In 1960, the Northamptonshire Regiment joined the Lincolnshire Regiment to form the 2nd (Regular) and 2nd (TA) Battalions of the new East Anglian Regiment, which became the Royal Anglian Regiment four years later. As of 2017, the two Army Reserve centres at Clare Street, Northampton, and St Mark's Road, Corby, both occupied by REME recovery units, are the only sites to have survived successive cuts, representing the Army's sole presence in the county.

Quebec Barracks in Wootton had become the HQ of the Royal Pioneer Corps as Simpson Barracks, but that, too, closed in the 1980s and was demolished around ten years later. Some new buildings were added at Clare Street; and in Corby, a new drill hall bearing the badge of the Northamptonshire Regiment, now a volunteer centre, was opened in Elizabeth Street in 1962, and an industrial building leased for a REME detachment. Oundle School CCF got a new armoury and the old Hythe-style butts at the rifle range were replaced by Bisley-type frames in 1994.

Corby: the drill hall that opened in 1962 now serves as the town's volunteer centre.

Air Defence and the Royal Observer Corps

The Brigstock army camp had been used by 928 Engineer Battalion, US Army, and had also housed Corby Steelworks employees, but from 1951–5, it became a US Army AAA training camp. By 1955, however, AA guns for home defence had been replaced by Bloodhound/Thunderbird guided weapons and the British AA Command had been stood down as the only AA guns remaining operational were those mobile weapons accompanying armies in the field. The ROC had remained in service after the end of the war, and in the early 1950s, building on the prototypes seen at Clipston or Sutton Bassett, a standard model of aircraft-spotting post had been developed for them. This was a rectangular concrete box, roofed at one end, which could accommodate the two or three observers who might be on watch together, affording them some minimal cover for their plotting table and instruments. If the location warranted it, then this box could be mounted around 6 feet (1.85 metres) off the ground on legs, and accessed by an integral ladder. Despite this attempt to make the observer's life a little less uncomfortable, contemporaneous with the demise of the fixed AA guns, it was realised that modern aircraft flew too fast for observers to identify and report them, so a new role would be found for them. The threat of a nuclear strike had implications for monitoring its effect and the established network of ROC posts appeared ideal for logging ground zero and also measuring and reporting the levels and directions of travel of radioactivity. ROC members, now absorbed into UKWMO, were trained to handle those rudimentary instruments needed to carry out these tasks. Each post was replaced by an underground bunker, equipped with food and water, beds, and a chemical toilet. This bunker would remain home to its crew until it was safe to come out if, indeed, there was anything to

Clipston (SP70258268) is an outstanding example of a ROC aircraft-spotting post, probably dating from the final years of the Second World War and remaining in use into the early 1960s, and an underground post, built in 1959, for monitoring radiation in the event of nuclear war.

Clipston: another view of the two components of this ROC post.

come out to. Some established locations were found to be unsuitable for sinking bunkers so, as at Chipping Warden, Oundle, and Duston, among others, new, better-drained sites were chosen. At Benefield and Cogenhoe, the posts were relocated on to, respectively, Deenethorpe and Denton airfields. By 1964, the county's twenty-one underground posts were operational. Like the earlier spotting post, the underground bunker was designed and built by Orlit, a firm specialising in small concrete structures. Entered through a trapdoor, leading via steel rungs down a 14-foot-deep (4.5-metre-deep) vertical shaft, it was basically a concrete box, roughly 20 feet × 8 feet × 8 feet (6 metres × 2.5 metres × 2.5 metres). On the surface, all that was visible was the entry hatch, a ventilator, and the tops of the bomb power indicator and the fixed survey meter probe. Posts were grouped in threes and fours and reported by telephone to a regional control room that aided the co-ordination of any military response and the deployment of civil emergency services. Constant reorganisations resulted in posts being assigned to different groupings and controlled from different centres until, in 1968, eleven of the county's posts were closed, followed by the remainder as part of the peace dividend following the break-up of the USSR of 1991. Throughout these years, under the auspices of the RAF, the dozens of ROC Observers remained civilian volunteers putting in shifts, taking part in exercises, and attending training sessions and camps.

RAF and USAAF Airfields

By June 1945, the winding down of RAF units was well under way. Sywell reduced its staff and intake; Polebrook was closed to flying; Chipping Warden took in No. 10 Air Navigation School for a few months; Deenethorpe became No. 11 Recruiting Centre for no more than a year; and Desborough was allocated to Transport Command for training Dakota pilots from Leicester East. Grafton Underwood and Spanhoe both served as vehicle depots until 1954 and 1947, respectively. Kingscliffe accommodated POWs, some of whom were sent to work at Desborough. Flying ceased at Croughton in 1946, which went into care and maintenance until 1951, when it was handed over to the USAF. Silverstone started its new life as a motor-racing circuit in 1948. Polebrook took on a new role under 273MU, for a year, refurbishing aircraft for sale to other air forces and for civilian use. Sywell became No. 6 Reserve Flying School, RAFVR, and resumed its function as home to the Northamptonshire Aero Club. In 1951, it also became No. 4 Basic FTS, training National Servicemen to fly and only ceasing RAF training activities in 1953.

The first development in Northamptonshire linked to the Cold War came in 1952 at Chelveston. Here, the airfield had been handed over to the redeployed US 3rd Air Force, and runways were extended to allow the jet bombers to operate. The B-47 Stratojets moved in on completion of the work in 1956. These 'Reflex Alert' aircraft of the US Strategic Air Command carried out three-week-long tours of duty sitting, fully armed on the tarmac, ready for a fifteen-minute take-off. Crews spent two weeks on high alert, with a week off in the middle, the days for their departure flights to the States alternating with the days for their reliefs' arrivals. This rolling provision kept at least twelve action-ready aircraft on station at all times. The NATO reorganisation necessitated by France's withdrawal in 1959 replaced the SAC bombers with RB-66

Destroyers of the Tactical Reconnaissance squadrons, which stayed until flying ceased in 1962. The operation of these aircraft had brought a range of improvements to the airfield. First had come the lengthening of one of its runways from 2,000 yards (1.85 km) to 3,400 yards (3.14 km); next, dispersed around the runway, thick concrete hard standings were laid as Operational Readiness Platforms (ORP) for the B-47s on alert and, in front of the old J-type hangar, an extensive concrete apron as an Aircraft Servicing Platform (ASP). Chelveston was one of the few airfields provided with igloos for the storage of atomic weapons. These were sunken concrete boxes, covered in earth and entered through a pair of bombproof doors. It was also given a new control tower on a steel lattice framework.

By the late 1950s, both NATO and the Warsaw Pact possessed nuclear weapons that could be delivered by jet bombers. These were vulnerable to a new generation of AA guided weapons, such as the Bloodhound/Thunderbird, which had entered service in Britain in 1958, so an alternative delivery system was sought. As a stopgap until an ICBM could be developed by the USA, the Thor IRBM was introduced, but its limited range of 1,750 miles (2,800 km) meant that many prime Russian targets could only be reached by missiles based in Britain. A total of twenty missile sites in four groups were established on old airfield sites down the eastern side of England under the code-name 'Emily'. Two sites in Northamptonshire—Harrington and Polebrook—were chosen within a group based on North Luffenham in Rutland. The project was a joint Anglo-US co-operation with separate areas of the secure missile sites under USAF or RAF control. Each site contained three hard-standings with conduits for power; fuelling points for the extremely volatile liquid oxygen, which powered the rocket motors; and solid L-shaped concrete blast-walls for shielding sensitive areas from the heat as the rockets were launched. Although there was a robust servicing and maintenance building on site, the rockets were stored in a horizontal position on trailers under canvas covers, only to be hoisted into the vertical immediately prior to launching. At Harrington, the base commander was provided with a new offsite house at 9 High Street, Harrington. As a result of the horse trading that followed the resolution of the Cuban Missile Crisis in 1962, the Thor bases were stood down, Harrington and Polebrook being among the last to close in August 1963 when the missiles were airlifted back to the USA. In 2017, Croughton remains a USAF centre for monitoring communications with its prominent golf balls. Replacement buildings, such as the three-storey medical and dental centre opened in 2015, are added as necessary. The Sywell and Buttocks Booth repair facilities took on all Brooklands Aviation's overhaul and maintenance work until their closure in 1977 and 1974, respectively. In the 1950s, a pipeline, terminating at RAF Bruntingthorpe in Leicestershire, was laid from the major reserve depot at Sandy in Bedfordshire to supply fuel direct to RAF Chelveston and the Kelmarsh distribution depot, by now provided with four 4,000-ton tanks. Kelmarsh continued in active use until 1990, when it was mothballed, a state that continues to the present.

Harrington: a structure on the Thor site, possibly a fire-tender garage.

Harrington: one of the three launch pads for Thor IRBM missiles.

Precautions Against the Threat of Nuclear War

Communications

The much-heralded 'Four Minute Warning' was symptomatic of an obsession with the speed of communications that identified a need to pick up signs of enemy activity as early as possible to intercept enemy signals and to pass military information around the country as quickly as practicable. The RAF communications station at Greatworth, manned from 1956–60 by 962 Signals unit, was a satellite of the central RAF signals HQ at Leighton Buzzard in Bedfordshire, and served as the transmitter for RAF Stanbridge. It consisted of brick buildings plus Nissen huts with a mess and NAAFI, and numerous aerials occupying a site covering 90 acres (36 ha). It was leased to the USAF, 1988–92, after which it was sold by the MOD, with many of the buildings remaining as an industrial estate. In contrast, Staverton Radio Relay Station outside Daventry has vanished. It moved from the RAF to the USAF and remained in service until 2012. Its communications tower was used by the USAF eavesdroppers at Croughton, until the structures were demolished in 2014. The BBC transmitting station on Borough Hill, Daventry, was operational until 1992. It is now managed by Arqiva Communications. Early warning installations such as Fylingdales in North Yorkshire would report via a network of microwave communications towers known as Backbone, dating from the 1960s, whose best-known example is the Post Office Tower on London's Tottenham Court Road. Charwelton Microwave Tower is a terminal for the line joining the London and Birmingham GPO Towers and Backbone's spine, which runs from Stokenchurch in

Charwelton microwave tower, part of the military 'Backbone' communications network.

Buckinghamshire to Copt Oak in Leicestershire, and thence to the rest of the country. Alongside these GPO microwave towers, the Home Office had its own network of radio stations, known as Hilltop for transmitting orders under a regime of martial law, using UHF. This would ensure that the police and the army would maintain order in the event of a nuclear attack by preventing looting and general civil disobedience. An example is Potcote, standing at 515 feet (158 metres) to the west of the A5. The masts at Honey Hill, Dodford New House Farm near Naseby, and Thenford Hill may also all have originated in these two networks.

Emergency Control Centres
In the event of decentralised government becoming necessary after a nuclear attack, Northamptonshire and Leicestershire together formed Region 3.2, administered from Nottingham. Although a number of existing facilities such as the underground ARP Centre at the Stewart & Lloyd Corby Steelworks continued in use as Civil Defence centres into the 1970s, mainly new control centres were being built right up until the 1980s. A county control was built under county hall following its relocation to Wootton Hall Park. The Corby CD centre was partially destroyed by fire in 1975 and was subsequently abandoned. There were other local centres such as that under Wellingborough Fire and Ambulance Station, built in 1962, and currently (2017) in use simply as cellarage.

The cellars of Wellingborough fire station were designed as an emergency control centre as part of a national network for activation in the event of nuclear war.

Military Roads

Plans for life in the immediate aftermath of a nuclear attack included the exclusive use of certain roads by the military. With the authority to shoot to kill if necessary, the TA would ensure that key routes remained open. 'A' roads and motorways including the M1 through Northamptonshire were designated as Essential Service Routes (ESR), and the government planners were very clear that these major routes would not be clogged by refugees. Other uncontrolled routes were available to the general public who were expected quickly to experience gridlock, unavailability of fuel, and mechanical breakdown. As well as the ESRs, the Army had its own Road Route System linking specific destinations. The M1 between London and Leeds, codenamed BAT, took traffic on via the M62 to the military port of Hull, connecting to a NATO presence in Rotterdam.

Appendix I

Pre-Conquest Fortifications

Prehistoric Camps and Linear Earthworks

Arbury Hill, near Badby, hillfort (SP541586)
Chipping Warden, Arbury Banks, hillfort, (SP494486)
Daventry, Borough Hill, hillfort (SP589632-585619)
Draughton, defended settlement (SP778775)
Duston possible site of an *oppidum* or tribal centre
Farthingstone, Castle Yard, hillfort, (SP617563)
Guilsborough, Burrow Hill, hillfort (SP673729)
Hartwell, Egg Rings, Salcey Forest, hillfort (SP802502)
Harringworth, circular enclosure of indeterminate age (SP941947)
Harringworth, similar to above, (SP939949)
Hunsbury, hillfort (SP738583)
Irthlingborough, Crow Hill, hillfort (SP9571)
Newbottle, Rainsborough Camp, hillfort (SP526348)
Rothersthorpe, The Berry, earthwork of unknown age and origin (SP715567)
Thrapston, possible ring fort (TL003782)
Whittlebury, Old Tun Copse, hillfort/settlement (SP7143)

Roman Defended Towns

Bannaventa (Whilton Lodge)
Irchester
Towcester

Saxon and Danish Fortifications: Church Towers, Halls, and Thegnal Enclosures

Brigstock, Saxon church tower and stair turret, late tenth or early eleventh century
Brixworth, Saxon church tower and stair turret, late ninth to early eleventh century
Chipping Warden, Arbury Banks, possible Anglo-Saxon or Danish camp
Church Stowe (Stowe Nine Churches) Anglo-Saxon church tower and earthwork
Culworth, possible pre-Conquest ringwork, with church in outer enclosure
Daventry, Burnt Walls, possible Anglo-Saxon or Danish camp (SP586613)
Earls Barton, pre-Conquest church tower and defensive earthworks
Geddington, traces of Anglo-Saxon work in nave and tower arch of church
Greens Norton, Anglo-Saxon nave of church
Harringworth, possible Danish camps (SP941947) and (SP939949)
Nassington, Prebendal manor house and church, possible late-Saxon structures
Northampton, St Peter's, Minster church and palace complex with halls
Northampton, tenth-century town defences with clay bank and timber revetment
Radstone, eleventh-century work in church tower
Rothersthorpe, The Berry, possible Anglo-Saxon or Danish camp (SP715567)
Sulgrave, pre-Conquest church and ringwork with stone and timber buildings
Wadenhoe, fortified site, possible Anglo-Saxon or Danish camp (TL009833)
Raunds, Furnells Manor, sequence of Danish and Anglo-Saxon halls and church
Weedon Lois, possible pre-Conquest ringwork
West Cotton/Stanwick, similar development to Furnells

Appendix II

Medieval Castles, Fortified Manor Houses, and Tudor Strong Houses

Alderton, The Mount, ringwork (SP741470)
Apethorpe, fortified manor house (TL023954)
Ashby St Legers, fortified manor house (SP573681)
Astwell, fortified manor house (SP609440)
Aynho, castle, location unknown
Barby, doubtful motte (SP543707)
Barnwell, quadrangular stone castle (TL049852)
Barton Seagrave, two moated complexes (SP886769 & 886771)
(Lower) Benefield, ringwork walled in stone (SP987885)
Billing Priory, fortified manor house (SP804618)
Boughton House, Kettering, fortified manor house (SP900815)
Brackley, motte (SP583364)
Bradden Manor, fortified manor house (SP648487)
Braybrooke, East Hall, moated stone castle (SP767845)
Canons Ashby, doubtful motte, probable garden feature (SP575509)
Castle Ashby, stone castle buried in later house (SP863592)
Clopton Hall, Tudor strong house (TL063802)
Collyweston, fortified manor house (SK995029)
Cransley, doubtful motte (SP825767)
Culworth, ringwork (SP545470)
Daventry, John of Gaunt's Castle, moated site, probable hunting lodge (SP581612)
Dingley, semi-fortified Tudor manor house (SP770877)
Drayton House, fortified manor house (SP963800)
Earls Barton, ringwork/motte (SP852638)
Easton Neston, fortified manor house (SP701493)
Farthingstone, Castle Dykes, ringwork or motte, and three baileys (SP619566)
Fineshade, Hymel/Hely, short-lived earthwork castle (SP972977)
Fotheringhay, motte and bailey castle rebuilt in stone (TL062930)
Grafton Regis, priory converted to fortified manor house by Woodvilles (SP752467)
Grafton Regis Palace, residence of Henry VIII (SP759470)

Gaultney (near Rushton), exact location unknown
Harlestone, possible tower house, on a motte (SP705645)
Harringworth, fortified manor house (SP918975)
Higham Ferrers, motte and bailey castle rebuilt in stone (SP961688)
Lilbourne, motte and two baileys (SP561774)
Lilbourne, motte of possible siege castle (SP553771)
Little Houghton, Clifford Hill, motte (SP806606)
Little Houghton, doubtful ringwork castle (SP803597)
Little Preston, ringwork or motte (SP589543)
Long Buckby, ringwork and bailey castle (SP625676)
Moor End Castle, Yardley Gobion, moated stone castle (SP756446)
Moulton, motte (SP786672)
Muscott, fortified manor house (SP625632)
Northampton, motte and bailey castle rebuilt in stone (SP748605)
Preston Capes, motte and bailey castle (SP577549)
Rockingham, motte and bailey castle rebuilt in stone (SP867913)
Sibbertoft, Castle Yard, motte and bailey castle (SP691832)
Southwick, fortified manor house (TL022922)
Sulgrave, Saxon ringwork developed as Norman castle (SP562456)
Thorpe Waterville, fortified manor house (TL022814)
Thrapston, possible site of lost motte and bailey castle (SP996788)
Titchmarsh, moated stone castle (TL025795)
Towcester, Bury Mount, motte astride Roman town wall (SP693488)
Wadenhoe, fortified site of indeterminate age (TL009833)
Warkworth, vanished stone castle (SP490397)
Weedon Lois, ringwork and bailey castle (SP603470)
Wollaston, Beacon Hill, short-lived motte and bailey castle (SP908629)
Woodnewton, former fortified manor house belonging to Fineshade Priory

Ecclesiastical Defensible Structures

Badby, moated monastic grange (SP561592)
Bradden Manor, preceptory of the Knights Hospitallers (SP646483)
Daventry Priory
Dingley, preceptory of the Knights Hospitallers (SP770877)
Hardwick, preceptory of the Knights Templars (SP852698)
Harrington, preceptory of the Knights Hospitallers (SP772804)
Higham Ferrers, Archbishop Chichele's College of 1422
Irthlingborough, tower of college founded 1354
Nassington Prebendal House
Northampton, St Andrew's Priory, St James's Abbey, Delapre Abbey, Whitefriars, and
   Greyfriars
Pipewell Priory

Licences to Crenellate

1301 Thorpe Waterville to Bishop of Coventry and Lichfield
1304 Braybrooke to Thomas de Latymer
1304 Titchmarsh to John Lovell
1306 Castle Ashby to Walter of Langton, Bishop of Coventry and Lichfield
1310 Barton Seagrave to Nicholas de Seagrave
1328 Drayton House to Simon de Drayton
1347 Moor End Castle, Yardley Gobion to Thomas de Ferrariis/Ferrers (SP756446)
1387 Harringworth Manor to William de la Zouche of Totteneys, confirmed 1431
1473 Boughton House to Richard Whetehille
1477 Bradden Manor to John Holcot
1499 Easton Neston to Richard Empson, including parkland
1512 Althorp to John Spencer

Town Defences

Northampton
Towcester

Moats

Aldwincle, moat with two rectangular islands and wide ditch (SP981855)
Aldwincle, square moat with scatter of building rubble and roof tiles (SP982855)
Arthingworth, manor of Catesby family; square level platform (SP756815)
Ashton, moat (SP764500)
Barnwell, moat (TL052842)
Brampton Ash, The Hermitage, a grange of Pipewell Abbey (SP783854)
Braunstonbury, square moat of manor house (SP533656)
Castle Ashby, Chadstone, a roughly square moat, originally around a manor, integrated into later fishponds (SP852587)
Chipping Warden, moat (SP502484)
Clopton, small rectangular moated site (TL061802)
Cottesbrooke, small square moat with traces of a former building (SP690746)
Daventry, John of Gaunt's Castle, probable hunting lodge (SP581612)
Dingley, earlier house, altered subsequently (SP773876)
Evenley, Astwick, wet moat supplied by stream (SP573344)
Faxton, Lamport, partial moat around medieval manor house site appearing to enclose site of former church (SP784753)
Great Harrowden, moat 90 × 60 metres with ditch 10 metres across (SP879707)
Grendon, moat 50-metre-square with 1-metre-deep ditch (SP881610)
Hemington, moat destroyed (TL089850)
Hemington, moated site enlarged as a water feature around Beaulieu Hall (TL095582)
Helmdon, Old Mountains, moated site and manorial earthworks (SP616430)

Higham Park, moat (SP982642)
Hinton-in-the-Hedges, moated manor house (SP563369)
Kingsthorpe, Polebrook, small square moat with 2-metre-deep ditch (TL080855)
Loddington Moat Lodge, moated farmstead (SP796781)
Luddington, ditched platform with ponds, probable manor house site (TL102837)
Marston Trussell, roughly square wet moat of Thorpe Lubenham manor (SP705868)
Muscott, moat east of Muscott House may have enclosed the house (SP627633)
Newton, rectangular enclosure, possible medieval moat, much altered (SP887833)
Orlingbury, Wythmail Farm, oval moat surrounding farm (SP842721)
Papley near Warmington, 100-metre-square moat modified as gardens (TL105888)
Pilton, 25-metres-square moat with ditch up to 20 metres wide (SP990869)
Quinton, a roughly rectangular moat (SP776541)
Stanion, moat 45 metres × 50 metres with 5-metre-wide ditch (SP924863)
Steane, two moats (SP555392 and 556391)
Stoke Albany, moat and fishponds of manor house (SP808880)
Stoke Albany, embanked site of building (SP807883)
Stoke Doyle, 30-metre-square moat; limestone slabs found (TL029860)
Stoke Doyle, irregular rectangle with ditch 2 metres deep and 15 metres wide (TL001866)
Stutchbury, moat (SP569438)
Thornby, moat reduced to L-shaped pond (SP673758)
Thrapston, possible moat (SP996788)
Thurning, moat roughly 50 metres square with shallow ditch (SP085829)
Thrupp Lodge, Norton, partial remains of moat (SP598650)
Walgrave, North Hall Manor, moat (SP802723)
Warmington, moated platform 20 metres × 15 metres, and higher platform 7 metres across (TL079914)
Weekley, Hall Yard, moat, possible site of the Old Hall manor house (SP890806)
Weldon, moat (SP923897)
Weldon, Hall Close, moat (SP926893)
Whiston, small rectangular moat (SP847606)
Winwick, moat 40 metres across (SP623740)
Yardley Hastings, moated farmstead at Biggin Lodge (SP858533)
Yelvertoft, moat now destroyed (SP602755)

Royal Hunting Lodges

Brigstock (SP945852)
Geddington (SP896831)
Kingscliffe (TL007971)
Kingsthorpe untraced
Silverstone possibly (SP668442)
Wakefield possibly (SP738426)

Keepers' Lodges

Beanfield Lawn at Corby (SP863881)
Cottingham (SP862904)
Harringworth Lodge (SP932953)
Higham Park, Newton Bromshold near Rushden (SP982642)
Rockingham Castle, Cottingham (SP862904)
Sudborough, Slipton Lodge, moated keepers' lodge (SP950812)
Wakerley Lodge, Oundle (TL011876)

Unfortified Medieval Stone Houses

Deene Park (SP952927)
Hardwick (SP852698)
Harrington (SP772804)
Yardley Hastings (SP864568)

Appendix III

Civil War Sites

Sites in *italics* doubtful or rejected.
Aynho-on-the-Hill (SP513330)
Banbury Castle, Oxfordshire (SP454404)
Canon's Ashby, house SP575506, St Mary's church (SP578505)
Daventry, Borough Hill, campsite (SP5862)
East Farndon, Hall Close, entrenchments (SP717851)
Fawsley Hall, garrison (SP561568)
Grafton Regis, Tudor palace, garrison (SP760469)
Kelmarsh, sconce (SP728801)
Northampton town defences
Rockingham Castle (SP867914)
Towcester, town defences
Towcester, Bury Mount (SP693488)
Walgrave, mound, possible Civil War battery (SP82439734)

Appendix IV

Regular, Militia, and Volunteer Forces, 1860–1918

Northamptonshire and Rutland Militia Amalgamated, 1860: Northampton

Northamptonshire Rifle Volunteer Corps 1859-80
1st Corps: Althorp
2nd Corps: Towcester
3rd Corps (4th and 5th) Corps: Northampton
6th Corps: Peterborough
7th Corps: Wellingborough
8th Corps Daventry
9th Corps: Kettering

Northamptonshire Militia Split into Two Battalions, 1874: Northampton

1st Administrative Battalion, Northamptonshire Rifle Volunteer Corps 1880–87
'A' Company: Althorp
'B' Company: Towcester
HQ + 'C-G' Companies: Northampton
'H' & 'I' Companies: Peterborough
'K' & 'L' Companies: Wellingborough
'M' Company: Daventry
'N' Company: Kettering

1st Volunteer Battalion, Northamptonshire Regiment 1887–1908
'A–N' Companies as above but three additional companies formed in 1900, and cadet
    companies at Wellingborough GS and Oundle School (1902)

Northamptonshire Regiment 1908
1st and 2nd Battalions Northamptonshire Regiment, alternate home or foreign postings
3rd Battalion Northamptonshire Regiment (formerly Militia), Gibraltar Barracks,
    Northampton

4th Battalion Northamptonshire Regiment (TF)
HQ: Corn Exchange, Northampton
'A', 'B', 'C', and 'D' Coys: Clare Street, Northampton and Daventry, Weedon, Althorp,
    Long Buckby, and Harpole
'E' Coy: Wellingborough and Finedon
'F' Coy: Kettering
'G' Coy: Desborough and Rothwell
'H' Coy: Higham Ferrers and Rushden and Irthlingborough

The Northamptonshire Yeomanry 1908
HQ and 'A' Squadron: Clare Street Northampton and Cottesbrooke
'B' Squadron: Peterborough and Oundle, Glinton and Thrapston
'C' Squadron: Kettering and Wellingborough, Rushden and Clipston
'D' Squadron: Daventry and Weedon, Blisworth, Blakesley, and West Haddon

Cadet companies, 1904–18
Northampton Boys' Brigade: six companies by 1904
Northampton School, Cadet Corps, Billing Road, from 6 February 1914
Kettering Grammar School Cadet Corps from 30 September 1916
Magdalen College School, Brackley, Cadet Corps, from 7 May 1915
Wellingborough GS Junior OTC: one infantry company in 1914
Oundle School Junior OTC: three infantry companies in 1914

Appendix V

Barracks and Army Camps

Pre-First World War

Boughton Park: camp for Norfolk Regiment cyclist battalion, 1913
Elmington Lodge, Rifle Range, 1904, for Oundle OTC (TL065891)
Nobottle Range, 600-yard range opened 1903 for Rifle Volunteer Corps (SP667626)
Northampton, Barrack Road, two-troop Cavalry Barracks built 1796
Northampton, Gibraltar Barracks, Northamptonshire Regimental Depot, 1881
Northampton, Ordnance Depot, *c.* 1806, disappeared
Northampton, Westbridge, listed in Northants HER as cavalry barracks, *c.* 1908
Weedon Barracks and Depot, 1790s; barracks and Pavilions demolished

First World War

Greatworth radio/telegraphy station (SP554433)
Hackleton rifle range (SP811558)
Nobottle rifle range (SP667626)
Northampton, Gibraltar Barracks, Barrack Road, Northamptonshire Regimental Depot
Northampton, Kingsley Park: 51 Reserve Park (HT) ASC, 1916-20
Northampton, Kingsley Park: No1 (HQ) Company (HT) ASC Train, 72 (HF) Division
Northampton, Kingsthorpe army camp
Northampton Racecourse (last race 1910) hutted camp, grandstand rebuilt 1930
Oundle, Elmington Lodge rifle range in use by OTC and VTC (TL065892)
Towcester: Nightingales Meadow, camp for Northamptonshire Yeomanry, 1914
Towcester, Plough Hotel: officers' mess Northamptonshire Yeomanry, 1914
Towcester, Dr Knight's School and houses: billets Northamptonshire Yeomanry, 1914
Weedon Barracks, Cadet School, RFA
Wellingborough, No. 4 Company (HT) ASC Train, 72 Division (Home Forces)
Wellingborough Camp, RE Motorcycle training camp, 1918 (SP895675)

Second World War

Apethorpe Palace: RHA, 1940; later Czech and/or Polish troops

Arthingworth, Hall Farm: 9 Support Group; infantry/tank firing range

Ashby-St-Legers: camp for 6th Bn Leicestershire Regiment

Barby Camp in Romney huts (SP542711)

Blatherwyke Hall, camp for Polish troops; A/T Troop of 1st Polish Independent Parachute Brigade, pre-Arnhem; hall damaged and demolished 1948

Boughton House Camp: 4th County of London Yeomanry, 2nd Armoured Division and 22nd Armoured Brigade REs; 43 acres of the Park from June–August 1940; Canadian troops, 1940

Boughton House estate office, Burdyke: Canadian troops, May 1940; AAF-596 US Army 26 Signal Construction Sqdn; General Stores & Medical Depot; 1541st QM Truck Bn. (Aviation); subsite of Q-101 QM Depot, Kettering

Brigstock Army Camp (SP955852)

Brigstock Army Camp built 1928 for emigrant preparation, closed 1930; reused from 1939 by Army, ATS and WLA; then by US 928 Engineer Bn (SP 935863)

Castle Ashby camp (SP863593)

Cottingham, Bury House, now Cottingham Hall: 11 Field Sqdn RE of 9th Armoured Division; also basement of factory in Rockingham Road

Deene Park: army camp for Greek, Polish, and Indian units, (SP949927)

Delapre Abbey, infantry training camp, 1944, satellite of Gibraltar Barracks

Easton Neston Lodge: HQ 257 Company, 72 Searchlight Regiment (SP704498)

Ecton Hall, billet for Canadian troops (SP829636)

Evenley Hall, East Riding Yeomanry, 27 Armoured Brigade, 1940–3 (SP588355)

Fawsley Hall: 27th Armoured Brigade (SP561568)

Finedon Hall: Free French troops (SP911720)

Flore House, billets for infantry unit (SP6460)

Greens Norton, Kingsthorn Woods, Canadian troop encampment, (SP660490)

Grendon Hall, Free French forces (SP880608)

Guilsborough Ho: HQ GHQ Reserve 9th Armoured & 43rd Infantry Divisions, 1940

Guilsborough Park Camp: camp for Overlord forces, 1943–4 (SP6672)

Haselbech Hall: Highland LI, King's Dragoon Guards, and 11th Bn. Worcestershire Regiment, 1st Heavy Regiment, RA (SP713773)

Kelmarsh: 2085 QM Trucks (Aviation), USAAF

Lamport Hall: billets for 'A' Company, 11th Battalion, Worcestershire Regiment, later for Czech troops (SP759745)

Litchborough: WI Room and Baptist schoolroom, billets for 13/18th Hussars

Nassington, Ring Haw Camp: camp for Overlord forces, 1943–4

Northampton, Clare Street drill hall: REME depot, 28th Armoured Brigade office

Northampton, Gibraltar Barracks: Northamptonshire Regimental depot

Northampton Racecourse, Talavera Barracks, hutted camp for Northamptonshire Regiment; No. 2 ITC; No. 1 ATS Training Centre; No. 3 Military Dispersal Unit

Northampton, Billing Hall: Czech troops and AA training camp

Northampton, Delapre Abbey: grounds requisitioned as ITC; pre-D-Day camp for 1st Czechoslovak Independent Armoured Brigade, 1944,

Oundle Rectory: RASC training unit and ATS unit
Overstone Park, camp for Overlord forces (SP816659)
Overthorpe Hall: FANY training centre (SP482418)
Rushton Hall, Kettering: RAOC OCTU (SP836827), expanded 1941 to Leicester
Spanhoe airfield: 505th Parachute Infantry, 82nd US Airborne Division
Thrapston Militia Camp: HQ 78 HAA Regiment, 1940; AA training (TL0078)
Thrapston: RASC/AAF-584 US Army 6 Medical Supply Platoon (TL013780)
Welford, The Hemplow: billets for a company of 11 Bn Worcesters, now demolished
Wellingborough Camp: AAF-580 QM Q-102 Truck, Post Office, Military Police
    (Aviation), etc. 1942–5
Wellingborough, Railway Club, Free French officers' quarters
West Haddon Hall, Royal Engineers (SP630716)
Weston Favell, Birchfield Road East (now Cherry Orchard School): tank training area
Woodford Halse, Hinton Gorse Hotel: billets for 4/7 Dragoon Guards, 1940 (SP5353)
Wootton, Quebec Barracks: begun 1941 as new Northamptonshire Regimental Depot

Post Second World War

Brigstock Army Camp: US Army AAA Training Camp, 1951–5, (SP 935863)
Northampton, Barrack Road, Gibraltar Barracks, Northamptonshire Regimental Depot;
    most of site sold to Royal Mail 1980; one nineteenth-century barrack block remains.
Talavera Barracks, hutted camp on racecourse, for Northamptonshire Regiment,
    demolished 1948, and returned to public use, 1953
Wootton, Quebec Barracks, Northamptonshire Regiment Depot; later as Simpson
    Barracks, Royal Pioneer Corps Depot; opened fully 1948, demolished 1990s.

Appendix VI

Drill Halls and
TA/Army Reserve Centres

NB: locations in *italics* demolished/disappeared/untraced

Althorp(e) Hall, Stable block is a possible location.
    In 1859, 1st Corps Northamptonshire Rifle Volunteers,
    In 1880, 'A' Company, 1st Volunteer Bn Northamptonshire Regiment
    In 1914, drill station for 'A' Company, 4th Bn Northamptonshire Regiment
Blakesley Hall
    In 1914, drill station for 'D' Squadron, Northamptonshire Yeomanry.
Blisworth
    In 1914, drill station for 'D' Squadron, Northamptonshire Yeomanry,
Brackley
    In 1914, drill station for Banbury-based 'C' Company, 4th Battalion, Oxfordshire and Buckinghamshire Light Infantry
Drill Hall, 20 St Peters Road, in use by 1938; now housing: 'Yeomans Close'
    In 1938, 2nd Northamptonshire Yeomanry
Clipston
    In 1914, drill station for 'C' Squadron, Northamptonshire Yeomanry
Corby
    1: Elizabeth Street, ex-TAC, 1962; T-shaped office/hall block, garages, workshops, 25-yard range, staff housing, etc.; now the town's volunteer centre.
    2: St Mark's Road, Army Reserve Centre, leased from 1962; hall, garages/workshops
        In 2017, 118 Recovery Company, REME (Volunteers)
Cottesbrooke Hall
    In 1914, drill station for 'A' Squadron, Northamptonshire Yeomanry.
Daventry: 8th Corps, Rifle Volunteers, formed November 1860.
    1: New Street, *Assembly Hall*, 1871, drill hall from 1873–1921; demolished 1980s
        In 1880, 'M' Company, 1st Volunteer Battalion, Northamptonshire Regiment
        In 1914, 'D' Squadron, Northamptonshire Yeomanry, and drill station for 'B' Company, 4th Battalion, Northamptonshire Regiment

2: Waterloo, ex-TAC, now Cadet Centre *c.* 1980–2; small L-shaped block and garage. Denton, Horton Road, Cadet Training Centre, in current use in modern buildings on former ordnance storage site

Desborough

Beech Close, *Drill Hall*, pre-First World War, demolished for old people's home.

In 1914, base for 'G' Company, 4th Battalion, Northamptonshire Regiment

Finedon no evidence of drill hall

In 1914, drill station 'E' Company, 4th Battalion, Northamptonshire Regiment

Harpole no evidence of drill hall

In 1914, drill station 'C' Company, 4th Battalion, Northamptonshire Regiment

Higham Ferrers no evidence of drill hall; used town hall or drill hall at Rushden.

In 1914, base for 'H' Company, 4th Battalion, Northamptonshire Regiment

Irthlingborough no evidence of drill hall

In 1914, drill station 'H' Company, 4th Battalion, Northamptonshire Regiment

Kettering: 9th Corps, Rifle Volunteers formed April 1867

1: York Road, Drill Hall, by 1899; addition for Freemasons, 1901; brick-built front block with entrance to left through to hall at rear; gabled addition to right; from 1928, Masonic and Drill Hall Co. Ltd, until at least 1940

In 1899, 'N' Company, 1st Volunteer Battalion, Northamptonshire Regiment; drill instructor at 29, Green Lanes Terrace, 1898

In 1906 and 1914, base for 'F' Company, 4th Battalion, Northamptonshire Regiment

In 1914, HQ 'C' Squadron, Imperial Yeomanry

In 1928, Northamptonshire Territorial Association

In 1930, base for 'D' Company, 4th Battalion, Northamptonshire Regiment

2: High Street, *Old White Horse Hotel*, HQ 'C' Squadron, Imperial Yeomanry; drill instructor at 24, The Grove, 1906;

3: Station Road, *Drill Hall*, 1936, brick, two-storey front block with cupola and hall to rear; 'tank store', and smaller building recorded prior to their demolition for new housing. A steel-clad garage and temporary brick office remained in an adjoining yard for a while afterwards

In 1939, base for 'A' Company, new 4th Battalion, Northamptonshire Regiment, and 403 Company, 50 AA S/L Regiment RA (TA)

In 1947, base for elements of 585 SL Regiment

Long Buckby

High Street, drill hall in use 1910; possibly Admiral Rodney PH, in existence by 1864; club-room in use by Home Guard in the Second World War

In 1914, drill station 'C' Company, 4th Battalion, Northamptonshire Regiment

Northampton

1: Market Place, Corn Exchange, built 1850, used as drill hall by 4th and 5th Corps, Rifle Volunteers, formed February and March 1860, and amalgamated in 1872; RVC Orderly Rooms in Corn Exchange, Dymchurch Lane, and Bridge Street, 1877 and 1890; classical frontage, large hall to rear, side entrance through archway (later PH) to small courtyard with possible armoury; in use until 1918; (Gaumont) Cinema by 1921

In 1887, 'C'–'G' Companies, 1st Volunteer Battalion, Northamptonshire Regiment

In 1914, 'B'–'D' Companies, 4th Battalion, Northamptonshire Regiment

2: Barrack Rd, Gibraltar Barracks, HQ of 1st Volunteer Battalion, Northamptonshire Regiment by 1898

In 1938, HQ of new 4th Battalion, Northamptonshire Regiment in *Isolation Hospital*

3: Clare Street, Drill Hall/Armoury built 1859 as militia armoury, at a cost of £7,000, and extended for use as a drill hall; built in brick with stone dressings as a mock medieval castle with gatehouse, corner towers, arrow slits, etc., and an added hall behind shown on map of 1921; extra land was acquired in 1937 to accommodate the mechanized machine-gun company of the 4th Battalion, Northamptonshire Regiment; new buildings and modifications to existing ones over the years; currently (2017) is in Army Reserve use by a REME unit

In 1890, HQ of both 3rd and 4th Battalions, Northamptonshire Militia

In 1914, HQ, Northamptonshire Yeomanry; HQ and 'A' Coy.4th Battalion, Northamptonshire Regiment; and base for East Anglian Divisional Transport and Supply Column, East Midland Brigade Company, ASC

In 1931–6, base for 25th (Northamptonshire Yeomanry) Armoured Car Company; HQ, 4th Battalion, Northamptonshire Regiment; HQ, 162 (East Midland) Brigade; Northamptonshire TA Association offices;

In 1938, base for 401 and 402 Companies, 50 AA S/L Regiment RA (TA)

In 1947, base for elements of 585 S/L Regiment

In 1952, HQ of Huntingdonshire and Northamptonshire Territorial Associations

In 2016, 104 Battalion, REME and 118 Recovery Company, REME.

4: 53 Sheep Street, Drill Hall; stone four-bay house with arch to rear courtyard;

In 1906 and 1914, HQ and 'A' Squadron, Northamptonshire Yeomanry

5: Langham Place, house used as temporary HQ for duplicate unit

In 1938, HQ of new 4th Battalion, Northamptonshire Regiment

6: Wootton Hall, used by 2nd Northamptonshire Yeomanry, 1940

Oundle

1: Benefield Road, Drill Hall, early twentieth-century two-storey block and attached house all in stone, formerly with brick hall to rear, garage, small-arms range, and a pair of Second World War explosives and inflammables stores; until recently, a museum; hall demolished and remaining buildings converted to residential

In 1914, drill station for 'B' Squadron, Northamptonshire Yeomanry

In 1927, base for 'B' Company of reorganised 5th Bn Northamptonshire Regiment

In 1939, base for 'B' Company, 5th Battalion, Northamptonshire Regiment, and temporary base for a battalion of the Leicestershire Regiment

In 1948, base for one company of 5th Battalion, Northamptonshire Regiment

2: Oundle School: cadet corps formed in 1902

The CCF Armoury and 25-yard range are still in use, with the Elmington Lodge full-bore range

In 1914, three companies of Junior OTC

Raunds

1: Marshall's Road, Temperance Hall saw formation of VTC unit (27 November 1915); then used by Home Guard in the Second World War; with cottages to rear, now a private residence

2: Rotten Row, 'Golden Fleece' PH; drill hall mentioned in use by Northamptonshire Regiment's new 4th Battalion in 1938–9; then by the Home Guard; likely the 'Golden

Fleece', consisting of a large clubroom, which may have once held a skating rink, with an annexe to one side and the PH itself to the rear, all now private residences

In 1903, base 'R' Company, 1st Volunteer Battalion, Northamptonshire Regiment, with local headmaster as their colour sergeant, so school may have been drill hall.

In 1938, base for 'B' Company, new 4th Battalion, Northamptonshire Regiment

In 1940, 'A' Company, 8th Battalion, Northamptonshire Home Guard

Rothwell

The Old Chapel in Well Lane is currently used as a drill hall by the ACF;

In 1914, drill station 'G' Coy 4th Battalion, Northamptonshire Regiment

Rushden

1: Church (now Newton) Street, *Drill Hall*, in use by 1910, on site opposite Carnegie Library; site redeveloped as PC and car-park.

In 1906, base for 'H' Company, 1st Volunteer Battalion, Northamptonshire Regiment

In 1910, base for 'H' Company, 4th Battalion, Northamptonshire Regiment and 'C' Squadron, Northamptonshire Yeomanry

In 1914, drill station for 'C' Squadron, Northamptonshire Yeomanry, 'H' Company, 4th Battalion, Northamptonshire Regiment

2: Victoria Road, Drill Hall, *c.* 1927; referred to as Territorial Institute in 1936; two-storey front block with gable and stone detailing; hall, garages, etc., to rear; staff house attached; may have accommodated units nominally based at nearby Higham Ferrers

In 1920, base for one company of 4th Battalion, Northamptonshire Regiment

In 1936, company transferred from 4th Battalion to 5th Battalion, Northamptonshire Regiment.

In 1938, 'D' Company, new 4th Battalion, Northamptonshire Regiment (returned from 5th Battalion)

In 1948, base for one company of 5th Battalion, Northamptonshire Regiment

Thrapston

King's Arms PH in use by 1910, but given up by 1958; demolished for library/shops

In 1910, one troop of 'B' Squadron, Northamptonshire Yeomanry

In 1933, in use by detachment of 4th Battalion, Northamptonshire Regiment

Towcester: 2nd Corps, Northamptonshire Rifle Volunteers formed October 1859

1: Town Hall, built 1866, housed armoury with 100 sets of weapons and equipment

In 1898, one troop of Royal Buckinghamshire Hussars Yeomanry in 1898

In 1887, 'B' Company, 1st Volunteer Battalion, Northamptonshire Regiment

2: Vernon Road, *Drill Hall*, (SP696483) described as large wooden structure, 1925

In 1938, one squadron of 2nd Northamptonshire Yeomanry

Weedon Royal Ordnance Depot

In 1914, drill station for 'D' Squadron, Northamptonshire Yeomanry, and 'B' Company, 4th Battalion, Northamptonshire Regiment

Wellingborough: 7th Corps Rifle Volunteers formed September 1860

1: *Corn Exchange* 1861, possible first drill hall; demolished 1958

2: Church Street, Drill Hall/Armoury converted from Methodist chapel, in, use by 1877 until not later than 1906;

In 1887, 'K' & 'L' Companies, 1st Volunteer Battalion, Northamptonshire Regiment

3: Great Park Street, Drill Hall, by 1906; two-storey front block with gable over entrance arch; hall behind with single-storey annexes; similar in appearance to Rushden but much earlier; sold 1957.

In 1906, 'K' & 'L' Coys 1st Volunteer Battalion, Northamptonshire Regiment

In 1914, drill station for 'C' Squadron, Northamptonshire Yeomanry, and base for 'E' Company, 4th Battalion, Northamptonshire Regiment

In 1914, 1920–30, base 'C' Company, 4th Battalion, Northamptonshire Regiment

4: High Street, Drill Hall; nineteenth-century Methodist manse; two-storey brick and ironstone, double-fronted house, with hall and extensive garages added on to rear; acquired by TAA, 1938; hall and garages part-demolished *c*. late 1990s. NB: Northants Record Office Accession No. 1968/50, TBF.172 (papers of Talbot, Brown & Fisher *c*. 1928): Riding School, Wellingborough Drill Hall, alterations and estimates but no plans and no date.

In 1938, base for 403 Company, 50 AA S/L Regiment and 'C' Company, new 4th Battalion, Northamptonshire Regiment.

In 1947, base for elements of 585 S/L Regiment

5: Wellingborough Grammar School, cadet corps raised in 1900; OTC in 1928

West Haddon

In 1914, drill station for 'D' Squadron, Northamptonshire Yeomanry

Appendix VII

Military Airfields and Other Aviation-Related Sites

Notes:

i: USAAF designated Station Number, where applicable, in brackets

ii: Air Ministry design numbers in italic: number after '/' denotes year of issue

e.g.:   343/43 = design number 343 in (19)43

Badby:	Pre-First World War Landing Ground used in annual manoeuvres.
Braybrooke:	223MU, RAF Forward Ammunition Depot, 1943; passed to USAAF (Station 521).
Chelveston (Station 105):	1941–62; built by Taylor-Woodrow with a J-type (5836/39) and two T2 (8254/40) hangars; a Watch Office (518/40) and concrete runways, soon to be lengthened, as an operational bomber base. Accommodation was in dispersed communal sites. A new 4,000-yard (3,700-metre) runway was laid by a US Army engineer battalion in 1956. Isolated on the northern part of the airfield near the bomb stores, a cluster of nine Nissen huts, numbered 137–145, and used for the storage of SAA, small bombs, and pyrotechnics, such as sea markers and flares, was recorded in 2011; four of them (Nos 141–4) are provided with intervening blast walls. A solitary Butler shed remains (2017) near the former entrance.
Chipping Warden:	1941–6; built with one J-type (5836/39) and four T2 (8254/40) hangars; a Watch Office (518/40) and concrete runways, as a base for OTUs and Beam Approach Training units. Most buildings on the airfield itself and on dispersed sites were tb. The hangars and several buildings such as the Crew

Procedure Centre survive (2017), and the village primary school occupies the Station Sick Quarters. On the north-eastern edge of the airfield, among a cluster of flight offices, an L-shaped range of semi-sunken Stanton shelters forming six rooms, entered by three sets of stairs, and furnished with two escape hatches, has been suggested as a Battle HQ.

Clipston: First World War Home Defence Landing Ground (SP717819).

Collywestom: *see* Easton-on-the-Hill.

Croughton: Opened in 1938 as RAF Brackley and designated an emergency LG in 1940 with a permanent flare path; built by Wimpey in 1940 as a grass field and renamed RAF Croughton in 1941 as a satellite of RAF Upper Heyford, with four T2 (8254/40) hangars and an all-purpose watch office (12779/41). The airfield was used by 16 OTU; No. 1 Glider Training School, 1942 until March 1943; No. 20 (P)AFU, and a Beam Approach Training unit until October 1944. In 1950, it became a USAF communications centre, and since 2005, 422 Air Base Group under command of Fairford has carried out monitoring of military and clandestine communications. The four hangars survive, surrounded by later buildings, but the defence area has gone.

Daventry: Automobile Association listed LG, during the 1930s (SP588605).

Deenethorpe (Station 128): 1943–6; built with concrete runways, two T2 (8254/40) hangars and an all-purpose watch office (343/43); communal sites were scattered between the airfield and Upper Benefield to the east. It served as an operational USAAF bomber station throughout its short life. The operations block remains, but other tb structures that survived into the 1990s are fast crumbling.

Denton (Brafield-on-the-Green): 1940–5; was initially established as a relief LG for Sywell FTS; the grass flying-field was ringed by two extra over (12532/41) and eight standard blister (12497/41) hangars. Nothing now remains.

Desborough: 1943–6; built by Tarmac with concrete runways, one B1 (11776/41) and four T2 (8254/40) hangars, and an OTU satellite watch office (13726/41), for 84 OTU, which remained throughout the war. Four T2s stand at Desborough: one was imported from Podington and occupies the B1 base (SP813865);

another came from St Athan (SP814856) while two originals (SP816867 and 809860) remain but the fifth hangar (SP825863) was destroyed by fire. A Gymnasium/Chapel (14604/40) and a number of Romney and Handcraft huts stand on a communal site astride the B669, plus a Standby-set house on the southern edge of the airfield.

Earls Barton: 1931–45, used as a Landing Ground for Tiger Moths of 6EFTS, particularly for aircraft flying from Sywell practising forced landings (SP862645).

Easton-on-the-Hill/Collyweston: 1917–19 and 1939–45; during the First World War, No. 5 TDS flew DH.6, R.E.8, F.2B, and Avro 504 aircraft; it had three pairs of GS Hangars and an ARS with rows of timber barrack huts; this was all demolished; in 1940, it was merged with the adjoining Wittering (now Cambridgeshire), which had retained its TDS buildings, but maintained a partially separate identity operating the enemy aircraft flight.

Grafton Underwood (Station 106): 1942–5; built by Wimpey, and opened in May 1942 as a USAAF bomber station with concrete runways, two T2 hangars (8254/40), and a watch office (15898/40) with attached operations room for bomber satellite stations. It was closed for five months at the end of 1942 for an upgrade, which included lengthening the runways. The operations block, Norden bombsight store, and a quadrant tower remain, along with the BHQ and two FC Construction pillboxes.

Harrington (Station 179): 1943–5; intended for use by an OTU, it was built by a US Army Engineering Aviation Battalion as a USAAF bomber base, with concrete runways, four T2 (8254/40) hangars and an all-purpose Watch Office (343/43). Only finally opening in March 1944, it was used by the Carpetbaggers flying clandestine missions to occupied France. Only the operations block, the machine-gun butts, and two brick pyrotechnic stores (5488/42) remain of the wartime airfield. From 1959–63, Harrington was a Thor IRBM base with three launch-pads, whose massive L-shaped blast walls may still be seen along with other specialised structures.

Hinton-in-the-Hedges: 1940–44; opened in late 1940 as a grass field, for use by 13 and 16 OTUs; concrete runways were laid later; the airfield had one B1 (11776/41) hangar and one T2 (8254/40), with a bomber satellite watch office (15898/40). From July 1942, flying radio stations were operated by the Signals Development Unit. The communal sites, consisting mainly of tb, Nissen, and Laing hutting, lay to the west.

Kingscliffe (Station 367): 1941–45; there had been a landing ground hereabouts in the First World War, but the precise overlap with the LG, which had been operating with Wittering's CFS and, from 1935, a FTS into the early months of the war, remains uncertain. Not until 1941 was work completed on the concrete runways and perimeter track, enabling it to function as a RAF fighter airfield. It had one Callendar Hamilton hangar (6649/37), a night-fighter watch office (FCW 4514), three extra over and nine standard blister hangars, all given the same drawing number (13084–7/41) on the AM plan. Many of the airfield's defences survive in good order with sleeping shelters (11070/40), one of which has been strengthened to support LAA guns (16142/41). The PBX (5648/41) is thought to be a conversion of an earlier BHQ. On a communal site to the north-east stands a gymnasium/chapel (14604/40), with other mainly tb huts. The airfield was handed over as a USAAF fighter station at the start of 1943.

Lilbourne: 1916–19; opened for use by training squadrons in 1916, and then as the Midland Area Flying Instructors' School, 1918–19. The grass flying field was south of Watling Street with a row of three permanent hangars, workshops and flight office. On the other side of the A5 was a hutted complex containing HQ, administration, and living quarters.

Litchborough: A pre-First World War landing ground used in the annual manoeuvres of 1913.

Northampton, Cliftonville: 'The Lindens', RAuxAF HQ, 1938–57.

Polebrook (Station110): 1941–5; built by Wimpey as a RAF bomber station with one J-type hangar (5836/39) and a watch office (518/40); two T2 hangars (8254/40) were added later. The RAF began operating the first B-17 Flying Fortresses to appear in British skies. The airfield was upgraded with lengthened runways later in 1942 to accommodate a USAAF Bomber Group. It finally closed in 1948 but in 1959 it was selected to serve, until August 1963, as a Thor IRBM base. The J-type hangar, one of the T2s, and the blast walls of the missile launch pads remain.

Silverstone: 1943–6; built by Mowlem to open in March 1943 as an OTU base, with concrete runways, one B1 hangar B1 (11776/*41*), four T2s (8254/*40*), and an all-purpose watch office (343/*43*). Administration and communal sites lay between the airfield and the A43 road. The watch office remains within the motor-racing circuit.

Spanhoe (Station 493): 1944–45; built as a bomber airfield with concrete runways, two T2 hangars (8254/*40*), a watch office (343/*43*), and tb and Nissen huts. It was used by USAAF Troop Carrier Command units flying C-47s and gliders, in both the D-Day and Rhine Bridges airborne operations.

Sywell: 1935–54; opened as a grass field in 1928 for club use and in 1935 as a RAF FTS run by Brooklands Aviation. In 1940, a CRU opened and Armstrong Whitworth established a factory assembling Lancaster bombers, which were flown off from the expanded field. The clubhouse of 1934 is still in use along with the adjacent pre-war hangars (one once serving as a gymnasium), behind which stand two side-opening aircraft sheds. Brooklands Aviation then added two large double-gabled sheds and a Bellman hangar (8349/*37*), before Armstrong Whitworth erected a pair of R-type MAP hangars. Finally, four extra over (12532/*41*) and thirteen standard blister hangars (12497/*41*) were built around the perimeter of the flying field. Most of the other buildings on site, such as the canteen, were constructed by local firms to one-off designs. The current watch office had been built by 1953, when the flying school closed.

Towcester: Pre-First World War landing ground used in annual manoeuvres.

Upper Stowe: Pre-First World War landing ground used in annual manoeuvres.

Wansford: First World War Landing Ground located near the later Kingscliffe airfield (TL028978).

Wicksteed Park: USAAF Quartermaster Company depot, 1942.

Second World War Anti-Invasion Defences

Pillboxes on Defended Searchlight Sites

Brigstock (SP949860)
Collyweston (TF019009)
East Carlton (SP824896)
Gretton (SP904953)
Little Oakley (SP897850)
Pipewell (SP840852)
Rothwell (SP821802)
Woodnewton (TL049951) (pillbox demolished)

Defended Airfields

Chelveston
Chipping Warden
Collyweston
Croughton
Grafton Underwood
Hinton-in-the-Hedges
Kingscliffe
Polebrook
Sywell

Roadblocks

DL = one of seventeen original inner roadblocks developed as defended locality.
NCC = roadblock constructed by county council early in the war.

Ashton TL048891

Barby SP541715

Boughton Crossing, Welford Road SP736652

Brafield on the Green SP819562

Chacombe SP471431 and 486437

Duston SP719613

Duston SP725623 one of original seventeen defending Northampton

Geddington, SP891826

Great Doddington, 216 recycled A/T cylinders reported at SP878636

Great Oxendon SP737823

Hardingstone SP781594 one of original seventeen, retained in 1941

Hardingstone SP761578

Irthlingborough SP952709 A/T cylinders reported beside road

Kelmarsh SP737792 and 746804

Lamport SP756745

Little Harrowden SP882720, 879720, 875719 A/T cylinders all *ex situ*

Long Buckby SP602665

Mears Ashby, Wood Lodge Farm, SP830681

Middleton Cheney SP483418

Moulton, Cross Street, Poplars Hotel, SP782662

Northampton, Welford Road, SP743639 'A' Coy 12 Bn abandoned 1941; one of seventeen

Northampton, Harborough Road, SP748644 'A' Coy 12 Bn abandoned 1941; one of seventeen

Northampton, Boughton Green Road, SP761644 'A' Coy 12 Bn until 1941; one of seventeen

Northampton, Kettering Road, SP777637 'A' Coy 12 Bn abandoned 1941; one of seventeen

Northampton, Weston Favell, SP786621 'A' Coy 12 Bn abandoned 1941; one of seventeen

Northampton, South Bridge Far Coton, SP754597 original then DL 'B' Coy 12 Bn.

Northampton, Billing Road, SP788611 12 Bn abandoned 1941; one of seventeen

Northampton, Wellingborough Road, Billing, SP801628

Northampton, Mereway Flyover, SP754581 12 Bn abandoned 1941; one of seventeen

Northampton, Towcester Road, SP742581 12 Bn abandoned 1941; one of seventeen

Northampton, Rothersthorpe Road, SP741590 12 Bn abandoned 1941; one of seventeen

Northampton, Malcolm Dr./Weedon Rd, SP736608 'D' Coy 12 Bn to 1941; one of seventeen

Northampton, Hopping Hill, SP725623 'D' Coy 12 Bn to 1941; one of seventeen

Northampton, Old Bants Lane Junction, SP735615 'D' Coy 12 Bn to 1941; one of seventeen

Northampton, Dallington, SP737619 'D' Coy 12 Bn to 1941; one of seventeen

Northampton, Kingsthorpe Rail Bridge, SP742626 'D' Coy 12 Bn to 1941; one of seventeen

Northampton, Buttocks Booth, SP783643, 784643, 783644, 783642, four roadblocks forming one of original seventeen; manned by 12 Bn until September 1941

Northampton, Kingsthorpe, Cock Hotel SP751633 DL, 'A' Coy 12 Bn

Northampton, West Bridge, SP746603 DL 'D' Coy 12 Bn from September 1941

Northampton, Spencer Bridge, SP747600 DL 'D' Coy 12 Bn from September 1941

Northampton, Abington Park, SP773618 unconfirmed DL

Northampton, St Peters Bridge SP781594 one of seventeen, designated DL 'C' Coy 12 Bn

Northampton, White Elephant/Kingsley Park Hotel SP765619 superseded Buttocks Booth roadblock, 'A' Coy 12 Bn

Oundle, TL048891 NCC
Pitsford, Springhill Farm SP750682 NCC
Pitsford, SP762669 AT rails and 2' diameter cylinders
Rockingham, SP866924 NCC
Rushton A6003 SP865812 NCC
Spratton Bridge, SP719682 NCC
Stoke Bruerne SP748491 NCC
Syresham SP652423 A43 NCC
Towcester, A5 SP688493 NCC
Upton Hall A45 SP716602 NCC
Warkton SP895791 and 891801 NCC
Warkworth SP478409 NCC
Weekley SP886808 and 887807, A43, NCC
Wellingborough, London Road, SP899666, NCC
(Wellingborough, SP895674, 127 A/T cylinders as revetment, Croyland Road)
(Wellingborough, SP890667, 183 A/T cylinders in Doddington Road corner of cemetery,
    opposite Kingsway & Royal Oak PH)
(Wellingborough, SP 890667 in cul-de-sac Abbotts Way, six A/T cylinders *ex situ*)
West Haddon, SP634716 A428, NCC
(Wollaston, up to 16 A/T cylinders *ex situ*)
Wootton/Hardingstone SP766572 B526 NCC
Wootton SP738573 north of bridge on old A43, NCC

Defensive Structures at Vulnerable Points

Brigstock Camp: Type DFW3/22 pillbox, one of originally three, SP935863
Daventry, Borough Hill: OP/guard post on BBC building
Great Addington: loopholes at SP95887504
Northampton, Mereway Flyover, SP754581, two loopholes in boundary wall
Northampton power station: two circular gun posts at SP765596 and 764597
Oundle, South Street: possible loopholes at TL043885
Oundle, Stoke Doyle Road: spigot mortar pedestal at TL03558811
Weedon COD: loopholed outbuildings, perimeter walls, pillboxes, etc.

Premises Used by
the Northamptonshire Home Guard

This list draws on information on Harrington Museum's list.
Aston le Walls, OP in church tower, SP497508
Badby House, HQ 10 Battalion, SP562611
Barby, OP in windmill, SP541695
Barnwell, range (Oundle Rifle & Pistol Club), Explosive & Inflammables Store
Billing Park, Pearces Factory, HQ 'A' Company, 11 Battalion
Blakesley, HQ 'A' Company, 13 Battalion
Blisworth, Caretaker's House at Bacon Factory, HQ 'B' Company, 13 Battalion
Bozeat, Bottrill & Sons, London Road, HQ 'D' Company, 8 Battalion
Brackley, 20 St Peter's Street, drill hall, HQ 14 Battalion
Brackley, 7 High Street, HQ 'B' Company, 14 Battalion
Braunston, OP in windmill, SP538662
Brixworth, RDC Offices, Spratton Road, HQ 9 Battalion
Brixworth, Harborough Road, Red Lion PH, alternative BHQ 9 Battalion
Bulwick, pair of Explosive & Inflammables Stores at SP963942
Burton Latimer, range at Croxen's Yard
Byfield, Church Institute, HQ 'D' Company, 10 Battalion
Chacombe, Chinner Farm, range for 14 Battalion
Chelveston Village Institute, drill space for 5 Platoon, 'A' Company, 8 Battalion
Cogenhoe, Church Street, Rectory, guardroom in coach house
Cogenhoe, OP in windmill SP822606 (demolished)
Corby Steelworks, HQs 6 Battalion and 'C' Company, 6 Battalion
Corby, Gretton Brook, HQ 'A' Company, 6 Battalion
Cosgrove, OP in church tower
Cottingham School, local HQ
Daventry, Borough Hill, BBC Company, 10 Battalion, SP588621
Daventry, Wheatsheaf Hotel, HQ 'B' Company, 10 Battalion, SP571623
Deanshanger, OP in water tower
Denton Vicarage, HQ No. 15 Platoon, 'D' Company, 11 Battalion
Desborough, Rushton Road, HQ 5 Battalion

Duston, Church Schools, HQ 'C' Company, 11 Battalion
Earls Barton, Fox & Hounds PH, HQ 'C' Company, 8 Battalion
Ecton Hall Old Riding School, indoor range No. 6 Platoon, 'C' Company, 8 Battalion
Everdon Rectory, BHQ No. 2 Sector (10, 13, and 14 Battalions) from 1943
Eydon, Wayside, HQ 'D' Company, 14 Battalion.
Farthingstone, live firing range, SP618565
Fawsley Wood, firing range with butts
Finedon, Round House, firing range for 7 Battalion's spigot mortars and Smith guns
Great Brington, training camp on Gawburrow Hill
Gretton School used by 6 Battalion
Guilsborough, Ward Arms barn, HQ 'A' Company, 9 Battalion
Harrowden Hall, used for camps by 'G' Company, 7 Battalion
Hardingstone Generating Station, 'A' Company, 15 Battalion made up of employees of the Northampton Electric Light and Power Company
Hardingstone House, HQ 'E' & HQ Companies, 11 Battalion
Harlestone, Old Chapel HQ 'C' Company, 9 Battalion
Harlestone, two compartment Explosive & Inflammables Store, SP701639
Higham Ferrers Town Hall, HQ 'F' Company, 8 Battalion
Irthlingborough, SA Hall, 7 Battalion
Kelmarsh, firing range for 2-inch mortars, SP739796
Kettering, 17 The Grove HQ (3) 5 Battalion (from 75 London Road)
Kettering, The Brickyard, London Road, HQ 'D' Company, 4 Battalion
Kettering, 75 London Road, HQ (2) 5 Battalion (from Rushton Road, Desborough)
Kettering, Lower Street, Tannery, weapons store in shed
Kettering, LMS Railway Station, HQ 'G' Company, 4 Battalion
Kettering, The Rectory, HQ 4 Battalion and HQ Company
Kettering, Royal Hotel, HQ 'E' Company, 4 Battalion
Kettering, Avenue House, Rockingham Road, HQ 'B' Company, 4 Battalion
Kettering, Stamford Road, HQ 'C' Company, 4 Battalion
Kettering, Millers Dance Academy, Trafalgar Road, HQ 'A' Company, 4 Battalion
Kilsby, George Hotel, HQ 'A' Company, 10 Battalion
King's Sutton, Astrop Hill Farm, HQ 'C' Company, 14 Battalion
Kislingbury, The Schools, HQ 'F' Company, 11 Battalion
Little Brington Saracens Head PH, 3 Platoon, 'C' Company, 9 Battalion, SP660637
Long Buckby, Church School, HQ 'C' Company, 10 Battalion
Long Buckby, Admiral Rodney PH clubroom used by 10 Battalion
Moulton, Spendlove's Cottage, HQ 'D' Company, 9 Battalion
Moulton, Artichoke Inn PH, used for training by 9 Battalion
Newnham, Romer Arms PH, HQ 'E' Company, 10 Battalion
Northampton, 127 Great Russell Street, HQ 12 Battalion despatch riders
Northampton, 10 Hunter Street, HQ (2) 12 Battalion despatch riders
Northampton, 21 Abington Grove, HQ 'A' Company, 12 Battalion
Northampton, 34 The Broadway, No. 1 Platoon, 'A' Company, 12 Battalion
Northampton, Advance Motor Works, HQ 2 Platoon, 'A' Company, 12 Battalion
Northampton, Bridge Street, Warwick Arms, HQ 'B' Company, 12 Battalion
Northampton, 60 Bridge Street, HQ 5 Platoon, 'B' Company, 12 Battalion

Northampton, West Street, Flower in the Hand PH, HQ 6 Platoon, 'B' Company, 12
    Battalion
Northampton, Station House, Cotton End, HQ 7 Platoon, 'C' Company, 12 Battalion
Northampton, 63 King Edward Road, HQ 'C' Company, 12 Battalion
Northampton, Bushland Road School, HQ 10 Platoon, 'C' Company, 12 Battalion
Northampton, Clarke Road, Brooke Factory, HQ 11 Platoon, 'D' Company 12
    Battalion
Northampton, Billing Road, Town & Country School, HQ 12 Platoon, 'D' Company,
    12 Battalion
Northampton, 111Adnitt Road, HQ 13 Platoon, 'D' Company, 12 Battalion
Northampton, The Rosery, Kingsthorpe, HQ 'D' Company, 12 Battalion
Northampton, 2 Upper Mounts, HQ 19 Platoon, 'F' Company, 12 Battalion
Northampton, 23 Hunter Street, HQ 20 Platoon, 'F' Company, 12 Battalion
Northampton, Craven Street, Working Men's Club, HQ 21 Platoon, 'F' Company, 12
    Battalion
Northampton, Victoria Road Schools, HQ 22 Platoon, 'G' Company, 12 Battalion.
Northampton, 45 Kingsthorpe Road, HQ 23, 24 & 25 Platoons, 'G' Company, 12
    Battalion
Northampton, 15 Kingsthorpe Grove, HQ 'H' Company, 12 Battalion
Northampton, 43 Kingsthorpe Road, HQ 26 Platoon, 'H' Company, 12 Battalion
Northampton, Oliver Street, HQ 27 Platoon, 'H' Company, 12 Battalion
Northampton, 61 Kingsthorpe Road, HQ 28 Platoon, 'H' Company, 12 Battalion
Northampton, Houghton Road, United Counties Depot, HQ 'B' Company, MT
    Regiment
Northampton, Derngate, Milton Chambers, HQ 11 Battalion
Northampton, Black Lion Hill, Brewery House, HQ 15 Battalion
Northampton, Abbey Works, Express Lifts Co. HQ Company 15 Battalion
Northampton, 74 Harlestone Road, HQ 'B' Company, 15 Battalion
Northampton, St Andrews Street, HQ 'C' Company, 15 Battalion
Northampton, The Mounts, Campbell Square police station, Keep; Gibraltar Barracks
    Keep; and Clare Road drill hall Keep; were all manned by 'F' Company, 12 Battalion,
    whose HQ was in the Lord Raglan PH.
Northampton, St George's Avenue, Duncan House, HQ of the original LDV
Norton, Manor Farm, local Home Guard base
Old Stratford, OP in Davenports Brewery tower
Oundle, Benefield Road drill hall: HQ 3 Battalion and 'F' Company, 3 Battalion
Oundle, Benefield Road drill hall: pair of Explosive & Inflammables Stores
Oundle School: HQ 'E' Company, 3 Battalion
Overstone Park, training camp, SP816659
Potterspury, OP in church tower
Quinton, Old Rectory, 11 Battalion company HQ,
Raunds, Parish Rooms, Temperance Hall and Golden Fleece PH, used by 'A' Company,
    8 Battalion
Raunds, CofE Infants School, HQ 'A' Company, 8 Battalion
Roade, Yew Tree Cottage (Pearces Factory), HQ 'B' Company, 11 Battalion
Rushden, HQ 8 Battalion

Rushden, Lovells Factory, HQ 'B' Company, 8 Battalion
Rushden, Swindalls, Station Road, HQ 'E' Company, 8 Battalion
Silverstone OP in windmill used by 13 Battalion, SP674444
Spratton Manor House, used by 9 Battalion
Stoke Bruerne Rectory, rooms used by 13 Battalion
Syresham, The Grove HQ 'D' Company, 14 Battalion
Sywell Aerodrome, HQ 'E' Company, 9 Battalion
Sywell, 600-yard rifle range
Thenford House, HQ 'A' Company, 14 Battalion
Tiffield Old Brickworks used as firing range by 13 Battalion
Towcester, High Street, Territorial Club, HQ 13 Battalion
Towcester, High Street, Pomfret Hotel, HQ 'C' Company, 13 Battalion
Towcester, Dunkley's House, HQ (2), 13 Battalion
Wadenhoe, Kings Head PH, used by 3 Battalion
Wellingborough, Old Drill Hall, HQ 'B' Company, 7 Battalion
Wellingborough, Elm Street, Church Room HQ 'A' Company, 7 Battalion
Wellingborough, 10 (with 7a as Reserve HQ) Eastfield Road, HQ 'E' Company, 7 Battalion
Wellingborough School, HQ 7 Battalion
Wellingborough, Castle Street, Evington House, Administrative HQ 7 Battalion
Wellingborough, Police Station, Battle HQ, 7 Battalion
Wellingborough, Regal Cinema basement, Battle HQ, 7 Battalion
Wellingborough, Dulley's Brewery, BHQ 7 Battalion, destroyed by bombs
Wellingborough, Church Street, Priory, BHQ 7 Battalion, 1944
Wellingborough, 34 Market Street, No. 3 Sector HQ (7, 8, and 11 Battalions.)
Wellingborough Station: two railway coaches for 'E' Company, 7 Battalion
Wellingborough, Sun Inn PH, HQ of Keep manned by 'B' Company, 7 Battalion
West Haddon, The Crown PH, used by 10 Battalion
Whiston, The Firs, rifle range used by 'D' Company, 11 Battalion
Whiston House (former rectory), used by 'D' Company, 11 Battalion
Wollaston, Baptist Schoolroom HQ 'G' Company, 8 Battalion
Woodford Halse: firing range for Fawsley Hall
Yardley Gobion, OP in water tower
Yardley Hastings, The Castle & Memorial Hall, HQ 'D' Company, 11 Battalion

Appendix X

Air Defence

Anti-Aircraft Defences: First World War

Warkworth Filling Factory: Overthorpe Lodge (SP484410) and Bodicote, AA batteries, each with a single 18-pounder gun.

Shire Lodge, Corby: AA battery with two 6-pounder Nordenfeldt AA guns, with searchlight site close by.

Anti-Aircraft Defences: Second World War

AA & S/L Sites
Abthorpe, SP646464, S/L site
Althorp, SP693650, S/L site
Barby, SP523709, S/L site, 425 Bty 58 S/L Regiment
Boughton, Northampton, SP747652, S/L site
Bozeat, Dungee Barn, SP926601, S/L site
Braunston, SP548651, S/L site, 425 Bty 58 S/L Regiment
Brigstock, SP949860, S/L site and pillbox 362 Bty 41 S/L Regiment
Brixworth, SP772706, AA and S/L site
Brixworth, SP777705 S/L site, 467 Bty 73 S/L Regiment
Brockhall, SP628614, S/L site
Broughton SP838752 and 835762, AA/S/L and S/L sites, 362 Bty 41 S/L Regiment
Burton Latimer, SP895755, S/L site, 362 Bty 41 S/L Regiment
Chacombe, SP467433, AA Bty 'H1' Hanwell, Banbury
Churchover, SP527807, S/L site
Clay Coton, SP596776, AA site
Clipston, SP703832, S/L site
Cold Ashby, SP649753, S/L site, 425 Bty 58 S/L Regiment
Collingtree SP748555, S/L site
Collyweston, TF019009, S/L site and pillbox, 362 Bty 41 S/L Regiment
Corby, HAA batteries: *see* Rockingham and Weldon

Corby, LAA sites defending steel works at SP879905, 870906, 896886, 901896

Cosgrove, SP796419, possible AA battery

Cottesbrooke, SP694748, S/L site, 425 Bty 58 S/L Regiment

Crick SP568740, LAA site protecting radio station

Daventry, SP564636, 'C' Bty with four 3-inch HAA guns in 1940

Daventry, Newnham Grounds, SP591602, Bty of four 3-inch HAA guns in 1940

Daventry, Newnham Lodge, SP603601, S/L site, 344 Bty, 58 S/L Regiment

Deenethorpe, SP977915, S/L site, 362 Bty 41 S/L Regiment

Denford, TL000762, AA site

Dob Hall, SP 790849, S/L site, 362 Bty 41 S/L Regiment

Dodford near Weedon Bec, SP625616, S/L site

Duston, SP715616, S/L site, 467 Bty 73 S/L Regiment

East Carlton, SP824896, S/L site and pillbox, 362 Bty 41 S/L Regiment

Farthingstone, SP594555, S/L site

Faxton, SP795753, S/L site

Finedon, SP920712, S/L site

Gayton SP694459, S/L site, 467 Bty 73 S/L Regiment

Grafton Underwood, SP919798, S/L site, 362 Bty 41 S/L Regiment

Great Billing, SP809631, S/L site

Great Oxendon, SP734855, S/L site, 426 Bty 58 S/L Regiment

Greatworth, S/L site

Grendon, Clay Hills, SP870612, S/L site, 467 Bty 73 S/L Regiment

Gretton, SP904953, S/L site and pillbox, 362 Bty 41 S/L Regiment

Hackleton, SP800556, S/L site, 467 Bty 73 S/L Regiment

Harlestone (Althorp), SP693651, site identified by AP as 467 Bty 73 S/L Regiment

Harrington, SP770796, S/L site, 425 Bty 58 S/L Regiment

Irchester, SP924661, AA Battery

Kelmarsh/Clipston Grange, SP715796, S/L site

Kelmarsh/Grasslands Farm, SP718802, S/L site, 425 Bty 58 S/L Regiment

Kettering, SP878803, AA & S/L site

Kilsby, SP576704, S/L site, 425 Bty 58 S/L Regiment

Kingscliffe, TL000967, S/L site, 362 Bty 41 S/L Regiment

Lamport, SP749757, S/L site, 425 Bty 58 S/L Regiment

Laxton, SP951960, S/L site, 362 Bty 41 S/L Regiment

Lilbourne, SP559774, S/L site, 425 Bty 58 S/L Regiment

Little Oakley, SP897850, S/L site and pillbox

Marston Trussell, SP695851, S/L site

Mears Ashby, SP844656, S/L site

Newnham, SP573601, S/L site

Northampton Town & Country School, SP775603, S/L site

Northampton, Old Racecourse, SP760616, S/L site

Northampton, SP747630, S/L site

Northampton, Park Avenue South, SP776609, S/L site, 467 Bty 73 S/L Regiment

Old Lodge, SP796753, S/L site, 425 Bty 58 S/L Regiment

Old Stratford, Windmill Field, SP779402, AA battery

Overstone, SP799656, S/L site

Oxendon Farm, SP738853, S/L site
Passenham, SP779402, AA Battery
Piddington, Hackleton, Hill Farm, SP801557, S/L site
Pipewell, SP840852, S/L site and pillbox
Pipewell, SP840845, S/L site, 362 Bty 41 S/L Regiment.
Preston Capes, Preston Fields Farm, SP556546, S/L site
Ravensthorpe, SP662695 and/or 672703, S/L site(s), 425 Bty 58 S/L Regiment
Roade, Ashton Lodge Farm, SP772510, S/L site
Rockingham, SP882912, Corby 'H2' HAA Bty, four 3.7-inch and GL Mk II Radar,
    517(Mixed) Bty 136 HAA Regiment (RA)
Rockingham, SP872909, S/L site, 362 Bty 41 S/L Regiment
Rothwell, SP821802, S/L site and pillbox, 362 Bty 41 S/L Regiment
Rothwell, SP816803, S/L site
Spratton, SP726703, S/L site, 467 Bty 73 S/L Regiment
Sulby, SP667802, S/L site, 425 Bty 58 S/L Regiment
Sulgrave, SP552452, S/L site
Sutton Bassett, SP773898, S/L site, 362 Bty 41 S/L Regiment
Sywell, SP819698, S/L site, 467 Bty 73 S/L Regiment
Thorpe Malsor, SP825800, S/L site
Thrapston, SP013782, LAA Bty
Thrupps Ground, SP594649, S/L site, 425 Bty 58 S/L Regiment
Titchmarsh, TL017806, AA & S/L Bty in Town End field
Upper Heyford, SP680596, S/L site
Wadenhoe, TL007840, AA & S/L site
Watford, SP615701, S/L site, 425 Bty 58 S/L Regiment.
Weekley, cSP882803, S/L site, 362 Bty 41 S/L Regiment
Weldon, SP898851, S/L site, 362 Bty 41 S/L Regiment.
Weldon, Oundle Road, Caravan Park, SP933891, Corby 'H1' HAA Bty, four 3.7-inch
    and GL Mk II Radar, 517 (Mixed) Bty 136 HAA Regiment (RA)
Welford, Downton Hill, SP624806, AA Battery and SP623804, S/L site
Wellingborough, Grange Farm, SP865694, S/L site, 467 Bty 73 S/L Regiment
Wellingborough, SP897673, AA Battery
Wellingborough, Mill Farm, SP892660, S/L site, 467 Bty 73 S/L Regiment
Westfield House, SP737742, S/L site
Whilton, SP636749, S/L site
Woodnewton, TL049951, S/L site and pillbox (demolished)
Yardley Hastings, Potters Clay, S/L site, 467 Bty 73 S/L Regiment
Yardley Hastings, SP857553, AA & S/L site
Yelvertoft, SP605752, S/L site, 425 Bty 58 S/L Regiment
Total of 103 sites (reference: List of 32 AA Brigade sites, TNA: WO166/7389, 1942)

Bombing Decoys for Northamptonshire Targets
KEY:
FL: factory lights
LG: locomotive glows
MY: marshalling yards

K: daytime airfield decoy
QL: night decoy with lights
QF: night decoy with fires
SF (Special Fires) or 'Starfish': decoy simulating urban area under attack

Alwalton (Cambridgeshire), K then Q for RAF Kingscliffe (and Wittering) (TL152949)
Little Gidding (Cambridgehire), Q for RAF Polebrook (TL116817)
Swineshead (Bedfordshire), QL for RAF Chelveston, (TL062635)
Warmington, QL for RAF Kingscliffe (TL080919)
Preston Capes, for Weedon, 1941–2, QF, 'A' Army Series (SP585559)
Cranford, for Kettering, 'C' Series Civil QL/QF, 1942–3; MY/FL for Kettering railway station; (SP914784)
Woodford, for Kettering, 'C' Series Civil, QL, 1942–3; MY/FL/LG for Islip factory; (SP962761)
Stanion, for Corby, 'C' Series Civil, QL/QF, 1942–3; MY/FL/LG for Stewart & Lloyd steel works; (SP911854)
Barby, for Rugby, 'C' Series Civil QL, then SF, 1942–3; (SP536712)
Claycoton, for Rugby, SF, 1941–3; (SP600783)
Knotting, for Wellingborough, 'C' Series Civil, QL 1942–3; MY/LG for marshalling yards; (SP990633)
Kislingbury, for Northampton, SF, 1941–3; (SP708586)
Hardingstone, for Northampton, SF, 1941–3; (SP802581)

ROC Posts
Note: posts in *italics* destroyed
Benefield, Deenethorpe airfield: SP960899, 1955 u/g
Blakesley windmill: SP623504, 1938, closed 1968
Brackley: SP584374, 1938, u/g; in use 1968
Brixworth: SP755709, 1938, u/g 1960, in use 1968
Chipping Warden: SP491481, 1939, 1943; resited 1960 u/g to SP505519
Clipston: SP703826, 1938, u/g 1959, in use 1968
Cogenhoe: SP822606, 1938; resited 1953 to Denton airfield SP817577, closed 1968
Corby: SP932906, 1938, closed 1968
Crick: SP579713, 1938 (between railway & M1), closed 1968
Daventry: SP577608, 1938, Newnham Hill, to Borough Hill SP587626, closed 1968
Duddington: SK991007, 1949, u/g 1961
Duston: SP717615, 1954, resited u/g 1962 to SP713604
Earls Barton: SP870648, 1953, u/g 1960
East Carlton: SP835887, 1949, u/g 1964, closed 1968
East Haddon: SP672678, 1938, resited SP671676, 1953, closed 1968
Kettering, Weekley, Glebe Road, SP874804, 1938, closed 1968
Oundle: TL037888, 1949, resited to TL033906, 1961, u/g 1964, closed 1968
Raunds: SP988746, 1938, u/g 1961, in use 1968
Roade: SP749518, 1938, closed 1968
Sutton Bassett: SP777907, 1938, u/g 1959, in use 1968
Wellingborough: SP879677, 1938, resited 1953 to SP869649 *Earls Barton*

Appendix XI

The Secret War, Intelligence, and Communications

Pre-1939

Daventry, BBC Transmitting Station, 1925, 1932, and 1935
Litchborough, memorial (2001) recording 1935 radar experiment

Second World War

Brockhall Manor: STS 1, one of six SOE depot schools, 1940–44; then NORSOG & OSS; Force 12 (enemy aliens), 1942
Daventry, Borough Hill: BBC transmitter
Finedon Hall: assembly point for SOE agents and Jedburgh teams, 1944
Greatworth signals station, Leighton Buzzard satellite, used by Bletchley (SP554433)
Grendon Hall SOE Free French section & FFI; OSS Country Area 'O', 1944–5
RAF Harrington: USAAF 'Carpetbaggers' base
Northampton, Cliftonville, Sunnyside House, SOE/OSS holding house for agents
Staverton, Radio Relay Station, 1940 (SP549610); earlier buildings accommodated staff of RAF Daventry, GEE Station on Borough Hill
Overthorpe Hall: FANY training centre

Post Second World War

Charwelton, 'Backbone' microwave terminal tower (SP513563)
Crick, Rugby Radio Station, main block 1955, aerials/masts spread into Warwickshire
Daventry, Borough Hill, BBC transmitter until 1992
Dodford, radio mast (SP608620)
Greatworth, RAF signals station (SP554433)
Honey Hill, radio mast (SP640768)
Potcote, Home Office 'Hilltop' radio station (SP664525)
Staverton, RAF & USAF Radio Relay Station (SP549610)
Thenford Hill, radio mast (SP523443)

Military Hospitals and Welfare

First World War Hospitals

Barnwell Manor Auxiliary Hospital
Blakesley Hall, Auxiliary Hospital 1914–18 (demolished)
Brackley Auxiliary Hospital
Church Brampton, Golf Club: Auxiliary Hospital
Cottesbrooke Hall: hospital and convalescent home, 1914–18
Dallington Hall War Hospital
Daventry, 36 High Street: hospital and convalescent home
Duncote Hall, Towcester: Auxiliary Hospital
East Haddon Hall and Institute: Auxiliary Hospitals
Everdon Hall: Auxiliary Hospital
Eydon Hall, Byfield: Auxiliary Hospital
Guilsborough Hall, Church Mount: Auxiliary Hospital
Higham Ferrers, Midland Road: Auxiliary Hospital, now library
Kettering General Hospital, Rothwell Road: ward for discharged soldiers, 1918
Kettering, London Road VAD Auxiliary Hospital
Kettering Sanatorium converted to war hospital from 1914–18
Lois Weedon: Auxiliary Hospital for Officers
Northampton Asylum, Billing Road: opened 1838, renamed St Andrew's Hospital 1887, military hospital
Northampton, Abington Avenue: former asylum, closed 1892, converted to military hospital, now museum
Northampton, Abington Avenue: Weston Favell Hospital, 1914–18
Northampton, Addison Villas: Auxiliary Hospital
Northampton, Berrywood: Northamptonshire County Asylum, built 1873–6, became Duston War Hospital in 1916; (until 1995, St Crispin's Hospital, Duston)
Northampton, Barry Road: town swimming-pool converted as auxiliary hospital
Northampton, Barry Road elementary school requisitioned as war hospital, 1916
Northampton, Billing Road: Northampton General Infirmary of 1793, in use 1914–18

Northampton, Castile House: Auxiliary Hospital
Northampton, King Street Emergency Hospital (St John's Ambulance HQ)
Northampton, Welford Road Hospital
Rushton Hall: hospital and convalescent home, 1915–18
Spratton, Broomhill: hospital and convalescent home
Staverton Isolation Hospital (SP549610)
Sulby Hall Auxiliary Hospital (demolished)
Thornby Grange, auxiliary military convalescent hospital
Thrapston, Corn Exchange: Red Cross hospital, 1914
Towcester Auxiliary Hospital
Wellingborough Auxiliary Hospital
Yardley Gobion Workhouse: auxiliary military convalescent hospital

Second World War Hospitals

Ashton Wold, Oundle: Red Cross hospital
Chacombe House (SP490436): Red Cross Convalescent Home/Auxiliary Hospital
Cottesbrooke Hall: Red Cross Convalescent Home/Auxiliary Hospital
Dingley Hall nursing home
Easton Neston House, convalescent hospital
Gretton House, High Street, Gretton: military hospital
Irchester, Knuston Hall: temporary hospital in grounds
Lilford Hall: US 16th Station Hospital, hutted hospital; nurses quarters in Lilford Hall; 303rd USAAF Station Hospital in park; railway siding at Barnwell for Nos 21, 43, and 45 Hospital Trains
Kettering General Hospital, Rothwell Road
Kettering, Rockingham Road: Smallpox Hospital
Northampton, Colwyn Road: St John Ambulance Brigade convalescent home
Northampton, Thornby Grange: Red Cross Convalescent Home/Auxiliary Hospital
Spratton, Broomhill: Red Cross Convalescent Home/Auxiliary Hospital
Whilton Lodge: nurses' residential training school

Second World War Hospitality and Welfare

Kettering, Carey Baptist Church: venue for Anglo-German Fellowship for POWs from Weekley Camp
Kettering, Corn Market Hall: WVS soldiers' recreation room and canteen
Northampton, Bridge Street, Plough Hotel, US Rest & Recreation centre
Northampton, County Hall: WVS clothing distribution centre
Northampton, Market Square, American Club
Oundle, Victoria Hall, service personnel social club
Polebrook airfield: Red Cross Depot

Munitions Production

First World War

Kettering: Allen & Caswell, boots for British, Italian, and Russian forces
Northampton, Bridge Street: Mulliners, military vehicles
Raunds: sixteen footwear factories with military contracts
Rushden: Cave & Son, boots
Warkworth (NFF No. 9 Banbury): shell-filling with lyddite, TNT, and gas

Second World War

Aircraft Production

Burton Latimer, Polwell Lane, A. E. Smith: MAP 'R'-type hangar for Wellington wings and ailerons
Daventry, Westbourne Engineering: Mosquito parts
Desborough, United Counties Bus Garage: Wellington fuel and oil tanks
Earls Barton, Abbott's & Abram's Garages: Wellington parts and servicing
Kettering, Carrington Street, A. E. Smith: Wellington wings and ailerons; also at Macrae's Garage in Rockingham Road
Kettering, Northampton Road and Victoria Street, Blanchflower's: Wellington tail units, flaps and cowlings
Kettering, Tresham Street, Thompson's Garage: Wellington parts
Northampton, Manfields and Cantilever Shoe Co.: Lancaster electrical wiring for supply to Ludlow Bros
Moulton, Northampton Road, Smith's Garage: Wellington parts
Northampton, Ardington Road, Co-operative Boot Factory: Wellington parts
Northampton, Bedford Road, Frecknall, Barnard & Scott: Lancaster parts
Northampton, Buttocks Booth, Vickers aircraft factory: Wellington fuselage and wing section repairs
Northampton, Far Cotton, Airflow Streamlines: Lancaster engine-cowlings

Northampton, Great Billing, W. Pearce & Co: Lancaster instrument panels
Northampton, Harlestone Road, Express Lifts: Wellington instrument panels
Northampton, Kettering Road, Butcher's Garage, and Corona Works, Ennerdale Road:
    Wellington wing section repairs;
Northampton, Kingsthorpe Hollow, Barratts: Lancaster parts
Northampton, St James, Corporation Bus Depot: Lancaster fuselage assembly
Northampton, St James, R. Whitton: Lancaster parts
Rushden, Bignells: propeller spinners
Sywell aerodrome, AWA and Vickers aircraft factory: Lancasters, Wellingtons
Wellingborough, Almarco: Mosquito engine bearers

Weaponry
Kettering, Catesby Road: Timson, Bullock, Barber Ltd (back-sight beds for rifles)
Kettering, Job Lee, Premier Engineering (parts for rifles)
Northampton, Hanwell Engineering Co. (parts for rifles)
Northampton, Harlestone Road, Express Lifts: 7.2-inch shells and parts for Oerlikon
    LAA guns
Rushden, Standard Rotary Machine Co. Ltd (magazine catches for rifles)

Other Manufacturers
Corby, Stewart & Lloyd, steel plant: piping for Pluto, 1942–4
Cottingham and Kettering, Wallis & Linnell: made 200,000 garments, many of them for
    the women's services: ATS, WAAF, etc.
Duston, British Timken shadow factory: roller bearings, 1941
Kettering/Burton Latimer & Corby: Kaycee made 500,000 garments for British and
    Allied military
Northampton, Haynes & Cann: 'escape' flying-boots convertible to civilian shoes
Northampton: ROF explosives factory; FF No. 20 planned but not built
Northampton, Wareings: military clothing

Depots

Munitions Storage and Distribution Depots in the Second World War

Aynho Park: fuel storage in the park, from 1940

Barby: MoS food depot taken over 1945 by RAOC Weedon (SP516703)

Barnwell: from 1939, AM Works Depot served by railway sidings

Barnwell: from 1939, RAOC Depot (TL043856)

Boughton Crossing: MoS double-shed food depot (SP736652)

Braybrooke: RAF 223MU, then AAF-521 for USAAF; Loatland Wood (SP777825) stored SAA, pyrotechnics; sleeping and communal sites (SP792835)

Broughton: RAF 209MU Equipment Park for supplying overseas units (USAAF)

Castle Ashby: No. 21 Vehicle Replacement Depot (SP861587); temporary storage of ammunition in Nissen huts at Parkhill Farm (SP869592)

Denton/Yardley Chase, from 1942, explosives storage in moated sheds served by rail-sidings; currently training area for adjacent ACF Cadet Centre

Easton Neston: Towcester Racecourse buildings used for military map storage

Great Billing; roadside ammunition storage in Nissen-type shelters

Irchester, Knuston Hall: transport depot for British and Canadian forces, 1940

Isham/Little Harrowden: ammunition storage facility (SP876727)

Kelmarsh: Air Force (Fuel) Distribution Depot (AFDD) supplied by rail and distributed by road tanker (SP747804)

Kettering, Wicksteed Park: Q-101 US Army QM Depot

Kettering: Allen & Caswell's footwear factory taken over as a depot by US forces

Kettering, Stamford Road, and RAF Grafton Underwood: RAF 236MU Mechanical Transport Reception, Servicing Unit and vehicle store, 1941

Kettering: RAF 263MU supply of fuel in jerry-cans; MT Disposal

Knuston Hall: British & Canadian military transport depot

New Duston, Harlestone Road: standard MoS triple-shed, 1941–6, for sugar storage

RAF Polebrook: RAF 273MU, long-term aircraft storage from 1945

Roade, Salcey Forest: RAF 72MU Ground Equipment Depot, in thirty-two large sheds; then disposal depot

Rushden, Harborough Road: RAF 204MU Equipment Park, issue of airborne stores for overseas units (USAAF)
Rushden: Ordnance Depot, 25th Ordnance Bomb Disposal Squadron USAAF
RAF Spanhoe: RAF 253MU, MT disposal, from 1945
Weedon Bec: COD with six out-stations: RAOC Sub-Depots or Relief Depots serving as overflow for Weedon COD, receiving and storing weapons at the end of the war, including Franklins Gardens, the Old Midland railway station, Martin's Brickyard all in Northampton; Heyford and Long Buckby brickyards; and Barby (Onley)
Whittlewood: temporary ammunition storage for RAF and USAAF
RAOC Home Industries Scheme Small Stores for collection and onward distribution
Crick, Blisworth, Daventry, Heyford, Little Houghton, Kettering, Rothwell, Thornby, Towcester, Watford, West Haddon

Women's Land Army Hostels

Desborough
Greens Norton, Towcester Road: WLA Hostel, POW camp, YHA (SP672501)
Naseby: WLA hostel became village hall; now demolished (SP688783)
Southwick
Titchmarsh: buildings in Church Field housed WLA
Woodford Halse, Byfield Road: sometime Hawkins Shoe Factory (demolished)
Yelvertoft, Clay Coton Road: village hall former WLA hostel (SP594758)

Cold War Munitions Storage and Distribution Depots

Desborough Airfield: Home Office Supply and Transport Stores
Kelmarsh, Harlestone Road: Air Force Distribution Depot (AFDD) (SP747804)
New Duston, Northampton: MAFF Depot 336N Sugar Store (SP715630)
Weedon Depot: Home Office Supply and Transport Stores

Appendix XV

POW Camps

Note: Average number of POWs held indicated in brackets

First World War

Boughton Park Internment Camp for Austrian & German POWs on site of C18 landscape feature
Brackley (forty)
Brixworth, Kennel Terrace, The Grange (forty)
Corby, Gretton
Creaton, Hollowell Grange (thirty-four)
Eastcote, Eastcote House (SP680541); 6 Birdshill Road (SP680540) camp hospital; (3,500 by 12 November 1918)
Easton on the Hill (515)
Gayton
Glendon, Glendon Hill Farm tented camp for ironstone workings (148)
Guilsborough Grammar School (seventy-six)
Oundle (over thirty)
Rothwell, Bunkers Hill Road camp for ironstone quarry workers (214)
Rushden House, Stables (eighty-five)
Upton Vicarage (fifty-five)
Winwick (thirty)
Yardley Gobion (forty)

Second World War

Barby, Hostel, Ware Road, village hall then demolished, (SP545706)
Boughton Park, POW Camp No. 35 for German working parties
Boughton House, New Ground Spinney, Camp No. 259 from August 1945–1948 for 300 German POWs

Byfield, Boddington Road, Camp Nos 87/151 (SP502534)
Daventry, huts of former HAA battery became German POW camp
Daventry, Braunston Road, POW camp
Denford, between Briggs Lodge and Denford village, camp for German farmworkers
Fineshade Abbey, POW camp, house damaged and demolished, 1956
Green's Norton, Towcester Road WLA Hostel became POW camp (SP672501)
Grendon, Lakeside Farm, camp until 1946 (SP874604)
Harrington USAAF communal site north of A14 became POW Camp No. 49
Haselbech Hall, camp east of Hall
Kettering, Weekley Glebe Road, POW camp
Kingscliffe airfield, Camp No. 702 from February 1946 until July 1947
Lamport (SP761747), hutted camp for Italian POWs
Litchborough: WI Room & Baptist schoolroom, after army vacated
Little Addington: Italian POW Camp No. 98 (SP961732)
Long Buckby, Station Road, German POW camp
Potterspury, Wakefield, Italian POW camp
Sulby Hall
Weedon Bec Camp No. 1010
Wollaston, Italian POW camp
Yelvertoft, Clay Coton Road, village hall, WLA hostel, POW Camp (SP594758)

Bibliography

Aberg, F., *Medieval Moated Sites* (York: CBA Research Report 17, 1978)

After the Battle, *PLUTO: Pipeline Under The Ocean* (Stratford: After the Battle 116, 2002)

Allcroft, A. H., *Earthwork of England* (London: Macmillan, 1908)

Allison, K., Beresford, M., and Hurst, J., *The Deserted Villages of Northamptonshire* (Leicester: Leicester University Press, 1966)

Arden, D., *A Bloody Elopement: the Daltons of Apethorpe and the Battle of Beams* (Northampton: Northamptonshire Past and Present 63, 2010)

Audouy, M., *Excavations at Berry Hill Close, Culworth in 1992* (Northampton: Northamptonshire Archaeology 25, 1993-4)

Bailey, B., Pevsner, N., and Cherry, B., *Northamptonshire* (Newhaven: Yale, 2013)

Belgion, H., *Titchmarsh Past and Present* (Titchmarsh: author, 1979)

Binder, J., *Life in a Northamptonshire market town during the Great War 1914–18; the diary of John Coleman Binder* (Oundle: Oundle Museum Trust, 2013)

Blades, B., *Roll of Honour* (Barnsley: Pen & Sword, 2015)

Bletsoe-Brown, M., *Sywell Aerodrome: the story of how they built the first concrete runway for 50 years* in Airfield Review 125 (Hoxne: ARG, 2009)

Bowyer, M., *Action Stations 6: Cotswolds & Central Midlands* (Wellingborough: Patrick Stevens, 1983)

Brown, A., *Higham Ferrers Castle Or Otherwise* (Northampton: Northamptonshire Past and Present V.2, 1974–5)

Brown, A., (ed.), *Roman Small Towns in Eastern England and Beyond* (Oxford: Oxbow, 1995)

Brown, A., and Alexander, J., *Excavations at Towcester 1954: the Grammar School site* (Northampton: Northamptonshire Archaeology 17, 1982)

Brown, J., and Soden, I., *Bury Mount A Norman Motte and Bailey Castle at Towcester* (Northampton: Northamptonshire Archaeology 35, 2010)

Brown, R. A., Colvin, H. M., and Taylor, A. J., *The History of the King's Works, Volumes 1 & 2: The Middle Ages* (London: HMSO, 1963)

Burley, P., *The Battlefield at Northampton* in Rotherham, I., and Handley, C. (eds.) *War and Peat* (Sheffield: Wildtrack, 2013)

Cadman, G., *Northamptonshire Bombing Decoys* (Northampton: Northamptonshire Archaeology 28, 1998–99)

Castle Studies Trust, *Visit to Fotheringhay, 17.3.2018* (Northampton: MOLA, 2018)

Chapman, A., *Excavation of the Town Defences at Green Street, Northampton, 1995–6* (Northampton: Northamptonshire Archaeology 28, 1998–99)

Chapman, A., *In search of Northampton Castle* in British Archaeology 135 (York: CBA, March April, 2014)

Chapman, C., *POW Camps in Northamptonshire* in Hindsight 21 (Northampton: June 2015)

Cocroft, W., *Dangerous Energy* (Swindon: English Heritage, 2000)

Cocroft, W., and Thomas, R., *Cold War: Building for Nuclear Confrontation 1946–89* (Swindon: English Heritage, 2003)

Compton, H., and Carr-Gomm, A., *The Military on English Waterways 1798–1844* (Mold: Railway & Canal Historical Society, 1991)

Crisp, G., *The Supply of Explosives and Ammunition to the RAF in WW2* in Airfield Review Vol. 10 Nos 1 (1988) and 2 (1989) and No. 124 (Thetford: ARG, 2009)

Delve, K., *The Military Airfields of Britain: East Midlands* (Ramsbury: Crowood, 2008

Downes, M., *Oundle's War* (Oundle: Nene Press, nd)

Everitt, A., *The Local Community and the Great Rebellion* (London: The Historical Association, 1973)

Foard, G., *The Civil War Defences of Northampton and its Suburbs* (Northampton: Northamptonshire Past and Present IX.1, 1994–5); *Naseby The Decisive Campaign* (Barnsley: Pen & Sword, 1995 & 2004); *Rockingham Forest, An atlas of medieval and early-modern landscape* (Northampton: Northamptonshire Record Society, 2009)

Francis, P., *British Military Airfield Architecture* (Yeovil: Patrick Stephens, 1996)

Francis, P., and Crisp, G., *Military Command and Control Organisation* (Swindon: in CD form for English Heritage, 2008)

Gibbs, L., *Conservation Plan for Storehouse Enclosure, Royal Ordnance Depot, Weedon Bec* (London: The Historic Environment Consultancy, 2005)

Gibson, M., *Aviation in Northamptonshire* (Northampton: Northamptonshire Libraries, 1982)

Giggins, B., *Northampton's Forgotten Castle* (Daventry: Castle Studies Group Bulletin 18, 2005)

Giggins, B., *Bury Mount Castle, Towcester* (Towcester: Towcester & District Local History Society, 2006)

Giggins, B., *Barnwell Castle Part 1* in Castle Studies Group Journal No. 32 (Daventry: CSG, 2018)

Greenall, R., *A History of Northamptonshire* (Chichester: Phillimore, 1979 & 2000)

Gurney, Lt-Col. R., *History of the Northamptonshire Regiment 1742–1934* (Aldershot: Gale & Polden, 1935)

Guy, N., (ed.), *Towcester Bury Mount* (news item and Wikipedia entry) (Daventry: Castle Studies Group Bulletin 21, 2007–8); *Alderton Mount* (news item and report of Time Team excavation) (Daventry: Castle Studies Group Bulletin 24, 2010–11); *Bury Mount, Towcester* (news item) (Daventry: Castle Studies Group Bulletin 24, 2010–11)

harringtonmuseum.org.uk/Military%20sites%20within2030%20miles%20of%20 Harrington%20Museum.pdf

Hatley, V., (ed.), *Northamptonshire Militia Lists 1777* (Northampton: Northamptonshire Record Society, Volume XXV, 1973)

hillforts.arch.ox.ac.uk

Holloway, B., and Banks, H., *Northamptonshire Home Guard* (Northampton: Northants Home Guard, 1949)

Hollowell, S., *Defending the Heart of England, Northampton 1940–44* (Northampton: Northamptonshire Archaeology 28, 1998–99)

Howarth, P., *Caxton Gibbet and Denton EFTS Relief Landing Grounds* in Airfield Review 126 (Hoxne: ARG, 2010)

Howarth, P., *Silverstone Bomber OTU Field* in Airfield Review 130 (Hoxne: ARG, 2011)

Jackson, D., *Excavation of the hillfort defences at Hunsbury in 1952 and 1988* (Northampton: Northamptonshire Archaeology 25, 1993–4); *The Iron Age Hillfort at Borough Hill, Daventry* (Northampton: Northamptonshire Archaeology 25, 1993–4)

Jackson, D., and Tingle, M., *An archaeological survey of the Hunsbury Hill-fort defences* (Northampton: Northamptonshire Archaeology 37, 2012)

James, Brig. E., *British Regiments 1914–1918* (Heathfield: Naval & Military Press, 1978)

Jervois, Brig. W., *History of the Northamptonshire Regiment 1742–1934* (Northampton: The Regimental History Committee, 1953)

Johnston, G., and Bellamy, B., *From Hillfort to Mansion: Excavations at Fineshade Abbey* (Northampton: Northamptonshire Archaeology 38, 2015)

Kenyon, J., *Castles, Town Defences & Artillery Fortifications in the United Kingdom & Ireland: a Bibliography 1945–2006* (Donington: Shaun Tyas, 2008)

King, D. J. C., and Alcock, *Ringworks of England and Wales* in Taylor, A. J., (ed.), *Chateau Gaillard III* (1966), (Chichester: Phillimore, 1969)

King, E., *King Stephen and the Empress Matilda, the view from Northampton* (Northampton: Northamptonshire Past and Present 67, 2014)

Klingelhoffer, E., *Rockingham Castle in 1250: Form and Function of a Royal Castle under Henry III* (Northampton: Northamptonshire Past and Present 7.1, 1983–4)

Knight, D., *An Iron Age Hillfort at Castle Dykes, Farthingstone* (Northampton: Northamptonshire Archaeology 21, 1986–7)

Liddiard, R., *Castles in Context* (Macclesfield: Windgather, 2005)

Metcalfe, A., letter re Major Mole in Northampton in English Civil War Times 52 (Leigh-on-Sea: Partizan Press, 1996)

McGlynn, S., *Blood Cries Afar. The forgotten Invasion of England 1216* (Stroud: History Press, 2011)

Nichol, N., unpublished list of First World War POW camps

Northamptonshire Libraries *Northamptonshire at War 1939–45* (Northampton: 1979)

The 1st and 2nd Northamptonshire Yeomanry 1939–45 (Brunswick: 1946)

Osborne, M., *20th Century Defences in Britain: the East Midlands* (Market Deeping: Concrete Publications, 2003); *Defending Britain* (Stroud: Tempus, 2004); *Always Ready, The Drill Halls of Britain's Volunteer Forces* (Leigh-on-Sea: Partizan Press, 2006); *Pillboxes in Britain and Ireland* (Stroud: Tempus, 2008)

Perkins, W., Northants Notes & Queries, Old Series, Volume III, items 456 and 458

Pevsner, N., *Northamptonshire* (Harmondsworth: Penguin, 1961) see Bailey *et al.*

RCHM, *Archaeological sites in central Northamptonshire* (London: HMSO, 1979)

RCHM, *Archaeological sites in north-west Northamptonshire* (London: HMSO, 1981)

RCHM, *Archaeological sites in south-west Northamptonshire* (London: HMSO, 1982)

RCHM, *Architectural sites in north Northamptonshire* (London: HMSO, 1984)

Renn, D., *Burhgeat and Gonfanon* in Liddiard, T., (ed.), *Anglo-Norman Castles* (Woodbridge: Boydell Press, 2003)

SUBTERRANEA BRITANNICA *www.subbrit.org.uk/rsg/sites*

Tate, W., *Inclosure Movements in Northamptonshire* (Northampton: Northamptonshire Past and Present 1.2, 1949)

Taylor, C., *Fieldwork in Medieval Archaeology* (London: 1974); *Moated sites: their definition, form and classification* in Aberg, 1978

Thamas, P., *Vagabond Soldiers and Deserters at Elizabethan Northampton* (Northampton: Northamptonshire Past and Present IX.2, 1995–6)

Tout, K., *Yeomen of England, Tales of the Northamptonshire Yeomanry from 1794* (Stroud: The History Press, 2012)

Treharne, R., *The Battle of Northampton, 1264* (Northampton: Northamptonshire Past and Present 2.2, 1955)

Turton, K., *Northampton in the Great War* (Barnsley: Pen & Sword, 2016); *Northampton at War 1939–45* (Barnsley: Pen & Sword, 2017)

Upson-Smith, T., *Building Recording of Nissen Huts at former RAF Chelveston* (Northampton: Northamptonshire Archaeology 37, 2012)

Webb, P., *Portrait of Northamptonshire* (London: Robert Hale, 1977)

Williams, A., *A bell-house and a burh-geat: lordly residences in England before the Norman Conquest* in Liddiard, R., (ed.), *Anglo-Norman Castles* (Woodbridge: Boydell Press, 2003)

Williams, J., *Four Small Excavations on Northampton's Medieval Defences and Elsewhere* (Northampton: Northamptonshire Archaeology 17, 1982)

Woodfield, C., *The Egg Rings: a defended enclosure in Salcey Forest* (Northampton: Northants Archaeology 15, 1980); *The larger Medieval houses of Northamptonshire* (Northampton: Northants Archaeology 16, 1981); *The defences of Towcester* (Northampton: Northants Archaeology 24, 1992); *New thoughts on town defences in the western territory of the Catuvellauni* in Brown, A., (ed.), *Roman Small Towns in Eastern England and Beyond* (Oxford: Oxbow, 1995)

Index